Moral
Development
and
Character
Education

THE NATIONAL SOCIETY
FOR THE STUDY OF EDUCATION

Series on Contemporary Educational Issues
Kenneth J. Rehage, Series Editor

The 1989 Titles

Moral Development and Character Education: *A Dialogue*, Larry P. Nucci, editor

Schools in Conflict: The Politics of Education, second edition, Frederick Wirt and Michael Kirst

The National Society for the Study of Education also publishes Yearbooks which are distributed by the University of Chicago Press. Inquiries regarding all publications of the Society, as well as inquiries about membership in the Society, may be addressed to the Secretary-Treasurer, 5835 Kimbark Avenue, Chicago, IL 60637. Membership in the Society is open to any who are interested in promoting the investigation and discussion of educational questions.

Moral
Development
and
Character
Education

A DIALOGUE

EDITED BY

Larry P. Nucci

The University of Illinois at Chicago

McCutchan Publishing Corporation

P.O. Box 774
Berkeley, California 94701

ISBN 0-8211-1308-9
Library of Congress Catalog Card Number 88-63921

This book is dedicated in memory
of Lawrence Kohlberg

Contents

Contributors

Victor Battistich, Developmental Studies Center, San Ramon, California
Dwight Boyd, The Ontario Institute for Studies in Education
Ann Higgins, Harvard University
Lawrence Kohlberg, deceased
Nona Lyons, Harvard University
Larry Nucci, University of Illinois at Chicago
Clark Power, University of Notre Dame
Kevin Ryan, Boston University
Eric Schaps, Developmental Studies Center, San Ramon, California
Daniel Solomon, Developmental Studies Center, San Ramon, California
Judith Solomon, Developmental Studies Center, San Ramon, California
Elliot Turiel, University of California, Berkeley
Herbert J. Walberg, University of Illinois at Chicago
Marilyn Watson, Developmental Studies Center, San Ramon, California
Edward A. Wynne, University of Illinois at Chicago

Preface

One of the more important educational issues raised by political conservatives is the role of the schools in developing children's moral values and character. Led by public figures such as former Secretary of Education William Bennett, the political right has called for a return to the direct teaching of traditional values through what is called "character education." Unfortunately, the politicized and sometimes strident tone of public discussion of this issue has tended to generate more heat than light. Many of the legitimate concerns of traditional educators have been overstated, while alternative views such as values clarification and developmental approaches to moral education have been subject to distortion and caricature.

This book emerged out of a conference sponsored by the Association for Moral Education, which brought together in November 1986 the principal researchers and scholars from the developmental and character education schools of thought. The purposes of the conference were to engage the participants in an open exchange of views, to uncover common ground, to clarify differences, and to outline directions for future research. This book contains chapters based on the major papers presented at the conference. The volume is divided into two parts. The first part contains chapters by proponents of character education; the second is composed of chapters by developmentalists.

The exchange of views contained in the book extends a debate over the nature of moral development and character formation that can be traced in Western philosophy at least as far back as Aristotle's *Nichomacean Ethics* and Socrates' *Meno*. It is the intent of this volume to help move that discussion beyond the simple reiteration of old positions to the presentation of new constructs and research that can constitute the basis for an informed approach to moral education.

A key participant in the conference was Lawrence Kohlberg. In many respects his ideas formed a touchstone for discussion, and the reader will find reference to his work in each chapter in this volume. It was Kohlberg's 1958 dissertation outlining stages of moral development that marked the resurgence of research interest in moral education in the United States. For it was Kohlberg's notions of moral development that provided the first meaningful research-based response to Hartshorne and May's findings in the late 1920s that children could not be divided up into those of strong or weak character. While Kohlberg's work is almost synonymous with developmental approaches to moral education, and although Kohlberg may be considered the most articulate and effective modern critic of character education, his later work on the "just community school" marked a rapprochement between those two schools of thought.

We did not know as we planned for the conference, and as I made initial arrangements for this book, that Lawrence Kohlberg's voice would be stilled on January 17, 1987. His chapter in this volume has been co-authored from his notes by his colleagues Clark Power and Ann Higgins. The book itself is dedicated in memory of him and his extraordinary contribution to research on moral development and moral education.

VOLUME OVERVIEW

The first four chapters of the book present the character education perspective. This perspective defines morality by the norms of the culture and its central moral institutions. Adherents to this perspective believe that the moral person is one who adheres to the values and traditions of the society and who possesses a set of presumably fundamental virtues such as honesty and loyalty. One develops good character (becomes virtuous), according to this school of thought, by exposure to role models and the exhortation of prosocial values by significant adults such as parents and teachers. The child develops a set of moral habits based on these values through the practice of right conduct aided by a system of social rewards and punishments.

Kevin Ryan begins the section with a defense of character education. Ryan argues convincingly that teaching values to children is a fundamental role of adults and institutions of any society. He takes issue with those who oppose the teaching of values on the grounds that in a pluralistic society there will be a divergence in the definition of morality. He contends that the removal of values education from the schools is a "dismantling of public education as we know it." At the heart of this "dismantling" is the failure of teacher education programs to prepare teachers to transmit social and moral values. In response to these concerns, Ryan proposes an approach to teacher education that would convey (1) a vision of the teacher as moral agent and (2) the process of teaching values.

Edward Wynne, in "Transmitting Traditional Values in Contemporary Schools," argues that in recent years there has been a significant increase in the disorderly conduct among young Americans that can be associated with a "diffusion of antitraditional values in education." Wynne contends that to correct this situation one need not wait for new theories and research on human development, but can simply examine and characterize the practices of schools where "more wholesome forms of transaction occur." These forms of transaction, according to Wynne, emphasize control and modification of student behavior. Wynne draws from observations of schools to describe the transactions that characterize his adult-centered, authoritative approach to values education.

Herbert Walberg and Edward Wynne, in "Character Education: Toward a Preliminary Consensus," extend Wynne's notion of character as entailing the delay of gratification to conjoin character development with academic goals. In their view, academic success stems from the student's ability to be committed and to push toward a significant accomplishment. That is, successful students possess the character trait of self-discipline and the protestant notion of hard work. Accordingly, Walberg and Wynne argue that schools that treat academic programs seriously contribute not only to academic success but to character development as well.

The final chapter in this section, by Marilyn Watson and her colleagues, serves as a bridge between the positions espoused by the character educators and those offered by the developmentalists in the next section of the book. The chapter describes a values education program that employs elements from both the character education and developmental perspectives. Their approach, in concert with character education, recognizes that adults play an active and important role in shaping the development of children's character. At the same time they reject the traditionalists' view of the child as a "blank slate," to be molded by society. Like the developmentalists, the authors of this chapter view the formation of the child's character and values to be interactive and largely a function of the child's own thinking and interpretation of experience. As a result, their program employs adult teaching and guidance toward prosocial values, and provision of opportunities for children to discuss, reflect on, and apply values.

The final five chapters compose the section on the developmental approach to moral education. Central to this tradition is the assumption that moral action is a function of moral judgment, and that reasoning or judgment undergoes development. Moral development according to this view is not a function of the straightforward acquisition of the norms of society, but emerges out of the child's efforts to resolve or take into account the competing claims or needs of persons. Accordingly, moral education, from the developmentalist perspective, emphasizes the role of reflection, perspective taking, conflict resolution, and autonomous choice.

The section begins with Dwight Boyd's chapter, "The Character of Moral Development." Boyd addresses the philosophical premises underlying Lawrence Kohlberg's theory of moral development to arrive at a definition of moral character. Boyd bases his position on Kohlberg's description of the highest stage of moral development. Boyd argues that since the moral principles embodied in this highest sixth stage cannot be established by appeal to the rules of conduct of a particular social system, one cannot correctly identify character as strong adherence to such a rule-based moral code. Instead, character traits such as courage are moral only to the extent that they facilitate and are congruent with the use of stage-six principles. Boyd concludes by suggesting that the aim of moral education should be the development of principled moral judgment and those character traits consistent with stage-six principles.

The chapter by Clark Power, Ann Higgins, and Lawrence Kohlberg, "The Habit of the Common Life: Building Character Through Democratic Community Schools," responds to the traditionalists' call for the teaching of moral habits. In the chapter they reanalyze Aristotle's views of virtue and moral habit, and conclude that Aristotle saw habit as the foundation for moral judgment rather than an end point, and justice as the master principle that integrates and gives moral worth to the other virtues. They offer the "just community" school as a way to develop a sense of collective responsibility in students, which Power, Higgins, and Kohlberg see as the underlying habit or basis for a moral (just) approach to life.

The next three chapters in the book present the views and supporting research of developmentalists who diverge from the Kohlbergian view of moral development. The chapter by Nona Lyons presents an approach to moral education that stems from Carol Gilligan's and Lyons's work distinguishing a moral orientation of care from a morality of justice. In the chapter Lyons illustrates each orientation, and describes how her program at the Emma Willard School integrates concerns for intimacy, nurturance, and affiliation with justice principles.

Elliot Turiel, in "Multifaceted Social Reasoning and Educating for Character, Culture, and Development," employs research and theory to demonstrate that social values, both at the level of society and at the individual level, do not entail a single orientation but reflect the coexistence of diverse social concerns and moral attitudes. At the level of the individual this diversity is reflected in the construction of distinct knowledge systems to account for moral considerations of justice and welfare, and concerns for maintaining social order, tradition, and convention. Unlike Kohlberg, Turiel treats these concerns as entailing separate knowledge systems rather than stages within a single system. As a result, Turiel argues for a more broadly defined social values curriculum that extends beyond the single aim of developing children's justice reasoning. At the same time he is critical of those who depreciate reasoning by asserting that morality is adherence to cultural values.

In the final chapter, "Challenging Conventional Wisdom About Morality: The Domain Approach to Values Education," Larry Nucci reviews research demonstrating that children's concepts of morality form a domain distinct from their concepts of societal convention. On the basis of that research, Nucci is critical both of the character educators who reduce values education to the teaching of social convention and of Kohlbergian developmentalists who reduce values education to moral issues of justice and human welfare. To support an alternative developmental approach, Nucci presents research on classroom applications of the distinction between morality and convention in values education. Finally, the chapter presents research on religious children's concepts of morality and religious rules to argue that morality may be taught in the public schools without violating Constitutional provisions regarding the separation of church and state.

Larry P. Nucci

Part I

Character Education

1

In Defense of Character Education

Kevin Ryan

Worrying about the young is probably genetically based. And those tribes or communities that do not worry about the young, or do not act sensibly, or do not respond well to their worries undoubtedly have a short history. It seems that recently Americans are worrying more about their young. In his book *An Inquiry into the Human Prospect*, Robert Heilbroner, an economic historian, sketches out the three catastrophic scenarios facing our species today—nuclear holocaust, worldwide famine, and destruction of the ecosystem. He then states what was really on people's minds as we entered the last quarter of the twentieth century. He believes that the great unease of the middle-aged population was because of "our inability to pass on our values to the young" (Heilbroner 1974, p. 15).

More recently, James Q. Wilson began his lead article in the twentieth anniversary issue of *Public Interest* with this statement: "The most important change in how one defines the public interest that I have witnessed—and experienced—over the last twenty years has been a deepening concern for the development of character in the citizenry" (1985, p. 3). And in that same paragraph he remarked about the growing awareness that "a variety of public problems can only be understood—and perhaps addressed—if they are seen as arising out of a defect in character formation." Anyone familiar with

3

Edward A. Wynne's statistics (see chapter 2, this volume) on changes in the rates of homicide, suicide, and illegitimate births among the young in the past four decades knows exactly why there is this public concern about character development.

While many are anesthetized to the plight of the young and have taken the moral confusion of youth as a price of progress, many others are being jarred awake. Even our political leaders seem to be sensing the public mood. Our leaders on the left, for example, Governor Cuomo, and on the right, ex-President Reagan, have urged the schools to teach traditional values more aggressively. The nation even received a lecture on the topic from Prince Charles at Harvard's recent 350th birthday party. These men are just giving voice to the public's views as registered in the 1975 and 1980 Gallup polls, wherein 79 percent of the respondents indicated they favor "instruction in schools that would deal with morals and moral behavior" (Gallup 1975, 1980). So, concern there is. But what do we do to teach morals and moral behavior? What to do to effect moral development positively? What to do to form good character? These are our issues.

Carl Bereiter (1973) has been urging public educators for some time to abandon this mission, claiming that in a pluralistic democracy the schools have no right to attempt to transmit moral values or to attempt to influence ethical considerations. Recently, Kurtines and Gewirtz (1984) suggested that the multitude of psychological models of moral functioning mirrors the moral pluralism in the country. The clear implication of this view, it seems, is to question the viability of the public schools. And, indeed, some members of our society are beginning such questioning. Recently, I was an observer at a small, invitational conference, chaired by the Protestant theologian Richard John Neuhaus and devoted to exploring the policy papers of a few leading Protestant thinkers concerned with this issue. The clear message I came away with is that behind the Moral Majority's sloganeering about the public schools infecting our youth with secular humanism is a solid core of Protestant intelligentsia who believe that the lack of moral training, on the one hand, and the atheological world view—if not antitheological world view—fostered by twelve years of largely compulsory education, on the other hand, are violations of First Amendment guarantees of religious liberty. In short, I believe that what they are suggesting is the dismantling of public education as we know it. And this drive to dismantle is being energized by the very issues central to this volume: moral education and character development.

THE EDUCATION OF TEACHERS

The issues and problems surrounding moral education and character education are many and varied. The concerns of this chapter are those of my own work, that of preparing elementary and secondary school teachers. As opposed to the professional work of most of the other writers in this volume, who are researchers and theorists, mine is very immediate, very involved with practice. And as will soon be clear, it is hardly the work for a purist.

But what has been the recent history of teacher education's efforts to prepare future teachers for their role as moral educators, as character developers? My own view is that the past twenty years have seen a quiet retreat. Teacher educators, sensitive and fidgety souls that we are, took quite personally the students' cry of the 1960s: "Don't trust anyone over thirty." As confused as anyone by the moral shifts of the period, we downplayed the future teacher's role as a transmitter of social and personal values and emphasized other areas. This same period has seen an enormous growth in research and writing on teaching techniques, strategies, models, and skills (Wittrock 1986). Teacher education has moved from the lecture hall and the library to the public school, to become more clinical—some students now have two or three semesters of clinical experience before they begin student teaching. Philosophy and history of education have been sacrificed on the altar of technique and practice (Tom 1984). And more and more the vision of the good teacher is as the good technician, the skilled craftsman who has acquired those behavioral skills and strategies that the "effective teacher" research claims are related to achievement. That "effective" is defined as the students' mastery of objective questions but without reference to higher-order intellectual processes or concern about the students' morals deeply troubles many educators.

While rarely exposed to philosophical views of the person, teacher education students are regularly exposed to a psychological view of man. If anything, educational psychology has become stronger in recent years. And, as is characteristic of this discipline, its focus is on man as an individual, separated from his social context. In these past decades, the three dominant schools of psychology—behaviorism, developmentalism, and self-actualization (or Third Force) psychology—have each offered to the teacher distinctly different metaphors of man, and each have used the "teacher-as-technician" motif. Behaviorism, at least in the form that it comes to teachers, has a few minutes in the curriculum about "reinforcing prosocial behavior." The developmental school offers a little more of the moral, providing the future teacher with a smidgen of Piaget and a dollop or two of Kohlberg. But the school of psychology that has the most influence in this area is self-actualization, with its offering of values clarification. In fact, values clarification influences more than only the educational psychology course—its relativistic assumptions have penetrated everything from discipline to curriculum. The focus of values clarification is to exalt process, and its effect on moral education and character education has been, by and large, to undermine to the point of making insignificant any notion of the school's passing on society's core values.

If teachers look upon their work with children as containing a moral dimension, this is something they bring to the classroom, not something they were taught in teacher education courses. This belief in the moral dimension of education comes from their religious and civil backgrounds. It comes from their lived experience as students and from their knowledge that their moral sensibilities were certainly affected by their own teachers. But whether or not prospective teachers come to teacher education with a well-formulated picture of themselves as moral educators, it is well recognized that they inevitably will have an enormous impact on students, from kindergartners to high school seniors.

What, then, should we do to prepare teachers for their responsibilities as character educators, as moral educators? While it is tempting to describe an ideal program of selecting and preparing moral educators, a West Point of Moral Education, if you will, I believe it is more useful to discuss what can be done now within the context of most teacher education programs. In effect, this means presenting certain ideas to the students and giving them opportunities to try out some of those ideas. First, then, is to give future teachers a vision of the moral agent, and, second, an understanding of how they can and will affect their own students as each struggles to become a moral agent and to develop character.

THE MORAL AGENT

The teacher needs a vision of moral man, some sense of the person as moral actor or agent. The view I will present is one that emerged from the "Foundations of Moral Education Project." The project has four committees: a philosophy committee, a psychology committee, an education committee, and a curricular materials committee. The work of each of the first three committees has been summarized in individual books. The philosophy and psychology committees have recently published volumes with University Press of America. The education committee's book is entitled *Character Education in Schools and Beyond* and was published in 1987 (Ryan and McLean 1987).

The education committee, composed of individuals several of whom (such as Tom Lickona, Ed Sullivan, Clark Power, Edward Wynne, Clive Beck) are well known to members of the Association for Moral Education, was party to much of the discussion and all of the papers of the other two groups. Out of the discussions of the education committee there emerged an integrated model of the moral agent. It is our contention that human character arises from the workings of three components: knowing, affect, and action.

Knowing

Man is a reasoning being, a knower. He has a natural telos to understand the world inside him and the world outside him. Also, and quite important, he exists in a community. Part of his community is a moral heritage. Each community has found certain patterns of behavior and certain human character traits and virtues necessary to sustain the life of the individual and the community. The moral person learns these values not simply in a rote, passive way but in an intellectual way. What is courage and when is it needed? What happens to me and to my community if I become irresponsible? What is kindness and what are the consequences of human kindness?

The moral agent also knows the behavioral referents to kindness. What does kindness mean within my family, or within my fifth-grade class? What does persistence mean in my life as a student, and later as a mate and parent? The emphasis on the moral agent's knowing means that students need to come to know their culture's moral wisdom, that is, what has been learned over the years. It means that they need to know the best literature and the most important aspects of its history. They need to know these stories and accounts not simply for form or for cultural literacy but for the moral lessons that are embedded in them. What is to be learned from Homer's steadfast journey? What is to be learned about courage and human frailty from the soldier's heroic roller coaster in *The Red Badge of Courage*? What can Ghandi's humble crusade tell us about the power of a moral idea whose time has come? Students need to know where we have been and what we have learned, not as the final word, but as the unfinished repository of our moral successes and failures. And this is why they need the best literature and the best history, rather than some hack attempt to socialize the young to their society's biases.

And, to ensure against moral passivity, the young need to know how to think morally and how to reason through an issue or problem rather than receive someone else's decision. The young must ask themselves questions such as: What is the good, the right in this situation? How do I choose between competing goods? What are the consequences of this course of action? To be moral agents, students need to become ethicists. They need to acquire during their years of education the skills of ethical thinking. Is this problem really a moral problem? What are the facts? What are the positive consequences for various courses of action? What are the negative consequences? Also involved here is the forming of the moral imagination, getting inside the world of the other, and considering possibilities without having to be presented with concrete events. And, finally, part of developing the moral agent is to develop the quality of good judgment, or what Aristotle calls "practical wisdom." We need to cultivate in our students a judicious style of judgment.

Affect

The moral agent is neither raw intellect nor disembodied reasoning but has feelings and emotions and passions that play a great part in the moral life. This affective component is one that many of us ignore or, at least, underestimate. I see it as an energetic, vital moral engine that frequently takes over the life of the moral agent, that drives the agent in directions his reason forbids, or that gives energy to decisions that the reason timidly points to. We all know those who can talk a good moral game, who can reason with the angels, but whose behavior is all too human. What I am suggesting is that we need to help the child acquire not simply intellectual skills, habits of the mind, but habits of the heart. We need to help the young learn to love the good. Pascal said it best: "The heart has its reasons, that reason does not know."

Part of this learning to love the good is developing commitments, but in particular a commitment to the moral life. It means developing a conscience, an inner voice, not of reason, but of affect, calling us in a certain direction. This voice should confront emotions such as greed, self-interest, and envy with a stronger desire to do the right, the good.

A part of this moral affect is love of self, concern for one's own well-being. The moral education of the affect involves the growth of self-love outward from the self to family and friends and to communities seen and unseen, to develop an ever-growing definition of what it means to love the good.

Affect has one other function, perhaps its most important. It is a bridge between knowing and the third component of character—action; in other words, affect is the link between thought and action.

Action

Here, in modern parlance, is where the rubber meets the road. Most would agree that any efforts at moral education or character development that fail to affect positively the child's behavior in some important way are doomed. Moral *action* is the bottom line. We see three elements or subcomponents of action: will, competence, and habit.

The word "will" has developed something of a bad reputation since the publication of Gordon Liddy's autobiography of the same name. Young Gordon strengthened his will by eating rats, which is not quite what we have in mind. Will is needed to mobilize and channel our moral energy. It provides us with the strength to push through our self-interest and laziness and fears. Will spurs us to moral action and carries us forward to do what our minds and hearts tell us we ought to do.

Competence refers to a repertoire of behaviors and skills the moral agent needs in order to act effectively in the world. A moral agent needs to be able to listen and understand, to empathize with the troubled, and to serve those in need. A moral agent needs to be able to lead others to see and do the good, and to stand up to injustice. And the agent must learn these competencies in the same way skills of decoding and encoding symbols are learned, in the same way the scientific method is learned.

Added to will and competence is habit. Good will and the capacity to act are not enough. Once learned, certain moral competencies must be habituated. Moral actions, such as telling the truth when a comfortable lie is handy or saying the right but unpopular thing when silence is easy, need to be practiced responses. One cannot stop and weigh consequences every time a moral event arises. Moral actions must be practiced, habituated responses to life situations.

This, then, is our integrated model of the moral agent, a person whose understanding, emotions, and behavior are fully developed. This is, we believe, an accurate, understandable, and usable model to be used as the basis for preparing teachers for their roles in moral education and character formation.

THE TEACHER AS MORAL EDUCATOR

Our second question, then, is: What should teachers be taught in order to fulfill this role of moral educator? This is a huge territory, which I have categorized into six areas in a somewhat labored alliteration: the "six e's of moral education and character development" (Ryan 1986). They are *e*xample, *e*xplanation, *e*xhortation, *e*nvironmental expectations (actually two e's here for the price of one), *e*valuation, and *e*xperience. I suggest that heightened awareness and training in these areas should be woven throughout teacher education.

Example

Example is perhaps the most obvious of the six e's and the one that makes us most uncomfortable. One of the facts of school life is that children watch their teachers to discover how grownups act. While I do not suggest that teachers must be saints, secular or otherwise, I do mean that they should be people who take the moral life seriously. Just as teachers should be models of persons using their minds, they should also be seen as models of persons responding to life in a morally admirable way.

But there is another aspect to this moral modeling. As I stated previously, many of our most important moral truths are embedded in our stories and in our history. The heroes and villains of our stories and our history need to be brought to the attention of our young. They need to know about Hester Prynne and Richard the Third. They need to know Adolph Hitler and Martin Luther King.

Explanation

Emile Durkheim, the French sociologist, is often cited as an apologist for the school's socialization of the young into the dominant values of society. He saw the school as a social vehicle to instill in the young society's values and rules of conduct. However, Durkheim insisted that these efforts must be rational. He said, "To teach morality is neither to preach nor to indoctrinate; it is to explain" (1925, p. 120). This teaching starts on the playground, when the teacher explains why we do not duel with sharp sticks, and it continues through the senior year, when the teacher explains to the soon-to-be high school graduates their duties to the Republic.

We need to educate morally through explanation; we must not simply stuff students' heads with rules and regulations but engage them in the great moral conversation of the human race. Indeed, it is the very existence of this conversation that makes us human. Thirty-five years ago, as an undergraduate at the University of Toronto, I was in a daze listening to Marshall McLuhan, a then obscure literature teacher, carrying on about "the medium is the message." I see now that his point is so relevant to schooling, so relevant to the moral education of children. Our continual explaining of the rules is, in and of itself, one of the most important messages of school.

Exhortation

While teachers' explanations are a crucial part of a child's moral education, their urgings and exhortations also have a place in the process. A child who is discouraged by academic failure or by having been cut from a team, a cast, or a musical group often needs something stronger than sweet reason to ward off self-pity. A student who is quietly and passively slipping through school may need a teacher's passionate appeal to inspire him or her to shape up and use the opportunity education offers. A youth who is flirting with racist ideas may not question this kind of sloppy thinking until he or she feels the heat of a teacher's moral indignation. A senior who has been turned down by a favorite college or denied entrance into an apprenticeship program may need more than the teacher's nuanced explanation that life is unfair. This student may need to be inspired or even goaded in order to endure and transcend such disappointment.

Exhortation should be used sparingly, and it should never stray very far from explanation. Nonetheless, at times teachers must appeal to the best instincts of the young and urge them to move in particular directions.

Environmental Expectations

A classroom is a small society with patterns and rituals, power relationships, and standards for both academic performance and student behavior. In a positive moral environment, students are respected and respect one another. The ability to establish a purposeful and civil classroom environment is what distinguishes the good teacher from the ineffective teacher. A central factor in a classroom environment is the moral climate. Are the classroom rules fair and fairly exercised? Does the teacher play favorites? Does good balance exist between competition and cooperation? Are individuality and community responsibility both nurtured? Are less able students protected but also challenged? Are ethical questions and issues of "what ought to be" part of the classroom dialogue?

I know of no handy guide to follow to establish and maintain an environment of moral expectation. And once established, such an environment is always moments away from collapse. But I have little doubt that a classroom's moral climate has a steady and strong influence in the formation of character and the students' sense of right and wrong.

Evaluation

It is perhaps here that I have stretched alliteration past the bounds of good sense. What I have in mind is the teacher's allowing the child to evaluate for himself, but also more. More than just allow, teachers must create opportunities for students to reflect on what they value, what they think is the good, what they believe is the right thing to do. If this sounds like a back door endorsement for values clarification, I must plead guilty. As someone who has done his share of bashing values clarification over the past two decades, I have along the way come to appreciate its power to involve students in the kind of moral and value issues that have meaning in their lives. I believe that I have been so opposed to the idea of values clarification attempting to carry the entire weight of the school's role in moral education that I have failed to see the substantial contribution it can make. When values clarification strategies and activities are used well and used within a total program of moral education and character education (as I suggest here), then they have a substantial contribution to make. And, of course, the same can be said for involving students in the structured discussion of ethical dilemmas.

Experience

In commenting on the enormous changes that have taken place in the world of children over two generations, James Coleman wrote "the modern generation of American youth is information rich and experience poor" (Coleman 1974). The world of U.S. children has been radically altered by changes in the economy, in the means of production, and in the size and structure of their families. Families today are smaller and less stable than families of two generations ago. Modern homes and apartments afford few tasks for children other than doing the laundry and the dishes, putting out garbage, and a few other light and brief chores. These are hardly routes by which to develop a sturdy self-concept. At the same time, by the standards of any previous generation, today's young people exist in a self-focused, pleasure-dominated world of turn-on escapism (through MTV, sexuality, drugs, or simply "hanging out"). Only rare and fortunate teenagers encounter the kinds of experiences that help them break out of this envelope of self-interest and learn to contribute to others.

Schools are increasingly responding to this condition by providing students opportunities to serve others both in school and out of school. Within such schools, students are encouraged to help teachers and other students. Older children often help young ones learn academic or physical skills; students also help teachers, librarians, or other staff members with routine clerical tasks. But out-of-school programs represent a larger departure from the ordinary. These programs enable students to provide services to individuals in need, such as a blind shut-in or a mother with a mildly retarded child. Other students work (usually without pay) in understaffed agencies, such as retirement homes or day-care centers. The school's staff members serve as trouble shooters and intermediaries between student volunteers and the individuals or agencies in need of assistance. Such service programs teach the skills of effective helping and enable young people to define themselves as individuals who are connected to others. Moral abstractions about justice and community take on immediacy. Students begin to appreciate the need to couple moral thinking with moral action.

Together these "six e's of moral education and character development" capture what I think preservice teachers should be prepared to do. Of course, these skills and competencies overlap and also are somewhat arbitrarily categorized, but together they represent what I see as the teacher's domain in the moral and character education of the young.

CHARACTER DEVELOPMENT: TOWARD A DEFINITION

In this last section I will suggest what I believe character development is and what it is not, what it represents as a movement, and how it differs from what I know of the cognitive-developmental moral education and other recent approaches.

Character development is quite eclectic, and appropriately so. Man is a complicated beast. We need all the sensible theories, all the angles of vision, all the illuminating metaphors we can find when it comes down to practice, to the questions of what schools and teachers can do to help a child become a morally mature person. Building practice on one metaphor from only one of many relevant disciplines, as for example, the cognitive-developmental metaphor of growth and stages seems to do, strikes me as loading more weight on the theory than the theory can stand. Character development is ready to select from many disciplines and use many metaphors—the growth metaphor, the Skinnerian metaphor, the fill-the-jug metaphor. Using so many metaphors from so many disciplines may get a little sloppy at times, but public education is not really for the excessively tidy, anyway.

Character development puts a heavy emphasis on culture. While it fully engages the transformational goal of schools, which is to make the student an active agent in the positive transformation of society, it places more emphasis on the traditional role of the school as transmitter of the culture. This emphasis springs from the conviction that civilization is a great human achievement, but a fragile one, and what we have learned must be conserved and vigorously passed on to the young, so that they will preserve and improve the culture. Students need not only to know how to work their will through Roberts Rules of Order, but also to know the lessons of history, about the dangers of banality and of wasting their lives on pleasure and self-indulgence, about human depravity, and about the need for human heroism. They have to learn that school is an enormous opportunity for them, that they have serious responsibilities to use the experience well and that there is life after high school, but that it favors only those with real skills and capacities like self-discipline and responsibility.

And, further, and George Counts notwithstanding, the public pays teachers not to devise schemes to change the social order, but to educate the young to a much more demanding idea, to teach the young the best of the past so that they might preserve it and build on it and thus extend it and improve on it. The vital and primary energies of the teachers and students should be centered around knowing what Edward Wynne (1985/86) calls the "Great Tradition": the stories, myths, and histories that represent our cultural heritage, and the heroes and villains, real and fictitious, who have the capacity to ignite the moral imagination of the young. Cultural literacy and the traditional content of school are of central importance in character development.

Character development is directive and sees the teacher in a more active role than does the cognitive-developmental tradition. Cultural transmission implies a flow of knowledge and skills from the culture through the teacher to the students. But I am not suggesting a vision of schools where teachers cram cultural heritage down the throats of passive students. On the contrary, character education means that teachers must vigorously engage students in the human story, helping them to discover not only the glorious achievements of mankind but also, in Henry Giroux's words, its dangerous memories. The teacher must help the student see the wisdom in Yeats's famous lines: "Things fall apart. The center does not hold."

Character development is more concerned with the collective life of the school, with providing a strong and positive environment for the student. It works hard to establish school spirit and a rich activity program for students. Expectations for students, both academic and social, are high. Prizes and awards are quite evident, and grade, classroom, and individual competition is encouraged. Students are expected to contribute to the welfare of the school, as a clear prelude to their responsibilities as adults to look to the welfare of their spouses, their families, their communities, and their nation.

In character development teachers are more authoritative and more of an authority. Not only do they know more, they have the responsibility to see that the students have a fair chance to learn what has been set out. The school and the classroom, therefore, is not a democracy. The rights and responsibilities of the students are quite different from the rights and responsibilities of the teachers. To counterbalance the demands for teachers to manage and channel the energy of the students and their diverse wills, teachers must have power. And, although they must use it justly, the classroom and the school have not been designed for one man-one vote, participatory democracy. In my view, the high burnout or dropout rate of teachers in experimental, "just community" schools is directly related to confusion over this very point.

And finally, character development seems to view the child, the student, in a somewhat different way than do cognitive developmentalists. It sees the child as malleable, needing formation, needing a strong environment. It sees the child as capable of good and evil. Frankly, it is not as optimistic as stage theory seems to suggest. It sees children as self-centered and needing to learn how to reach out beyond themselves. It sees character development as cognitive, but also as deeply involving the emotions of the child. It sees, too, the need for action, the need for schools and teachers to give students the opportunity to practice the virtues essential to a good life in a good society (of which democratic decision making is important, but only one virtue among many). A priority is training in virtues such as responsibility, consideration, and honesty that support a good life in a good society. And, since character education draws quite heavily from Aristotle, I will end with his famous answer to the question, How does a man become virtuous? "We become just by performing just actions, self-controlled by exercising self-control. We become virtuous by performing virtuous acts."

REFERENCES

Bereiter, Carl. *Must We Educate?* Englewood Cliffs, N. J.: Prentice-Hall, 1973.
Coleman, James. *Youth: Transition to Adulthood.* Chicago: University of Chicago Press, 1974.

Durkheim, Emile. *Moral Education: A Study in the Theory and Application of the Sociology of Education.* New York: Free Press, 1925.

Gallup, George H. "The Seventh Annual Gallup Poll of Public Attitudes toward the Public Schools," *Phi Delta Kappan* 57 (December 1975): 227–41.

Gallup, George H. "The Twelfth Annual Gallup Poll of Public Attitudes toward Public Schools," *Phi Delta Kappan* 62 (September 1980): 39.

Heilbroner, Robert. *An Inquiry into the Human Prospect.* New York: W. W. Norton, 1974.

Kurtines, William, and Gewirtz, Jacob. *Morality, Moral Behavior, and Moral Development.* New York: Wiley, 1984.

Ryan, Kevin, "The New Moral Education," *Phi Delta Kappan* 68 (November 1986): 228–33.

Ryan, Kevin, and McLean, George, eds. *Character Education in Schools and Beyond.* New York: Praeger, 1987.

Tom, Alan. *Teaching as a Moral Craft.* New York: Longman, 1984.

Wittrock, M. C., ed. *Handbook of Research on Teaching*, 3d ed. New York: Macmillan, 1986.

Wilson, James Q. "The Rediscovery of Character: Private Virtue and Public Policy," *Public Interest*, no. 81 (Fall 1985): 3.

Wynne, Edward A. "The Great Tradition," *Educational Leadership* 43 (December 1985/January 1986): 4–9.

2

Transmitting Traditional Values in Contemporary Schools

Edward A. Wynne

One of the most important responsibilities of adults is to transmit proper values to succeeding generations. Without strong adult engagement with the young, the culture of any particular human society will decay or expire. Despite such potential for social decline, most societies have managed to transmit their central values. This proposition obviously applies to American society, which has persisted more than two hundred years. This persistence argues for the vitality of certain patterns of so-called traditional values and of the systems involved in transmitting those values. In this context, "traditional values" means the panoply of virtues connoted by phrases such as the work ethic and obedience to legitimate authority and by the important nonreligious themes articulated in the Ten Commandments. Sometimes these are characterized as the Judeo-Christian ethic, but I do not want to define my priorities so as to exclude the nonreligious who believe in such virtues.

In the recent past, many researchers and some educators have favored approaches that have lessened the impact of traditional values throughout formal education, and their rationales for such antitraditional perspectives have been multifold. The views I express in this chapter are, however, frankly sympathetic to many traditional perspectives.

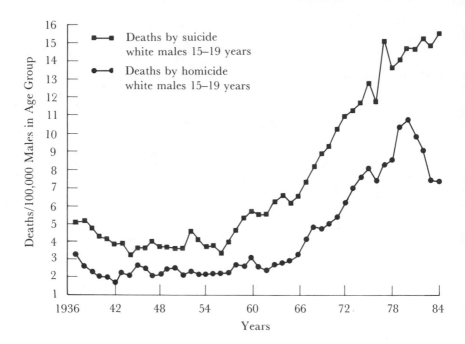

Figure 2-1.
Changes in the Rates of Homicide and Suicide
Among White Males, Ages 15–19
(1936–84)

RELEVANT DATA

One reason for such sympathy is that there are considerable hard data showing substantial long-term increases in the disorderly conduct of young Americans (Uhlenberg and Eggebeen 1986). Some of these trends are presented in the accompanying graphs (Wynne and Hess 1986). Based on the most recent data, the graphs show notable increases in the rates of adolescent death by homicide and suicide (Figure 2–1), and in the rates of out-of-wedlock births (Figure 2–2). The data focus on whites—our more advantaged population—to emphasize that such shifts are unrelated to race or to the more extreme levels of poverty.

Figure 2–2 shows that the rates of out-of-wedlock births have steadily increased since the first national data were compiled in 1940.

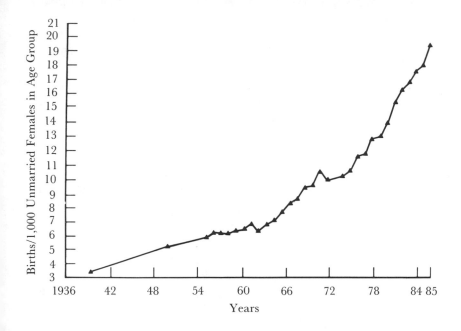

Figure 2-2.
Changes in the Rates of Illegitimate Births
Among Whites, Ages 15–19
(1940–85)

Figure 2–1 reveals that death rates of males by suicide and homicide also show powerful patterns of increase, but have somewhat moderated in the recent past. Between the early 1940s and 1984, the rates of death by homicide and by suicide among male adolescents increased, respectively, 441 percent and 479 percent. Between 1940 and 1985, the rates of out-of-wedlock births to adolescents increased 621 percent. In the last decade, all these rates attained the highest points in our history.

The rise in out-of-wedlock births occurred during an era when birth control materials, sex education, and abortion were all made more available to adolescents. These trends might have led one to forecast a decline in out-of-wedlock births—the opposite of what happened. While the data on homicide do not tell us who the murderers are, other research discloses that most murders are committed by persons of the same age as the victim. The relationship between suicide and morality may seem more problematic. But we are not in an age where most adolescents are subjected to extraordinary poverty or enormous work demands. The typical interpretation of the increase in suicides would be that many young persons lack the determination and self-control typical of earlier generations; and surely the decline in such characteristics has moral implications.

Reference should also be made to drug use by youth. National surveys disclose that in 1969, 21 percent of the high school seniors admitted to "ever using" marijuana. The comparable figures for 1980 and 1985 were 60.2 percent and 54.2 percent (Wynne and Hess 1986). It is likely that the equivalent figure for 1960, if it were available, would be far lower than 21 percent. As in the homicide and suicide data, we have recently seen a modest decline in youth drug use.

The precise relationship between such spreading youth disorder and the diffusion of antitraditional values in education is necessarily a matter of dispute. It would unfairly burden this chapter to offer a detailed explication of that relationship. However, there is a group of authorities who would undoubtedly argue for attributing a form of causal relationship to shifts in values and the aggravated youth disorder. Those authorities will be directly referenced and briefly discussed later in this chapter; their opinions form the justification for the frankly protradition position underlying this chapter.

MODES OF ADULT INTERVENTION

Adult intervention is needed to help young people grow up. Consequently, an important threshold question arises: How shall adults develop conceptual structure to direct and evaluate their systems of intervention? If we want to do something to improve youth conduct, what forms of research and theory building should we apply to plan our intervention?

One technique would be to hypothesize about certain human developmental and psychological characteristics. Then, we might gradually collect experimental and natural data. Our aim would be to invent some efficacious and novel means of intervention. The assumption underlying this approach is that all existing techniques are seriously deficient; our challenge is to develop a dramatically new and more effective device.

environments

An alternative technique is to observe youth-youth and youth-adult interaction in a variety of existing environments. We could then identify the environments in which more wholesome forms of interaction occur. The assumption underlying this approach is that some existing techniques are relatively efficacious. Our need is to identify those techniques and then to discover how such good techniques can be disseminated and further improved.

Points of Difference

The two proposed techniques are not mutually exclusive, but they differ in obvious ways. Without unduly extending the issue, one might consider that the tensions between the techniques have some relevance to the observations of Edmund Burke (1966). In his reflections on the French Revolution and in his other writings, Burke was deeply concerned with the sympathies of the revolutionaries for large-scale, dramatic efforts to change radically the nature of society or groups of human beings. He contrasted such sympathies with more incremental reform, largely based on the application of preexisting principles and traditional wisdom. For Burke, the more dramatic effort had the attraction of novelty, and it provided special prestige for intellectuals. However, far too often such efforts were distorted by utopian visions. As a result, they led to aggravated disorder and the abuse of authority. There are notable parallels between Burke's critique and the recent tendencies of some reforms (affecting moral education) to prescribe dramatically novel approaches in order to raise students' moral sensibilities to unprecedented levels.

In supervising my students' research in school, I have tacitly taken a position akin to Burke's. That position assumes that some educators are now doing good things, and that we should avoid pursuing novelty for novelty's sake. Thus, my students have tried to identify the ways that some existing schools are now effectively shaping pupil behavior in constructive fashions.

The concept of character is another theme underlying this research. The word "character" is rooted in the Greek verb "to mark." As R. S. Peters (1963) observed, the theme of marking reminds us that character is basically composed of observable conduct or words—or of refraining from certain conduct or words.

Despite this stress on observation, the concept is not purely behaviorist. Most thoughtful persons would recognize that a person's character is strongly affected by his state of mind. However, despite this recognition, the emphasis underlying the concept is on conduct that can be seen and heard. The modes of observation are basic. We do not need to administer questionnaires or conduct subtle in-depth interviews; all we need to do is watch and listen to people during everyday life. Certainly, some observers of character are more skilled than others. And often issues arise that deserve careful discussion. Still, there is a continuum of citizen involvement in character analysis—from the student council member or McDonald's employee evaluating his or her peers to Plato's reflections in *The Republic*. They all are participating in the ancient and honorable pursuit of character assessment.

Following up on the theme of observation, we should note that the "acts" that reveal character are usually tied to very simple values: telling the truth in the face of temptation, practicing delayed gratification, obeying legitimate authority, displaying helpfulness, and so on. In other words, the acts are only an extension of the traditional Boy—or Girl—Scout virtues. Of course, a good character, as just defined, does not satisfy all moral challenges that confront the young, or adults. But if we could regularly get most persons to display "good character" as it has been defined, we would probably raise the level of morality in the world. After all, when marriages fail for "inadequate" reasons, or crimes are committed, or persons in high office abuse their trust, the roots of such conduct are properly perceived as character related. And so substantially improving human character seems a notable attainment. It is also true that the practice of good character by pupils does not ensure they will display good character as adults, or even always display it away from school. Still, if we could help substantially to improve the character displayed by pupils in and around schools, it would be a notable attainment.

THE ROLE OF THEORY

The concept of simply engaging in "raw" observation, without some form of theory, is naive. Any complex environment, such as a school, is too large and diffuse for us to encompass all the phenomena that occur. To ensure that the observers ask the right questions, we must have a theory or a basis to provide perspective for our research. It should be noted that the perspective of my research has been rooted in the work of such theorists as Burke (1966), Emile Durkheim (1973), George Homans (1950), Orrin Klapp (1969), Sigmund Freud (1930), B. F. Skinner (1971), and James S. Coleman (1961), who throughout their works have recurrently stressed themes such as the nature and quality of social life in environments, the tangible and symbolic incentive systems prevailing, the virtues of conducting cross-environmental comparisons, and the need for persons who have authority to apply it with imagination, determination, and vigor.

These apparently diverse authorities are related by their some-what pessimistic views of human nature, and by their acceptance of the necessary role of hierarchy in human life. Their writings represent persisting intellectual themes. The fact that such a medley of authors offers such a coherent body of conclusions is striking evidence of the persisting and intellectual vitality of their positions. Given that vitality, it is not surprising that such critiques are again rising in urgency in our own era, particularly with reference to education. For example, a recent national report on moral education, widely publicized by the Association for Supervision and Curriculum Development, gave considerable emphasis to the work of Durkheim, whom most practicing educators would view as a relatively esoteric source (Ryan 1988, p. 17).

Putting the matter hypothetically, the authorities would propose that "good" youth environments—including schools—will place young persons into persisting, relatively stable groups under general adult direction and monitoring, providing the members of such groups with significant collective and individual responsibilities, and maintaining systems of values, symbols, and reinforcement that encourage group members to move toward traditional adult life. Conversely, youth environments that do not satisfy the hypothesis will be more generally characterized by disorder and withdrawal.

Touching on the matter of academic disciplines, one might say that my authorities are more concerned with sociology than psychology—with the group opposed to the individual. None of them is a totalitarian, or against all forms of personal development. But it is true that, compared to many psychologists, they place more weight on the development of wholesome groups than on the development of wholesome individuals. If they were defaulted for their diminishment of individual development, they would probably say that on the whole, it is realistic to imagine that we will develop many sound people without sound groups. Furthermore, many pro-individual efforts are so inimical to wholesome group formation that we end up with both unsound groups and unsound individuals.

Another characteristic of my authorities also deserves note: their support for pupil discipline, that is, the suppression of "bad" conduct. Indeed, to Durkheim, discipline was the first element of moral education. Perhaps this interest in discipline is related to concern for wholesome groups: it is impossible for groups to persist unless their members observe codes of discipline. Furthermore, the authorities would all recognize that the maintenance of discipline is rarely something to be taken for granted. As Freud observed, citing Hobbs, "Man is the wolf to man." Thus, they would see as naive policies that treated discipline as the easy by-product of making pupils happy, or as the outcome of skillfully managed discussion groups. On most occasions they would assume that maintaining discipline also involves attention to well-drafted codes of prohibition, occasional reiteration of rules, uniform patterns of serious enforcement, and the application of consequential punishment.

Some passing reference should be made to the research directly affecting public policy about character development. Leming's view of this research is informative (1981). In the late 1920s—at a time when many academics were seriously interested in "character" as a research and policy issue—Hartshorne and his colleagues developed a body of research that undercut such concerns. (Hartshorne and May 1928, 1929; Hartshorne, May, and Shuttleworth 1930). The general tenor of that research was that particular techniques of character training—such as in-class discussion, or even practicing helping activities—bore little or no significant relationship to pupils' later general patterns of moral conduct. These findings helped lead to a decline in interest in character as a research and policy issue. However, recent and more sophisticated research (and further analysis of the original data of the 1920s) has led many researchers to conclude that there is a reasonable degree of generalizability to character-related instruction and activities: people trained to practice a virtue in one context are likely to continue to practice adaptations of that virtue in other contexts (Rushton 1984). Further, we now understand, much better than was understood in the 1920s, how difficult it is to affect normal human conduct by any means. The process of moral shaping is enormously incremental, cumulative, and complex. To prove that any particular approach produces persisting, statistically significant effects on observable conduct is a notable accomplishment. Indeed, many of the systems of moral shaping popular in the recent past have failed to satisfy that test.

A PATTERN OF RESEARCH

I have developed a relevant pattern of research by means of a semiheuristic process (Wynne 1980), which was partly influenced by my former legal training. For instance, my knowledge of the rules of evidence led me gradually to give considerable weight to diverse school documents (e.g., discipline codes, faculty handbooks, materials posted on walls and in hallways). My students brought the originals, or copies, of such texts back to the college class. There they were examined, analyzed, and compared to equivalent documents from other schools. Inquiries were then made in the school about the circulation of such materials. When the documents enunciated policies, we watched school activities to see if the policies were observed. The documents also provided useful cross-checks to my students' field observations: if their observations disagreed with the documents, such conflicts were carefully examined.

Eventually, a relatively uniform process evolved. I provided graduate and undergraduate students with in-class instruction in school observation. Such instruction involved teaching the elements of a "good school checklist" (Wynne n.d.). Grounded on the theories and authorities cited earlier, the list includes about 150 items arranged in a hierarchy of categories and subcategories. In other words, it translates the principles articulated by theorists and researchers into a body of concrete school practices and policies.

For example, most of my authorities are sympathetic to ceremony and tradition. Thus, they would regard school assemblies as important occasions for articulating and emphasizing the moral values of a school. I therefore asked my students to report on the frequency, length, and nature of the assemblies in the schools they studied. If possible, they were to observe one or more assemblies. My students found schools, obtained access, and produced written reports of their observations, including appendices with documents (and sometimes photographs).

This comparatively elementary plan was blessed by a fortuitous circumstance. The students often went back to schools they had attended, or to those their children were attending, or to where they were working as teachers. And, my students come from an extraordinary variety of circumstances; thus I have collected information on almost every kind of school: ghetto elementary school, suburban flagship high schools, so-called free schools, traditional Catholic high schools, exclusive and costly private secular elementary and high schools, evangelical Christian academies, Hebrew day schools, and even a Lithuanian-American Saturday School. I have reviewed about four hundred such reports over fifteen years. Furthermore, some of the reports have covered the same school five times over a number of years.

The basic data for the reports were derived from simple listening; interviews of students, parents, teachers, and administrators; visual observation; and collecting public and semipublic documents about the school. All these data provide evidence about the values practiced and reinforced in the school. One can also learn much about a school's moral environment from reading a high school student newspaper; one will learn even more from reading five such papers from different schools.

Immediate Conclusions

Schools differ enormously in their policies on pupil discipline and character development. Similarly, the patterns of pupil discipline and of character displayed vary widely among different schools. These differences not only are affected by the institutional structure of the school—that is, whether it is public or private, suburban or urban, or elementary or secondary—but also are shaped by community variables and by the values of the principal and faculty.

In one Chicago public elementary school, the teachers gather each Friday in the teacher's lounge and end the work week by having coffee and pastries together for fifteen minutes during the school day. During this time the classes (K through 7) in the school—which is not in an affluent neighborhood—are all watched by the eighth graders, and excellent order prevails. In another Chicago public elementary school, each teacher keeps the door to his or her classroom locked during the day, to protect himself or herself and the class from dangerous intruders. At the end of the day, faculty and pupils flee the building as if they were leaving a sinking ship. In one suburban elementary school, my students observed that on Saturday afternoons it was common to see teachers' cars in the parking lot; the teachers spend a weekend day organizing their bulletin boards and doing other uncompensated in-room decoration. In another suburban elementary school, the teachers were bitterly angry with the principal, hostile and mistrustful of each other, and interested in having only minimal school responsibilities.

My intuitive conclusion, based on my student's work and my own analyses, is that (a) schools vary widely in the forms of procharacter and discipline practices they apply, (b) average levels of good character displayed by pupils in separate schools vary considerably, and (c) allowing for socioeconomic variables, good or bad school policies strongly affected the average character of pupils in a school. There is perhaps a normal curve of distribution that describes the quality of pro- or anticharacter policies applied in different schools. Most schools are near the middle of the curve in their efficacy, some schools are very bad, and some are very good.

One important test of a school's effectiveness in character development is the quality of relationships among the faculty (and between the faculty and other adults in authority) in the school. Student character development is the outcome of relationships of trust, dedication, good humor, and obedience prevailing among the faculty. It is true that these important general values must be transformed into policies and practices ultimately to affect students. However, the base for such policies is first a foundation of adult harmony.

To explore further the apparent differences among schools regarding character-related policies, I worked with many Chicago-area educators to develop a school recognition program—the "For Character School Recognition Program" (Wynne 1983, 1985, 1987). That program identified and recognized public and private Chicago-area elementary and secondary schools doing an exemplary job in developing pupil character and increasing academic achievement. The basic instrument of the recognition process was a form containing about seventy-five items. The form essentially asked the school to estimate the frequency with which certain patterns of desirable conduct occur around the school. These conducts were (a) acts of helping behavior, often simply participation in extracurricular activities, (b) rewards and recognition provided for individuals or groups for such conduct, and (c) acts of faculty cooperation, teacher-administrator engagement, and faculty-parent contacts.

"Better" schools were ones whose forms disclosed higher levels of such conduct than other similar schools (e.g., ghetto public elementary schools were compared to other public elementary schools in poor areas). Finalist schools were visited to cross-check the accuracy of the data on their entry forms. The program has just completed its third cycle. It has reviewed, over three cycles, the applications of about 290 schools and, after a relatively elaborate screening process, finally identified 53 winners. These winners represent a variety of schools serving different communities and age groups. The winning schools are environments wherein visitors see humane relationships accompanied by efficient and purposeful academic learning. Many site visitors—usually experienced educators—who have evaluated such schools have voiced similar conclusions.

As suggested, the "virtues" found in winning schools necessarily vary, depending on many circumstances. But some general themes can be indicated:

High levels of communication exist among the faculty, and among faculty, pupils, and parents.

Good pupil discipline, and the encouragement of helping conduct (e.g., pupil-to-pupil tutoring, extracurricular activities, pupils as teacher aides, fund raising by pupils) are both high priorities in the school.

Elaborate systems of recognition exist to foster both prosocial conduct and academic learning.

The adults are not clock watchers, but rather model strong engagement.

People generally enjoy their work; levels of burnout are low .

New faculty are quickly socialized to the existing supportive environment (or hired due to their evident sympathy with it), or are encouraged and compelled to leave.

Let me illustrate these themes with an example. I am currently doing site research in one of the winning public elementary schools that is located in a moderately difficult environment (i.e., an area where more than 50 percent of the families of students were at or below the poverty line as defined by the federal government). The school does not always succeed with its pupils. But one thing that is evident is that the faculty does not give up easily.

I asked one eighth grader how she felt about the school:

"It's a good school."
"Why?"

"Because they get you to learn."
"How?"
"Mostly by making you do your homework, and showing you how to do it. I went to another school 'til fifth grade, and the teachers didn't care if you even did your homework. Here, if you don't do it, they get mad and yell at you."

The relationship between pupil character and academic learning in the excellent schools is relevant. It is especially important since many theories of moral development—which offer prescriptions to educators —say little about academic learning. But the traditional concept of character sees it as closely related to academic commitment—at least while the young person is acting as a student (as compared to while playing baseball or babysitting). Students with good character are not necessarily extraordinary in academics, but they typically give academics a "good try." Similarly, teachers who help students develop good character also treat academic learning as important. Academics and character are coincident, since persons with character are by definition industrious. While they are students, the young should be industrious about the business of the school—academic learning. Similarly, the adults in schools, to model good character, must strive to help pupils learn. Of course, some poor students, and even some unindustrious ("lazy"?) students may still possess, or later develop, good character. But the basic assumption regarding academics is that students are not helped to develop good character by a school that is not true to its proclaimed purpose, which is to encourage students to learn academics.

At this time, pursuant to a grant from the U.S. Department of Education, my colleagues and I are analyzing the data we have collected in the For Character program, plus supplementary data. We are testing the hypothesis that schools that stress character development will simultaneously tend to give greater emphasis to academics (as measured by various indicators) than do schools that do not emphasize pupil character. Our preliminary analysis tends to confirm this hypothesis.

Tentative Conclusions

Schools that effectively assist pupil character development apply— both deliberately and intuitively—a relatively traditional body of practices and theories. In particular, these schools are

Directed by adults who exercise their authority toward faculty and
   students in a firm, sensitive, and imaginative manner, and who
   are committed to both academics and pupil character development;

Staffed by dedicated faculty who make vigorous demands on pupils
   and each other;

Structured so that pupils are surrounded by a variety of opportunities
   for them to practice helping (prosocial) conduct;

Managed to provide pupils—both individually and collectively—with
   many forms of recognition for good conduct;

Oriented toward maintaining systems of symbols, slogans, ceremonies, and songs that heighten pupils' collective identities;

Dedicated to maintaining pupil discipline, via clear, widely disseminated discipline codes that are vigorously enforced and backed up
   with vital consequences;

Committed to academic instruction and assign pupils significant
   homework and otherwise stress appropriate academic rigor;

Sensitive to the need to develop collective pupil loyalties to particular
   classes, clubs, athletic groups, and other subentities in the school;

Sympathetic to the values of the external adult society, and perceive it
   as largely supportive and concerned with the problems of the
   young;

Always able to use more money to improve their programs, but rarely
   regard lack of money as an excuse for serious program deficien-
   cies;

Open to enlisting the help, counsel, and support of parents and other
   external adults, but willing to propose important constructive
   changes in the face of (sometimes) ill-informed parent resistance;
   and

Disposed to define "good character" in relatively immediate and
   traditional terms.

Implications

I presented in the beginning of this chapter data about the long-
term rise in certain forms of disorder among young Americans. It is
possible that one of the several causes of the increase has been the
declining power of American schools to stimulate good character
among youth. At least, sophisticated readers would probably agree
that American schools are less likely now than in the past to apply the

character-development policies identified in this paper. Whether these policies are good or bad, they are less common than they once were. The causes for that shift are multifold.

The authority of principals over faculty and pupils and the authority of teachers over pupils have both been lessened by court decisions and by changing intellectual opinion. Principals' authority has also been weakened through the spread of teachers' unions and through growing school bureaucracies. As schools have become larger, more segmented, and more secularized, human relations have become more transitory and diffuse. Furthermore, developing pupil character obviously requires faculty members to work hard and display commitment. Such traits are always scarce and valuable. However, it is still my impression that for numerous reasons far too many teachers today are prone to substitute formalism for deep engagement with their pupils. And, as Willard Waller (1932) observed, "Formalism is psychically cheap" (p. 433). Finally, parental counsel, support, and monitoring have become less available to educators as various programs and technological improvements have distanced schools from their community roots.

Something should also be said about the multifold "causes" of such changes. These changes have occurred partly through the single-purposed pursuit of certain goals—often admirable—without regard to the effects the goals will have on other activities. Thus we have had school consolidation and the creation of magnet and areawide schools to tap broad catchment areas and to advance economies of scale, desegregation, and certain forms of school specialization. In addition, at different times the formation of teachers' unions was encouraged to foster school reform. Many philosophic factors have also had influence (e.g., the rising appreciation of individualism, or the aggravated hostility toward the practice of vital authority). And court decisions have had a variety of constraining effects. But whatever the multifold motives for the innovations, it is safe to say that the outcomes have often shifted far from the original intentions of the innovators. Whatever the effects of those shifts, it is true that the "innovations" have by now collected their pool of vested supporters. Thus, even while their charm has diminished, they have the resilience of being "established."

But it is still provocative to realize that despite these many changes many schools still apply traditional—and apparently effective—procharacter policies.

Thus, wholesome policies persist—or sometimes even revive

phoenix-like from the ashes—because they satisfy certain basic human needs. Adults who routinely deal with children and adolescents are gradually driven to recognize that adult-child relationships in schools cannot and should not be governed by so-called democratic theories. Perhaps such theories can be applied in transitory relationships; however, persisting adult-child relationships will tend to be based on more realistic concepts. In self-defense, the adults will exercise their inherent authority. Again, despite the bureaucratic structures that shape too many teacher-pupil contacts, many of the adults involved are gradually provoked to shape relations on more human, engaged principles. They simply find bureaucratic forms too sterile.

The truth is that certain homeostatic forces come into play in persisting adult-youth relationships. Traditional principles revive themselves. Basically, the adults begin to act like grownups, and the children are expected to act like children—and to be treated that way. This is partly what is meant by the remark, often reiterated to the young, that "You will feel different when you have your own children."

A typical example of such "normal" engagement came to my attention in a winning school where I am doing fieldwork. The assistant principal told me of a thirteen-year-old pupil who was in "deep trouble." She then listed the gruesome details of this trouble and easily convinced me that her phrase was not overstated. As an incidental part of her story, she remarked that in a desperate effort to raise the student's morale and increase his meager academic skills, she had arranged for her (the assistant principal's) sister, a mature woman, to come to school as a volunteer to tutor the pupil. The sister does not live in the neighborhood, but she has occasional free time and likes to help the assistant principal on special projects. I am certain that if I asked the assistant principal why she was going so far beyond the call of duty she would probably say, "One can't just sit there and give up on a thirteen-year-old. We may fail, but we have to make a real try." And many adults, with reasonable reinforcement, are disposed to act in such an engaged fashion. But such charity cannot be mobilized by appealing to job descriptions.

The Role of Researchers and Educational Leaders

The preceding analysis suggests researchers and educational leaders are provided with a marvelous opportunity and challenge. Many good things are now underway in schools. But probably the majority of schools and colleges—and my analysis is also even more applicable to higher education—are falling distressingly short of their potential in fostering character development. Furthermore, there are innumerable obstacles to the improvement of the present situation. Thus, the challenge is to

Define what we mean by character;

Identify the characteristics of good schools and policies that foster good character in pupils;

Discover and analyze the many barriers to improvement in less-than-satisfactory schools; and

Try to discover ways good policies can be improved.

The challenge is very ambitious. However, it is moderated when we recognize that our responsibility is not so much to discover and disseminate some new product but is instead to identify the policies applied by our allies—the many educators now concerned with character development in students. Then, we must work with those allies to spread and improve these practices. This concept of alliance—compared to simply delivering our enlightened word to the benighted and uninformed—is congruent with the profound traditions associated with the word "character." For, after all, persons of good character must be prepared to solicit the counsel of others and to display humility and deference, especially to those actually on the firing line.

REFERENCES

Burke, Edmund. *Reflections on the Revolution in France*. New Rochelle, N. Y.: Arlington House, 1966.

Coleman, James S. *The Adolescent Society*. New York: Free Press, 1961.

Durkheim, Emile. *Moral Education*. New York: Free Press, 1973.

Freud, Sigmund. *Civilization and Its Discontents*. London: Hogarth Press, 1930.

Hartshorne, Hugh, and May, Mark A. *Studies in the Nature of Character*. Vol. 1 *Studies in Deceit*. New York: Macmillan, 1928.

Hartshorne, Hugh, and May, Mark A. *Studies in the Nature of Character*. Vol. 2. *Studies in Self-Control*. New York: Macmillan, 1929.

Hartshorne, Hugh; May, Mark A.; and Shuttleworth, F. K. *Studies in the Organization of Character*. New York: Macmillan, 1930.

Homans, George. *The Human Group*. New York: Harcourt and Brace, 1950.

Klapp, Orrin E. *The Collective Search for Identity*. New York: Holt, Rinehart and Winston, 1969.

Leming, James S. "On the Limits of Rational Moral Education," *Theory and Research in Social Education* 9 (Spring 1981): 7–33.

Peters, R. S. "Reason and Habit: The Paradox of Moral Education." In *Moral Education in a Changing Society*, ed. W. R. Niblett. London: Farber and Farber, 1963.

Rushton, Philip. "The Altruistic Personality." In *Development and Maintenance of Prosocial Behavior*, ed. Erving Staub, pp. 271–90. New York: Plenum, 1984.

Ryan, Kevin, ed. *Moral Education in the Life of the School*. Washington, D. C.: Association for Supervision and Curriculum Development, 1988.

Skinner, B. F. *Beyond Freedom and Dignity*. New York: Alfred A. Knopf, 1971.

Uhlenberg, P., and Eggebeen, D. A. "The Declining Well-Being of American Adolescents," *Public Interest*, no. 82 (Winter 1986): 25–38.

Waller, Willard. *The Sociology of Teaching*. New York: Wiley, 1932.

Wynne, Edward A. *The Good School Checklist*. Chicago: Character, Inc.,n.d.

Wynne, Edward A. *Looking At Schools*. Lexington, Mass.: Heath Lexington, 1980.

Wynne, Edward A. *Chicago Area Award Winning Schools, 1982–83*. Chicago: Regan Communications, 1983.

Wynne, Edward A. *Chicago Area Award Winning Schools, 1984–85*. Chicago: College of Education, University of Illinois at Chicago, 1985.

Wynne, Edward A. *Chicago Award Winning Schools, 1987*. Chicago: College of Education, University of Illinois at Chicago, 1987.

Wynne, Edward A., and Hess, M. "Long-term Trends in Youth Conduct," *Educational Evaluation and Policy Analysis* 8 (Fall 1986): 294–308.

3

Character Education: Toward a Preliminary Consensus

Herbert J. Walberg and Edward A. Wynne

As many of the chapters in this volume attest, a variety of philosophical, psychological, and other approaches may be taken in defining, and in attempting to enhance, student character. Our approach has been to attempt to identify principles, policies, and practices for which a reasonable degree of consensus can be found among citizens, experts, and practicing educators. In the first part of this chapter, we describe a project to call attention to the importance of character education in schools and to develop some specific policies for which a consensus of opinion could be found among a group of sociologists, psychologists, philosophers, and policy analysts. In the second part, we present a list of school practices believed by experts and practitioners to contribute to the development of character.

A REFORM REPORT ON CHARACTER

Many education reform reports issued within the past five years have been deservedly preoccupied with increasing student achievement. But nearly all have ignored character. For this reason, we, together with a number of other educators and citizens, wrote and published the policy statement, *Developing Character: Transmitting*

Knowledge (Wynne and Walberg 1984). In the report, we define "character" as "engaging in morally relevant conduct or words, or refraining from certain conduct or words." Character, good or bad, is observable in one's conduct. Of course, character and conduct are significantly affected by our feelings and values. But an important test of good or moral feelings is whether we act in an appropriate fashion.

One unique element of our statement is its joint focus on the educational goals of character development and academics. These two goals are not mutually exclusive, but complementary (Wynne and Walberg 1985). We will first amplify this matter of goal complementarity and then briefly outline the report's recommendations.

Good character development in students is unlikely to occur unless the school treats its academic program seriously. This means that teachers should assign significant homework, test students and evaluate them in other ways (appropriate to their age level), provide a sound curriculum, and view teaching and academic learning as important. Without such academic activities, students will correctly see that their school time is not being spent in a purposeful fashion and that their teachers are not working very hard. From these observations, students might conclude that their time in school is not spent in a way that adults think profitable, and that their teachers are irresponsible employees. Thus, if teachers do not provide academic activities, students might learn "bad" lessons about character.

Of course, if asked what they want in school, many students would say they want little homework, nondemanding teachers, freedom from exams, and so on. Some schools and teachers would thus excuse their academic laxity by pointing out that they are satisfying students' wishes for lessened academic pressures. However, developing good student character requires more than pandering to the young. An important element of acquiring character is learning how to be committed, and how to push toward significant accomplishment. If students perceive school as a lackadaisical experience, they may develop lackadaisical approaches to other areas of character expression. They will seek easy ways out, become clock watchers, and otherwise display poor character traits. Many former students believe that they were not worked hard enough during their school years. For example, 67 percent of all freshmen entering college in the fall of 1984 agreed that the grading standards in their high schools were "too casy" (Astin 1984).

Academic work and the pursuit of excellence are also relevant to another aspect of character. Good character development, even viewed solely from an affective perspective, requires hard work by both students and faculty. It is not easy for students to learn and practice good behavior, nor for faculty to press students in this direction. If a school is focused on character development and students and adults are both working hard, it is unlikely that those educators have acquiesced to both a lax and an indifferent academic program. What we would expect is that teachers who work hard helping character development—who do not watch the clock, who develop and carry out significant activities, and who make serious demands on students—will simultaneously insist that their students become literate, learn mathematics, and engage themselves in the academic aspects of the school.

Academic work is also relevant to character development because many traditional approaches to character development have partly relied on academic techniques and materials. Poems, plays, and other literature have been read, discussed, and memorized to develop good character. History and biography have been used to provide role models, strengthen group identification, broaden students' time horizons, and increase their capability to delay gratification. Student-to-student tutoring and other forms of assistance to learning have been applied to develop helping conduct in and around school. Many elements in a cognitively demanding curriculum can be used, and often have been, to assist character development. But if the curriculum is given low priority or is presented in an undemanding fashion, then it has little potential to promote character development.

Good character also requires obedience to legitimate authority. This trait is obviously learned partly through habit and practice. Teachers are the most prominent extrafamily authority figures that students meet. The formal academic program is a central area in which teachers exercise their authority. Teachers and school administrators should insist that students arrive on time, pay attention in class, apply themselves to recitation, and otherwise display commitment. If teachers do not make such demands on students and monitor their compliance, important opportunities for building character are slighted.

Character May Help Academics

Character development may be as important for the academic program as academics are for character. Accepting discipline is one important part of character development. And yet it is well known that many teachers, when trying to teach academics, find much of their energies dedicated to maintaining student discipline. Thus, academics often proceed poorly because too much time is spent on discipline matters such as student disruptions of class, cuts and late arrivals, gross student inattention, cheating, and public disrespect for teachers. To become academically successful, schools must master the matter of student discipline. But the relationship between student academic learning and character goes even deeper, though the issue is somewhat complicated. The underlying matter is the topic of students' group life. And, since displaying good character essentially involves our relationships with others, schools that "teach" character must be concerned with the nature of students' group life.

Researchers such as James S. Coleman (1961) have demonstrated that many students find the grading structures used in many schools frustrating. To attain good grades, students must participate in highly individualistic academic competition; they must display excellence in academics by demonstrating their superiority over other students. Coleman concluded that many students resent the more successful students, who sometimes implicitly "put down" the less successful students. Some potentially able students may even withdraw from such divisive competition. Thus, high school students often segregate themselves into various cliques, and many of these cliques are hostile to the academic goals of the school. In many high schools, perhaps only 20 to 30 percent of the students are seriously enlisted in the school's academic programs. The others may only be "coasting."

Some of these cliques, or peer groups, pursue goals (e.g., athletics) that are indifferent to the school's academic goals. And some of the groups even pursue goals (e.g., delinquency) that are actively hostile to the school's declared purpose.

Citizens, educators, and parents determined to improve student character must monitor and influence the quality of students' peer groups. If possible, destructive peer groups must be suppressed. And peer groups must be formed—or redirected—to pursue goals in harmony with the school's formal goals: academics and character development. Coleman and his scholarly successors proposed that schools should devise more academic activities that could be conducted by groups of students working together, although competition among groups of students might be constructive. The International Society for the Study of Cooperation in Education is one outgrowth of this proposal. And many forms of cooperative learning activities—

some relatively "traditional" and others novel—have been identified and developed to foster such cooperative purposes (see chapters by Slavin and by Johnson in Walberg 1979).

Individualistic academic competition may overwhelm or otherwise discourage some students, and may lower overall school learning rates. Well-designed cooperative learning can overcome some of these difficulties. Cooperative learning can also facilitate the formation of student groups that build social skills and embrace teamwork. Cooperative groups can incidentally encourage the students to practice politeness, tact, loyalty, and many other virtues that constitute good character, and those virtues can be harnessed to meet academic ends while their development is simultaneously monitored and guided by classroom teachers.

The Larger Perspective

It may be helpful to consider the analysis just presented in an overall perspective. Lately, diverse forms of affective education have been proposed and tried that have apparently not helped improve student conduct, have been generally unrelated to school academic programs, or may have even been hostile to such programs. We have in mind values clarification and many forms of sex and drug education, although the elements of these programs have varied. There is little or no evidence that these programs have improved student character by conduct-related measures. Indeed, evidence shows that student conduct has suffered a long-term decline and that, during this same period, academic demands on students have generally slackened. Many affect-oriented approaches for improving character were tried during an era of slackening academic demands.

In sum, in American education during the recent past, both affective education and academic education tended to reduce demands on students. But it appears that neither student character nor academic learning was enhanced. Our view is that character and academic education must concurrently make significant and complementary demands on students.

Some foreign schools, for example, stress academics and student character development simultaneously. And "character" means practicing good discipline and being positively helpful to one's peers and to all adults. For instance, Japanese elementary schools are famous for their academic focus. They require much homework and have a long academic year. At the same time, these schools stress student helpfulness, character-developing extracurricular activities, firm discipline, and teacher-led discussions stressing the transmission of traditional virtues (U.S. Department of Education 1987). We might add that the Japanese enjoy some of the lowest rates of crime and delinquency.

But it is not solely a matter of foreign educational patterns. In fact, a number of American public and private schools have approximately equivalent priorities. Edward Wynne is involved in a school-recognition program in the Chicago area that identifies and honors public and private schools that stress both academics and character development. The advisory board of the program includes many practicing educators and administrators. Through three successive recognition cycles, hundreds of schools have chosen to solicit recognition. After careful screening, including site visits by teams, fifty-three schools—public and private, secondary and elementary, and suburban and urban—have been publicly recognized for their exemplary attainments.

The elaborate descriptive data developed by the program are convincing evidence that many practicing American educators do successfully pursue the twin goals of academics and student character. Indeed, it is probably no accident that many of the schools recognized had already established noteworthy reputations among educators as good schools. In other words, if we pay serious attention to the qualities that many educators now praise or try to attain, we will discover that some schools are already deeply engaged in encouraging both academic learning and good character.

The Statement's Recommendation

There has been an alarming, long-term rise in many serious forms of youth disorder. These alarming trends in national indicators of character pathologies include American youth from all races and economic backgrounds. The schools are surely not the sole cause for problems among the young, but educators, working with citizens, parents, and others, can do some things to diminish such problems. Our report identifies some of the most promising efforts:

1. Students, at all grade levels, should more frequently be assigned group responsibilities for academic and school-related
   activities. The assignments should stress both individual and

group accomplishment and should be evaluated through grades and other forms of recognition. The activities should emphasize service to others. They might include student activities with classmates, with students in other classes, and with or for community members. Typical activities include student-to-student tutoring; "team" academic projects; student authority over other students (e.g., hall guard, class monitor); many forms of extracurricular activities; and cooperative within-group, school-to-school, class-to-class, and row-to-row academic competitions.

2. School and community service projects appropriately monitored by adults can be conducted by students in all grade levels. In the longer run, such projects may moderate some education costs. We envisage current service employees not as being terminated but as being gradually phased out through turnover and retirement. States and districts might make such service a requirement for high school graduation.

3. Schools should maintain a relatively higher continuity of relationships among students and among students and teachers. Denmark offers an interesting example: A teacher and his or her students often stay together for elementary and much of secondary schooling.

   It is true that for most Western societies increasing discontinuity may be more appropriate as students mature. However, it is desirable, through high school, that each student be able to identify a supportive base group that is frequently engaged with the same responsible adult. This adult should ideally act as a teacher for this group, leading them in significant intellectual and cooperative activities. Some schools now maintain homerooms, which, if properly managed, can help attain this end. But schools within schools, discrete programs in schools, and various extracurricular activities can also be appropriate ways to keep students connected with responsible, caring adults.

4. The subject matter taught should ensure that students learn the basic facts of American civics, geography, and history. They need to know the dates and sequences of important events, major figures and controversies, and the common experiences and diverse contributions of our ancestors, older contemporaries, and ethnic groups. They also need to know

about the components and functions of American government
and the locations of major places in the United States and in
the world. As they mature, students will be expected to analyze
and evaluate such information. But it is first essential that they
learn a core of information.

5. Schools should maintain frequent and high-quality ceremonial
activities. These activities should stress the importance of
group cooperation and individual effort. They should also
focus on the theme of "contribution," including the contributions students have received from past and present Americans
and those that students are making and will be making to our
society and the human race. The occasions should be managed
with taste and imagination, just like any semiaesthetic activity.
The adults involved should participate with enthusiasm and
sincerity—basic requirements for good role-modeling.

6. The management of many recommended activities will usually
be handled at the classroom, local school, and district level.
But many "external" forces maintain policies that constrain
such activities. Some court decisions, for instance, restrict
public schools from considering student character as a criterion for graduation. Tenure laws and union contracts make it
harder to require teachers to display strong commitment. State
regulations may inhibit necessary flexibility in managing extracurricular activities. Public opinion sometimes confuses
effective extracurricular programs with frills (though the distinction is occasionally tricky).

To improve the situation, a combination of local initiative
and external facilitation is necessary. Schools must strive to act
to improve student character. Where there are external constraints, educators must solicit the agencies involved to recon-
sider their policies.

Thus, as our report indicates in greater detail, a number of general
character-development policies can be identified on which some
consensus can be found. We will next report a second effort and
analyze a set of still more specific suggestions for school practices
made by experts and practitioners specializing in character programs.

RATINGS OF SCHOOL CHARACTER PRACTICES

The 91,000-member Association for Supervision and Curriculum Development invited eight national expert scholars and educational practitioners to help identify practices that would contribute to student character or moral education. This organization is, of course, one of the most influential in education, since many of its members are superintendents, principals, curriculum developers, and supervisors.

With permission of the ASCD staff, we listed the fifty potentially desirable practices that emerged from the deliberations and asked the eight members, six of whom responded, to rate their desirability on a five-point scale from "strongly disagree" (to be rated 1) to "unsure, neutral, or don't know" (rated 3) to "strongly agree" (rated 5) on three aspects of each practice:

1. Research Support was defined as the extent to which research supports the effectiveness of the practice in enhancing moral learning.
2. Philosophical Soundness was defined as the degree to which the practice is supported by principled ethical and moral views.
3. In-School Feasibility was defined as the extent to which the practice can be implemented in public elementary and secondary schools.

Inspection of the ratings showed that practices rated highly on one aspect also tended to be rated highly on the other aspects. Therefore, we took the median of the three ratings by each person of each practice before taking the median of ratings by all those responding. This overall rating of each item (reported below) can be viewed as an indication of "overall desirability" by the six members of the expert and practitioner group who responded to our request.

Different groups might yield different ratings, of course, and those we report here are merely exploratory indications. Furthermore, the median ratings we have computed do not reveal the range of agreement and disagreement among the experts themselves. The median ratings are, nonetheless, of some interest. First, most practices received substantial agreement, and a considerable number received strong agreement. Second, the set provides a provisional list of recommendations from which policymakers and practicing educators can select for analysis and implementation, or possibly do their own ratings. Third, it seems that the list might form the basis of more exhaustive research.

We will group the practices into these categories: group and team approaches; ethical and moral approaches; teaching practices; and student cognition, to serve the purpose of discussion, although they might be grouped in other ways.

Group and Team Approaches

The first set of practices appear to have the common element of exploiting the forces of student groups to bring about character development. The practices, in order of the median overall ratings of desirability by the six experts, are as follows:

Extracurricular activities, 5
Community service (including within the school), 5
Promoting good sportsmanship, 5
Cooperative learning, 5
Building community, 5
Appropriate competition, 5
Peer tutoring, 4.5
Home-school partnerships, 4.5
Cross-class activities, 4
Appropriately managing ceremonies and symbols, 4
Bonding to small, knowable groups, 4
Cross-generational interaction, 4
Cooperative governance and cooperative planning, 4
Student support groups, 4
Team competitive activities, 3

Competition among teams was given only a neutral or unsure overall rating, but appropriate competition was given the highest possible rating. Some members of the expert group may have been distinguishing excessive, destructive, or unfair competition from moderate, team, or other forms of constructive competition.

Several practices among students appear to depend on altruism, teamwork, and mutual interest, such as peer tutoring, cooperative learning, extracurricular activities, and sportsmanship. Others such as community service, home-school partnerships, cross-generational interaction, and community service depend on and build extramural bonds and cooperation with adults outside the school.

Ethical and Moral Approaches

Many of the practices in the ethical and moral cluster depend on democracy and an exemplary social or moral order:

Generate caring and love, 5
Strong top commitment to values, 5
Expecting moral behavior, 5
Developing and publishing codes of values, 4.5
Developing moral sensitivity, 4
Common agreement on general principles, 4
Just community, or the "the moral school," 4
Moral dilemma discussions, 4
School organization that promotes continuity in moral education, 4
Moral debates, 3
Creating environments of choice, 3

Several practices are intended to build character on values, caring, and shared commitments. Several are attempts to build character from experiences in rational discussion and decision making to develop an explicit and common understanding within schools.

Moral debates and environments of choice were given low ratings. Perhaps, like competitive team activities, they were given lower ratings because they have the potential to get out of hand. They may, for example, pose conflicts between school and home values and between common shared understandings and subgroup or individualistic preferences.

Teaching Practices

Perhaps because the experts were all professionally interested in moral education or character development, they gave teaching practices somewhat lower ratings on the whole than other approaches:

Using traditional subjects to teach values, 5
Shaping behavior (discipline, rules, expectations), 4.5
Modeling, 4.5

Direct teaching of moral reasoning, 4
Advocating, 4
Teacher authenticity, 4
Empathy training, 4
Rewarding good conduct and punishing bad conduct, 4
Role reversal strategies, 4
Training in persistence, 4
Appropriate confrontation, 4
Dealing with less athletic child on playing field, 4
Reducing emotional frustration, 4
Advisory programs, 3
Clarifying responses, 3

The only practice to get the highest possible rating was the use of the traditional subjects to teach values.

The median rating for many of the other practices, however, was 4 (which corresponds to "Agree" rather than "Strongly Agree"); so their importance should not be dismissed. What might be called inculcation, as well as teaching by personal example, received general agreement as to soundness, support, and feasibility. The teaching practices ranged also from explicit or direct teaching to "insight" methods such as clarifying responses and asking students to act or argue in a role in the reverse of their real beliefs in order to gain an understanding of the views of others.

Student Cognition

The final cluster of practices seems to be "student-centered" in the sense of transferring responsibility and skills to students themselves so that they can think and act in moral and ethical ways—perhaps including their own ways (what psychologists might call intrinsic motivation):

Holding students responsible for their behavior, 5
Developmentally appropriate communication, 5
Prizing diversity and individual differences, 5
Conflict resolution, 4
Training kids to manage their impulses, 4
Problem-solving training, 4
Training in anticipating consequences, 4

Encouraging balance in thought, feeling, and action, 3.5
Developing an inner wisdom, 3

Unimpressive ratings were given to the last two practices concerning balance and wisdom. Perhaps they are too ambitious. Schools may find it more acceptable to increase knowledge and understanding— society is, indeed, calling for it—than to change the balance of inner values and behavior, which are more private, less testable human characteristics. Balance and inner wisdom may sound like virtues of middle or old age—not something the schools can easily accomplish.

CONCLUSIONS

It appears to us that some degree of consensus can be gained among experts and practitioners about issues and practices in moral education and character development. The reform report as well as experts' nominations of superior schools and ratings of character practices show that a fair amount of agreement can be reached about constructive policies and practices.

Most of the experts evidently favor a variety of approaches to character development, since the majority of approaches received agreement. Many of the approaches, moreover, can be used simultaneously and may reinforce one another. Peer tutoring and extracurricular activities, for example, may promote wholesome, constructive friendships.

Like other committee and consensual approaches, however, the issues and practices are not defined with philosophical and psychological rigor; perhaps they gain consensus at a cost of some vagueness. Neither the issues nor the practices have the virtues of other schemes in which the categories are both comprehensive and nonoverlapping. The issues and practices are incompletely specified from either a research or a practical standpoint. For that, the voluminous conceptual, research, and practical literature on the issues and practices— many of which are cited in other chapters in this book—must be consulted.

A consensual approach, nonetheless, may have some practical virtue. Not in two millennia have philosophers agreed on fundamental questions of virtue, values, character, and morals—although many will agree that this set of educational outcomes has been neglected, and that educators, parents, and students can do better (as the ancient Egyptians and Greeks also said). Psychologists may not have gotten much further with a scientific approach. Perhaps it is useful, in the absence of philosophical and scientific consensus, to enumerate the value issues and to develop a list of ends as well as some means that seem likely to accomplish them.

Such an exercise gives policymakers, educators, and students an opportunity to consider a reasonably comprehensive set of issues and ends. The exercise provides them with a knowledge base from which to work; they may add to the list, and define terms rigorously when it suits them; and they can make their own rankings. They may also consider which means are most effective, sound, and feasible.

Common sense and many of the practices themselves suggest that when those most directly involved make these decisions themselves, they are likely not only to have more timely and accurate information but to benefit from the process of decision making. Thus, perhaps the enumeration and lists we have provided here offer not ending but starting points.

REFERENCES

Astin, Alexander, et al. *Annual Report of National Norms for Entering Freshmen: 1984*. Los Angeles, Calif.: Cooperative Institutional Research Program, 1984.

Coleman, James S. *The Adolescent Society*. New York: Free Press, 1961.

U. S. Department of Education. *Japanese Education Today*. Washington, D.C.: U. S. Government Printing Office, 1987.

Walberg, Herbert J. *Educational Environments and Effects*. Berkeley, Calif.: McCutchan Publishing Corporation, 1979.

Wynne, Edward A., and Walberg, Herbert J., eds. *Developing Character: Transmitting Knowledge*. Posen, Ill.: ARL, 1984.

Wynne, Edward A., and Walberg, Herbert J. "The Complementary Goals of Character Development and Academic Excellence," *Educational Leadership* 43: 4 (1985): 15–18.

4

The Child Development Project: Combining Traditional and Developmental Aproaches to Values Education

Marilyn Watson, Daniel Solomon,
Victor Battistich, Eric Schaps, and
Judith Solomon

What can or must a democratic society do to build and maintain a commitment to the common good among its citizens? This question is being asked with increasing frequency in our society. In the 1950s the launching of Sputnik gave impetus to a renewed investment in scientific education; the current impetus for education reform is the declining concern among citizens for the welfare of others in our society.

Funded by the William and Flora Hewlett Foundation, the project described in this chapter was initially formulated as a result of the ideas and efforts of Dyke Brown (Brown and Solomon 1983).

Important contributions to the initial specification of the program and the design of the evaluation were made by Nancy Eisenberg and Joel Moskowitz, and by an Advisory Panel consisting of Marilyn Brewer, Martin Hoffman, Marian Radke-

This is causing educators (e.g., Honig 1985), politicians (e.g., Cuomo as reported by Schmalz 1986) and business leaders (e.g., Akers 1988) to call for renewed emphasis in our schools on the teaching of values and the preparation of children for citizenship in a democracy. In California, a state that often influences the content of textbooks used across the nation, new state frameworks in language arts and social studies explicitly mention the importance of teaching children about core social values such as fairness and concern for human rights and dignity (California State Department of Education 1987, 1988).

Efforts to provide character or values education through school-based programs have been increasing in response to this widely felt need. While all such programs begin with some variation on the question "How can we raise children of good character?" the way they respond to this question depends on their assumptions about how "character" is acquired. Most current programs on values education have been derived from one of two general perspectives about the origins of character: the traditional socialization perspective or the cognitive-developmental perspective.

In this chapter we will describe the Child Development Project (CDP), a longitudinal program focused on the prosocial development of elementary school children that is being conducted in three schools in a suburban middle-class community in Northern California. This program shares some underlying assumptions and classroom procedures with each of the above perspectives, but also differs from each in important ways. The project was initiated after a review of the theoretical and empirical literature on the antecedents of caring, responsible behavior (e.g., Hoffman 1978; Mussen and Eisenberg-Berg 1977; Staub 1978, 1979; Zahn-Waxler, Radke-Yarrow, and King

---

Yarrow, and Ervi Staub. David Johnson, Roger Johnson, Thomas Lickona, and David Weikart have also made helpful contributions. The adaptation or development of instruments and procedures, the training of research workers, the coordination of data collection, and the collection and coding of data was done by Jane Deer, Allyson Rickard, Marc Rosenberg, Carol Stone, and Margaret Tauber. Work on specifying and refining program components, developing specific program activities and approaches, and helping teachers, principals, and parents to understand, support, and implement the program was done by Carole Cooper, Patricia Tuck, Wendy Ritchey, Sylvia Kendzior, Carolyn Hildebrandt, Stefan Dasho, Gail Mandella, Rita Davies, and Lynn Murphy. Kevin DeLucchi has been responsible for substantial portions of the data analysis.

1979) suggested that a long-term and comprehensive school intervention program, delivered primarily by classroom teachers but with
considerable parent involvement, was both feasible and likely to
produce widespread and long-lasting changes in children's prosocial
attitudes, motives, and behaviors.

In the following pages we will describe the underlying assumptions
of the traditional socialization and cognitive-developmental perspectives, compare these assumptions with those that underlie the CDP
program, discuss the process by which the CDP program was developed, and describe the major elements of the program in some detail.
We will then briefly describe the design of the intervention and
summarize our major findings to date concerning program implementation and student outcomes.

UNDERLYING ASSUMPTIONS OF VALUES EDUCATION PROGRAMS

"Good character," according to the traditional socialization perspective, is imparted; that is, children are directly instructed in the
rules and values that a society holds important, and these values are
modeled and reinforced by the significant adults in children's lives.
Programs based on this approach (often called "character education"
programs) usually involve explicit teaching of how to distinguish
"right" from "wrong," explicit and public systems for rewarding
desirable behavior and punishing undesirable behavior, the use of
such important adages as the "Golden Rule," and the provision of
examples of morally correct behavior through either literature or live
models. The traditional socialization perspective is more consistent
with social learning theory and a behaviorist tradition than with the
other major psychological theories of human development (i.e., psy-
choanalytic, humanistic, or constructivist).

The cognitive-developmental perspective sees good character as
resulting from the construction of a personal moral system through
interpersonal interaction and moral reflection and analysis. Programs
that apply this perspective, which derives from the work of Piaget
(1932) and Kohlberg (1969, 1976), generally refer to themselves as
"moral education" or "just community" programs. Educators implementing such programs refrain from moralizing or telling children
what they should think, and stress the importance of natural peer

interaction for the gradual development of moral judgment (Berkowitz 1985; Blatt and Kohlberg 1975; Hersch, Paolitto, and Reimer
1979; Youniss 1980). It is assumed that children in voluntary equal-
status associations who initially act for their own self-interest will,
through the interaction process, come to appreciate the importance of
fairness and justice first for themselves and eventually for all. Once
they arrive at this understanding, they will be inclined to act fairly
and justly. Specific educational programs based on this perspective
usually involve children in discussions of moral dilemmas—either
hypothetical, real, or from literature (Berkowitz 1985; Blatt and
Kohlberg 1975; Power 1979; Rest 1983)—and have more recently
begun providing children with the power to decide about school or
class rules and how justice and fairness will be maintained in their
school community (Power 1979).

The Child Development Project draws its answer to the question
"How can we raise children to become prosocial individuals?" from a
theoretical perspective that overlaps in part with both the traditional
and the cognitive-developmental perspectives. We help teachers and
parents to enhance children's "prosocial" behaviors and attitudes
with a program that is shaped by three general propositions. The first
is that adults must play an active and important role in shaping the
development of children's character; this is consonant with the traditional perspective. The second proposition, shared with the developmental perspective, is that character develops from within the child
on the basis of the child's own thinking and experiences. The third
working assumption is that given an adequate family environment,
children will be disposed to be concerned about others as well as
themselves. This proposition can be viewed as somewhat contrary to
the blank-slate, traditional perspective, and as a slight extension of
the developmental perspective. These assumptions about character
development have led us to combined emphases, in our program, on
both adult teaching and guidance regarding prosocial values, and on
provision of opportunities for children to discuss, reflect on, and apply
these values. Teaching, in other words, is supported with the kind of
practice that we believe will strengthen children's developing prosocial tendencies.

The interventions selected for the CDP program were designed to
influence three different but interrelated systems—affective, cognitive,
and behavioral. We assumed that each of these is important to the
development of prosocial orientations, and that each can be in-

fluenced by several factors. We chose interventions that would alter the school and home environments in ways that: (a) are likely to have effects on the development of all three systems, (b) have strong empirical and theoretical support within one or more theoretical perspectives, and (c) constitute a coherent and mutually reinforcing set of practices when viewed within the context of our propositions about the nature of the child and the social environment (Solomon et al. 1985). For a detailed discussion of the ways in which extant theories and research findings influenced the development of the CDP program, see Battistich, Watson, Solomon, Schaps, and Solomon (forthcoming).

HOW THE CDP PROGRAM CHARACTERIZES THE GOALS OF SOCIALIZATION

The Role of Adults

Children depend on adults for guidance on how to regulate their social interactions, and also for moral wisdom. Many moral decisions involve weighing concerns about the well-being of fellow group members against concerns for the self. It is not always easy or straightforward, however, to know how to balance these concerns in particular situations. As societies determine ways to achieve this balance for different situations, this accumulated moral knowledge can be explained to others and passed on to the next generation, just as with accumulated knowledge about mathematics or the causal order of the world. Thus, once the child has acquired basic cognitive and self-regulating capacities, the main tasks of the "socializer" are to help the child understand the wisdom of the culture, including the ways of his or her social group, and to understand and commit to the complex set of rights and responsibilities inherent in group membership. Socialization is thus essentially teaching in its largest sense, not simply indoctrinating or controlling; and becoming socialized is learning, not simply accepting without question.

The human capacity to develop a moral system that balances individual needs with the needs of the group does not imply that everyone will successfully develop such a balance. Certain environmental conditions may be necessary for this to occur. The CDP program represents one attempt to structure part of the child's environment so as to maximize these conditions.

The Need for Internalized Moral Orientations

No society, not even the most totalitarian, can operate exclusively on the basis of external control and coercion. Surveillance and sanction systems can never be sufficiently ubiquitous to cover all, or even most, situations, and thus every society seeks to develop a citizenry that is able and willing to maintain the common good without promise of reward or threat of punishment. This is, of course, especially true in societies in which the effort is made to keep external control to a minimum (as is the case in democratic societies). For these reasons, an important goal of our program is to help children develop an internalized commitment to maintaining the common good and the personal strength to act on that commitment.

We focus on providing children with experiences and environmental conditions that, according to theory and research, would be likely to build their intrinsic commitment to learn and adopt our society's values. We do not believe rewards and punishments are effective means of increasing such commitments, although they may have some usefulness as "stop-gap" measures for children who, for a variety of reasons, arrive in school with little or no moral knowledge or intrinsic motivation to be concerned about the welfare of others. Numerous studies have found that when rewards and punishment are stopped, the behavior they were contingent on reverts to previous levels (Grusec and Mills 1982). A growing body of research indicates, further, that under certain circumstances children actually devalue behavior that has been rewarded or coerced (Connell and Ryan 1984; Grolnick and Ryan 1987; Koestner, Ryan, Bernieri, and Holt 1984; Lepper and Greene 1978).

THE EXPERIENCES THAT FORM THE BASIS OF THE CDP PROGRAM

In the following paragraphs we present the five kinds of experiences we see as important for the development of children's prosocial orientations.

Supportive Adult-Child Relationships

We believe that children are inclined to emulate adults with whom they have positive relationships and to reciprocate the ways they are treated, and thus we try to help parents and teachers to form warm and supportive relationships with children. Several studies indicate that children whose relationships with their parents are characterized as warm and supportive are more likely to behave in prosocial ways (Baumrind 1967, 1971; Lewis 1981; Maccoby and Martin 1983; Pulkkinen 1982; Radke-Yarrow, Zahn-Waxler, and Chapman 1983; Sroufe 1983). Regardless of one's theoretical perspective, one would hypothesize that such relationships are important for prosocial development. From our perspective, being the recipient of warm and supportive care is central to developing empathy and moral affect.

Exposure to Societal Values

We see the child as needing to learn from adults not only social customs and conventions but also the accumulated moral wisdom of adult society. A number of studies indicate that exposing children to prosocial models and stating or explaining the reasons for moral action (or the importance significant adults place on it) increase children's tendencies to value moral and prosocial behavior and to behave prosocially (Bandura 1969; Bryan 1975; Hoffman and Saltzstein 1967; Radke-Yarrow, Zahn-Waxler, and Chapman 1983; Zahn-Waxler, Radke-Yarrow, and King 1979). Thus, our program incorporates ways to help children develop more complex and sophisticated understandings of prosocial values and how they are manifested.

Opportunities for Peer Interaction and Prosocial Action

Our program includes many opportunities for peer interaction and prosocial action because we think that these help children to develop self-control, increase their moral and social understanding and concern for their fellows, and learn the various skills involved in prosocial behavior. A number of studies indicate that the opportunity to engage in prosocial action and to be a contributing member of a just and benevolent peer group are conducive to caring about fellow group members (Aronson 1978; Cook 1978), to the development of more altruistic attitudes (Whiting and Whiting 1973, 1975), and to a greater tendency to engage in spontaneous prosocial behaviors (Staub 1975).

Opportunities to Think About and Discuss Moral Issues

The work of structural developmentalists (e.g., Kohlberg, Turiel, Nucci, and Berkowitz) has demonstrated that children strive to develop coherent moral systems, and that this is fostered by providing opportunities to discuss and think about moral situations. From our view, it is important that children develop their capacity for autonomous moral reasoning so that they will be able to make moral decisions when faced with new and unanticipated situations. Additionally, as many developmental psychologists have noted (Cowan 1978; Erickson 1950), as children approach adolescence their trust in adult authority weakens and they strive for independence. At this stage they will need to have reasons for moral action that they regard as their own. Thus, our program involves opportunities for children to discuss and reflect on norms, rules, regulations, and social/moral situations. These opportunities are designed to help children develop their capacity for moral reasoning and to understand that behaviors that benefit the group are desirable not only because adults value them but also because they are consistent with their own developing social/moral systems.

Experiences That Promote Understanding of Others

It is necessary that one be sensitive to the needs of others before one can effectively take those needs into account. Children and adults vary greatly in their ability to understand the needs and perspectives of others; we therefore include experiences designed to enhance this ability as part of our program. The ability to take the perspective of others has been proposed by cognitive-developmental theorists as a central ingredient of prosocial action (e.g., Chandler 1973; Selman 1971). We do not assume that cognitive understanding of the perspectives and needs of others will automatically result in prosocial action (Schantz 1975). However, our position is similar to that of the cognitive-developmentalists in that we do assume that for *most* children such knowledge will *usually* result in prosocial action if the action is not contrary to the perceived self-interest of the child, and is within the child's capacity.

Limiting Conditions on the Prosocial Effects of Social Understanding. Several scholars have suggested that social understanding can also lead to the reverse of prosocial action such as exploitation and advantage-taking (Hoffman forthcoming; Shantz 1975). We propose that there are three major conditions under which knowledge of others might lead to exploitation rather than prosocial action.

An Insufficiently Caring Family Environment. If a young child does not have a caring family environment, then we would expect to see in him or her an excessive self-orientation and perhaps the beginnings of sociopathy (Sroufe 1983). We suspect that such children might be helped to become more prosocial only if they first experienced the kinds of supportive relationships that they have lacked in their families. Our assumption, however, is that most children have experienced a sufficient amount of caring and support in their family setting so that they develop a prosocial orientation to fellow group members.

An Insufficiently Caring Community. We would also not expect a child to behave prosocially in a community that is not meeting his or her needs, including the needs to feel competent and autonomous and to experience loving or respectful relationships (Erickson 1950; Maslow 1970; White 1959). When such needs are not being met, the demands of self-protection could lead the child to simply withdraw from the community, thereby removing the possibility of the community's influence on the child or the child's commitment to the community. Thus, we encourage teachers to shape the classroom consciously so that each person's needs are met in a balance that children are likely to see as fair.

When Others Are Seen as Members of an "Out-group." We would not expect a child's knowledge of the needs, feelings, or situation of others to result in prosocial concern if the child did not consider the others to be part of his or her social group. The tendency to fail to apply one's moral principles to those not considered to be part of one's group has been demonstrated many times in human history. We assume that children have to be taught to apply their social/moral system to individuals who are not part of their immediate social group. Since one of our goals is to teach children the importance of treating all people equally and respecting individual differences, activities developed to enhance social understanding also focus on extending the boundaries of the social group.

THE CDP PROGRAM

Our goal was to create a comprehensive set of home and school activities and practices that would incorporate all of the above-mentioned experiences: warm and supportive adult-child relations; highlighting and explaining the importance of prosocial values; practice at collaborating with others and acting prosocially; discussion of and reflection on the reasons for moral actions; and understanding, discussing, and reflecting on the feelings, motives, and needs of others. It was also necessary that our program be learned by average teachers and parents within the constraints under which schools operate, and that it fit easily within the normal routines of the classroom and the home.

For a variety of reasons both our school and home programs underwent substantial change during the process of development and implementation. Sometimes these changes resulted from our developing understanding of the practical limitations imposed by the fact that parents, teachers, and school administrators are very busy people and simply did not have the time to engage in all the activities that we and they deemed worthwhile. Sometimes these changes resulted from our becoming clearer about our own theoretical perspective and better able to translate that perspective into classroom and home activities. As we worked with teachers and parents, designed specific school and home activities, observed aspects of the program in action, and reflected on our experiences, we more carefully articulated our theoretical perspective and understood its relationship to school and home activities. What follows is a description of the school program as we currently conceive it. This is an idealized description; it is the conception that we present to teachers and that shapes the activities and materials we develop. The program in practice was sometimes far from ideal. After describing our ideal conception, we shall describe ways in which the actual implementation of the program met and failed to meet our ideal conception.

THE SCHOOL PROGRAM

Although we see the CDP program as an integrated whole, we have designed and taught it as five mutually consistent and somewhat overlapping components:

1. *Developmental Discipline*—an approach to classroom management that involves a concerted effort to create a caring community in the classroom in which each child's needs for autonomy, competence, and affection are balanced with the needs of the community in order to maximize the learning and well-being of all.

2. *Cooperative Learning*—an approach to academic instruction in which children work together to help one another learn and have opportunities to experience and practice such prosocial values as fairness, helpfulness, responsibility, and considerateness.

3. *Helping*—activities that provide children with opportunities for prosocial action both in the classroom and beyond.

4. *Understanding Others*—a focus on helping children understand and empathize with the situation and experience of others through literature, discussion, and direct experience.

5. *Highlighting Prosocial Values*—a focus on explaining the importance of prosocial values and helping children see the relation of values to actions through exposure to characters and events in literature and history and through personal example.

Developmental Discipline

We view the classroom as having four main functions: helping children learn a specified set of academic skills, concepts, and facts; fostering their love of learning; helping them learn a set of social skills, values, and expectations; and fostering their commitment to those values. The classroom management practices that a teacher uses must be consistent with all four goals. The teacher is inescapably engaged in socialization as well as education. Most current classroom management systems have been designed to serve the academic function only (e.g., Association for Supervision and Curriculum Development 1980; Canter 1976; Jones 1979). In fact, a recent review of classroom management research (Doyle 1986) does not even mention the possible socialization function of classroom management.

The socialization practices we advocate assume that most school-age children are disposed to learn and adopt the values of their community, to construct a personal moral system, and to act to benefit others as well as to satisfy personal needs. In contrast, many discipline systems are predicated on a view that children, particularly children who seem inclined to misbehave, need to have good character imposed on them. Such approaches are designed to show children that doing the "right" thing is in their self-interest. The only incentive invoked by such approaches is student self-interest—the knowledge that their behaviors will increase or decrease their receipt of positive or negative consequences. In such controlled classrooms, compliance can indeed be achieved by increasing the promise of external rewards or the threat of negative consequences. Such control may allow the teacher to achieve an environment conducive to academic learning (although probably not an intrinsic orientation to learning), but it does not teach a commitment to prosocial values.

Our program holds that socialization must focus on developing an internal disposition toward prosocial action. Developmental discipline attempts this in four somewhat overlapping ways:

1. Building a warm and supportive relationship between the teacher and each student.
2. Building a community in the classroom in which the stated learning goals are being achieved and in which each child's personal needs for competence, autonomy, and respect or affiliation are being met.
3. Assisting children to refine their own cognitive moral systems and their understanding of how those systems apply to everyday classroom life.
4. Using both proactive and reactive control techniques that enhance (or at least do not undermine) the above goals; that is, techniques that effectively control behavior but at the same time help or allow children to

    See themselves as well-intentioned (i.e., as morally competent),

    Understand how expectations or rules are consistent with their own sense of fairness or kindness,

    Understand how behaviors affect the well-being of others,

    Feel some autonomy in compliance (by experiencing the least coercive control method possible),

    Retain their belief in the affection and good will of the authority (by experiencing means of control that are nonpunitive, that focus on solving the problem at hand, and that appear to be fair), and

More easily satisfy the norm or expectation (by being taught a needed skill or being given tasks that require less skill or self-control).

Building Warm Teacher-Child Relationships. As stated earlier, we see warm and supportive adult-child relationships as central to the development of a child's motivation to be concerned about the welfare of others. It is not a simple task for a teacher to establish a personal relationship with each of thirty-plus students, especially when also charged with maximizing students' academic learning. In addition to increasing teachers' awareness of the importance both of the teacher-child relationship and of using informal opportunities to talk with students about mutual interests, we recommend that teachers use standard academic learning situations to build these relationships. For example, teachers can introduce stories by telling a related personal experience and inviting students to tell about their own related experiences, writing assignments can be about personal experiences or viewpoints, and children can learn interview skills by interviewing the teacher. In direct contrast to the "don't smile until Thanksgiving" approach, we advise teachers, especially at the beginning of the year, to take opportunities to perform kind or helpful acts for their students in order to let them know that the teacher is personally concerned about their individual needs.

Developing Children's Cognitive Moral Understanding. Children have much to learn about what constitutes fairness and kindness and about the reasons for the many rules and procedures necessary for regulating life in a social group. Teachers' needs to assert their power in order to maintain classroom control will be lessened if the children understand the moral principles that are being enforced.

In addition to offering explanations when stating expectations and correcting misbehavior, teachers can enhance children's moral understanding by involving them in developing class rules and norms and in the responsibility for seeing that the rules and norms function well. At all grade levels teachers begin the year by asking the children to think about and talk with one another about "the way we want our class to be." The children are specifically asked to think about things they do and don't want to happen in the class. The teacher then helps the children see that these things can be fit under a few general norms or values such as "be fair," "don't hurt," "be kind," and "be responsible." The norms are chosen to be general enough to cover a wide range of behaviors, and thus obviate the need for dozens of prescriptive and proscriptive rules. Regular class meetings are held throughout the year to assess how well the teacher and children are following the norms and, perhaps, to devise some procedures to help in areas where improvement is needed. We see this as a way of increasing children's understanding of such general values as kindness, fairness, and responsibility and of their application in the school and classroom setting.

Creating a Caring Community. As we argued above, children will be more inclined to adopt the values of their community and respond to community members in a caring way if their own needs are being met there. We focus on three psychological needs—autonomy, competence, and belonging. Many different activities go into creating a classroom community that meets or addresses these needs. Each child's sense of competence, for example, can be enhanced by using individual mastery rather than normative standards to evaluate learning, by avoiding competitive learning techniques such as spelling bees and the public display of differential levels of achievement of individual class members, and by using cooperative learning structures and multiple-ability tasks to help all children find avenues to success.

Personal autonomy is always restricted in a group setting, and the classroom is no exception. However, teachers can satisfy most children's needs for autonomy by providing opportunities for choice in the timing and content of academic work, by encouraging children to develop and work toward their own personal learning goals, by relying more on explanations than external control to induce children to meet academic and behavioral expectations, and by awakening children's intrinsic interest in the learning tasks.

In addition to needing a sense of competence and autonomy, children need to interact with and feel understood and liked by their fellow class members. Our program encourages teachers to conduct a number of classroom activities that promote children's interaction while learning, and to build a sense of belonging and friendly feelings among children. These include cooperative games in which children work together or help one another, activities involving products (such as class books or murals) to which all class members contribute, and partner and small-group activities in which children have opportunities to exchange personal information.

Classroom Control Techniques. While many think of classroom discipline as synonymous with gaining children's compliance through adult control, control techniques are only a part of developmental discipline. In fact, if not exercised with restraint, the use of external control can undermine the development of prosocial motivation. However, the teacher's careful and respectful exercise of control is a necessary aspect of a classroom in which children acquire a prosocial orientation.

Setting Expectations. We ask teachers to consider both the conditions that cause them to feel a need to exert control and the kinds of control to use when they feel it is needed. Teachers vary in the range of behaviors they feel they must control, and different teachers may react differently to the same student actions (Solomon and Kendall 1975). Often the amount of effort a teacher has to spend exerting control can be lessened by a careful analysis of what behaviors are important to a well-functioning classroom and developmentally appropriate for the particular group of children. We ask teachers to analyze their classroom procedures and expectations with the goals of eliminating unnecessary regulation and adjusting expectations to the developmental levels of the children in the class. Is it necessary that the children complete a learning activity exactly as prescribed? Is it reasonable to expect first-graders to sit quietly for over an hour? For third-graders to keep a class meeting interesting and well-paced? For fifth-graders to handle problems of peer rejection on their own? When control is needed, we recommend that teachers use approaches that will not undermine children's sense that they are competent, cared for, and autonomous.

Indirect Control. Control can be exercised in several ways. Indirectly, the teacher may organize the environment to encourage positive behaviors and discourage negative ones. Common examples of this type of teacher control are separating the children engaged in noisy tasks from those doing tasks requiring quiet contemplation, eliminating unnecessary distractions, and using a calming activity to help children make the transition from an exciting, energetic activity to a contemplative one. Indirect control is commonly used by effective teachers and is indispensable to maintaining a productive and enjoyable learning environment.

Reminders. A second type of control involves the teacher more directly, but the "force" behind the control is the child's recognition and acceptance of the teacher as a legitimate authority. This form of control often serves more as a reminder than as a threat. For example, a teacher's glance or frown can be seen by both teacher and child as a quiet way of reminding the child that he or she is not attending to the task at hand. The exercise of such control implies that the teacher believes that the child shares the underlying understanding and will willingly comply. This type of control implies mutual trust, and when such trust exists in a classroom it can take the place of more coercive forms of control.

Teaching Social Behaviors. A third type of control involves teaching or guiding children to more acceptable ways of behaving. This is similar to the ways teachers respond when children make mistakes in academic areas. For example, a teacher might intervene in an argument by demonstrating more tactful ways of stating opinions, or by suggesting a fairer way to reach an agreement. Such forms of control are often seen by children as helpful rather than coercive. For example, three first-grade children were pushing one another and arguing about who had the right to be first in the lunchroom line. A CDP staff member who was standing by suggested that the children guess a number and whoever was closest would be first. The children agreed, made their guesses, and the argument was settled. The next day, upon seeing the staff member again, one of the children exclaimed, "Hey, I remember you. You're the lady who helped us solve our problem." This type of control can be an important means of helping children understand and live up to prosocial values, but it can be time consuming and difficult to exercise. It requires that the teacher understand the problem from the children's perspectives and understand children well enough to know what solutions to suggest or how to help them discover a fair or kind solution.

We believe that the above three forms of control are key to managing a classroom without an undue reliance on manipulative and power-assertive techniques. We encourage teachers to think of most child misbehavior as they would think of academic errors: as opportunities to teach. What is taught will depend on what skill or knowledge the child appears to be lacking: verbal self-instruction for children lacking in self-control; specific social skills such as being able to explain feelings or resolve conflicts for children lacking in such skills; and provision of the moral or practical reason for a rule or expectation for children who do not see its importance.

Power Assertion. Of course, not all misbehavior is the result of children's lack of knowledge, self-control, or skills. Sometimes children misbehave even when they know better. If such misbehavior is more frequent than can be explained as momentary lapses in effort, we advise the teacher to see if there is some important need that is not being met in the classroom. Is there a warm and trusting relationship with the teacher? Are there sufficient opportunities for autonomy? Are there sufficient opportunities to demonstrate competence? If any of these is lacking for a child, a group of children, or the whole class, the teacher is advised to alter the situation, if possible, to better satisfy the children's needs. Figure 4-1 is a chart that we use to help teachers understand the many factors that should be considered in their decisions about whether and how to respond to children's misbehavior.

While most children can be helped to behave better by the use of these non-power-assertive techniques, some children, for one reason or another, will not respond to them, and it will be necessary to resort to the use of power assertion. Indeed, because time is frequently short in classrooms, and the need for immediate control is sometimes pressing, most teachers occasionally will find it necessary to use power-assertive techniques even with generally well-behaved children. When power assertion is used, we suggest ways to lessen the sense of coercion without lessening the effectiveness of the control.

Coercion is frequently less painful if the child has room for some choice or if the authority figure expresses sympathy for the child's situation (Koestner et al. 1984). For example, a teacher can send a disruptive child from the room but allow the child to determine when to return. A teacher may tell a disruptive group that he or she knows it is hard to work quietly, while still insisting on quiet. A child's sense of self can be preserved even in the face of serious misbehavior if the teacher attributes the best possible motive to the child consistent with the facts, while simultaneously stopping or even punishing the action. The following incident is an example. Some sixth-grade boys, while trying to play a practical joke, accidently broke a girl's wrist. When the principal had finished explaining to them the pain they had caused the girl, the boys were in tears. The principal told them that he knew that they were sorry and that they had not realized the harm

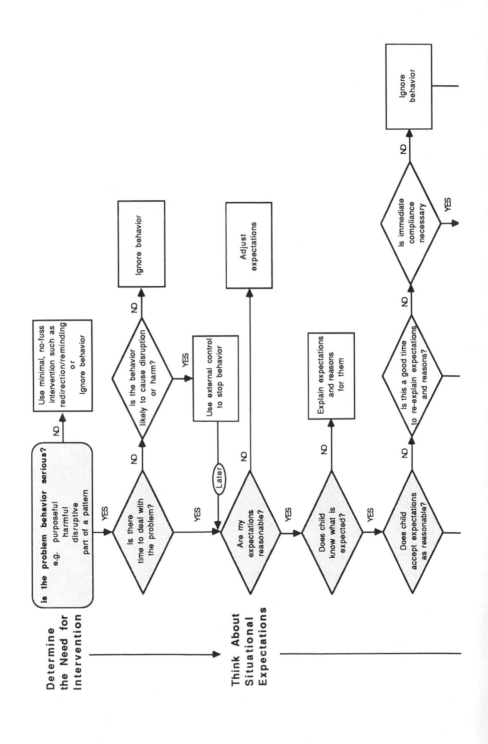

Determine the Need for Intervention

Is the problem behavior serious?
e.g. purposeful
harmful
disruptive
part of a pattern

NO → Use minimal, no-fuss intervention such as redirection/reminding or Ignore behavior

YES ↓

Is there time to deal with the problem?

NO → Is the behavior likely to cause disruption or harm?

    NO → Ignore behavior

    YES → Use external control to stop behavior → (Later)

YES ↓

Think About Situational Expectations

Are my expectations reasonable?

NO → Adjust expectations

YES ↓

Does child know what is expected?

NO → Explain expectations and reasons for them

YES ↓

Does child accept expectations as reasonable?

NO → Is this a good time to re-explain expectations and reasons?

    NO → Is immediate compliance necessary?

        NO → Ignore behavior

        YES →

YES →

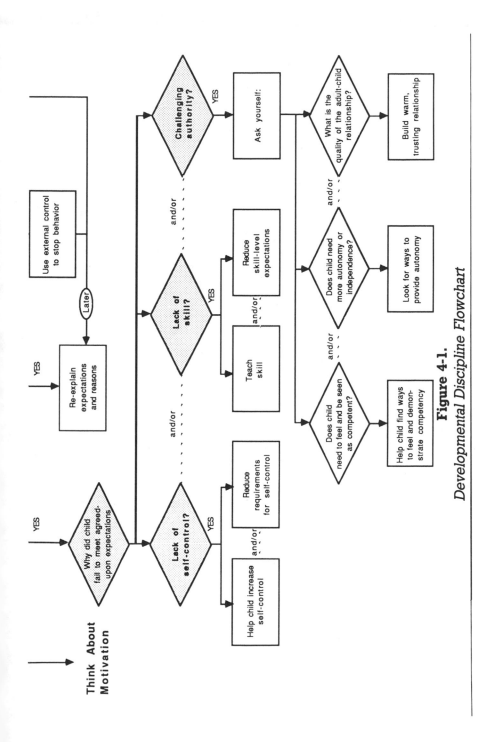

Figure 4-1.
Developmental Discipline Flowchart

they could cause. He then explained that he would have to suspend them from school for a day as a message to them and the community that what they had done was serious. The boys, on their own initiative, brought flowers to the girl. This example illustrates what we regard as a constructive approach to the use of power. We do not have a specific formula for its use, but simply advise teachers that when they find it necessary to assert power, they should try to be fair and nonpunitive, and to focus on solving the problem at hand.

The Importance of the Teacher's View of Children. In the course of training teachers in developmental discipline and providing them with techniques and activities for accomplishing all four of its aspects, we have found that many hold a view of children as self-centered, manipulative, and lazy. If one sees children this way, the logical way to prevent or respond to misbehavior is to use threat or punishment, and the logical way to get children to behave well is to use rewards. We try to help teachers see children not just as self-interested but also as prosocially oriented. If one believes children are interested in learning and want to please and to be fair and kind, then the appropriate response to misbehavior is to find out why the child was not able to do the right thing, and to provide the necessary help. The way to get children to behave well is to be sure they know what is expected, have the skills required, and can see that it is a reasonable, fair, responsible, or kind thing to do.

Cooperative Learning

Cooperative learning involves small groups of children working together to complete classroom learning tasks. Specific cooperative learning systems differ markedly depending on their educational purpose, the age of the children they are intended for, and their assumptions about children's motivations and about how children learn. Systems differ, for example, in the degree of structure they impose on the group work, the types of incentives they employ to increase children's motivation to achieve maximum social or academic performance, the degree and type of interdependence experienced by group members, and the degree to which instruction in social interaction skills is part of the lesson (Aronson 1978; Burns 1981; Cohen 1987; Graves and Graves 1985; Johnson and Johnson

1975; Kagan 1985; Minuchin and Shapiro 1983; Sharan and Sharan 1976; Slavin 1983).

Our approach to cooperative learning derives, in part, from the work of Johnson and Johnson (1975) and of Cohen (1987), but it differs from these and other approaches in several important ways. What follows is an abbreviated description of our approach. For a more detailed description of this approach and its relationship to other approaches, see Solomon, Watson, Schaps, Battistich, and Solomon (forthcoming) and Watson, Hildebrandt, and Solomon (in press).

Theoretical Rationale for Cooperative Learning as a Component of CDP. Participation in cooperative classroom interaction can provide children with several kinds of opportunities likely to enhance their commitment to prosocial values. Such interaction allows them to experience the democratic process (Dewey 1916), exchange viewpoints, and struggle to apply their developing conceptions of fairness in a noncoercive environment (Piaget 1932; Kohlberg 1969), and experience being treated fairly and kindly by others (Kohlberg, Kauffman, Sharf, and Hickey 1974). Cooperative learning also helps children learn to accommodate to others, develop appreciation for others' contributions, feel part of a cohesive group, and learn consideration and concern for others' needs and feelings. It provides the teacher with an opportunity to increase children's awareness of democratic and prosocial values, to help them translate these values into social behavior, to monitor peer interaction to increase the likelihood that it will be noncoercive, and to stimulate children to higher levels of moral thinking. For a more detailed description of empirical and theoretical reasons for assuming that cooperative learning will have a positive effect on children's socialization, see Battistich, Watson, and colleagues (in press).

In our system, the teacher both highlights and engages children in discussion of relevant prosocial values—specifically fairness, consideration, helpfulness, and social responsibility—and teaches needed social skills. This is because we see prosocial interaction as requiring both social skills and knowledge of and commitment to prosocial values, and because we see children as needing to learn both specific skills and conventions and the accumulated moral wisdom of our culture. We also encourage teachers to allow groups of children to work independently, struggling to solve problems that emerge. At the same time we stress the occasional need for teachers to intervene in the group work with guidance and instruction. This is because we see learning as involving both instruction and construction, therefore requiring explanation and guidance, independent discovery, and trial and error. We do not use extrinsic motivators, but rather focus on reminding children of intrinsic reasons for learning and for engaging in kind and fair interaction, and we help them to act on those reasons. From our perspective, cooperative activities provide a kind of "laboratory" for practicing and experiencing prosocial values and social skills while also pursuing academic learning.

Cooperative learning gives children opportunities to practice acting in noncoercive and helpful ways with their peers in a setting that is safer and more controlled than most others, including the playground. In our program, cooperative lessons provide formal instruction, guided discovery, and supervised practice in peer interaction. Less formal opportunities to interact in the classroom, on the playground, and elsewhere provide opportunities for independent discovery and practice.

Helping

Participation in home and classroom chores and cooperative learning activities provide children with many opportunities to be helpful to other members of their immediate social group (i.e., family members and classmates), but the helping component is also designed to provide children with wider opportunities for prosocial action. Cross-age buddies and tutoring programs provide older children, even those not skilled enough to provide much help to their classmates, with opportunities to help younger children. Schoolwide clean-up and beautification projects give children opportunities to help the entire school community, and community service projects allow children to reach out beyond school to the larger community.

Opportunities to help in the classroom and school are regular and quite frequent. Community service activities occur much less frequently—one to four times a year, depending on community need and the effort required to provide help. Such activities should be frequent enough for children to understand that they have a responsibility to help outside their immediate environment, but not so frequent that they feel this help to be a burden. Community services might be responses to ongoing needs, such as "trick or treating" for

UNICEF, recycling projects, or performing at a convalescent hospital; or they might be responses to emergencies, such as raising money for earthquake victims.

Buddies—An Example of a Typical School Helping Activity. Buddies activities are conducted with entire classes and involve older children helping younger ones. Older buddies might help younger buddies with a craft project, learning playground games, feeling comfortable in the school, or academic learning. These activities are designed to provide younger buddies with models of helpfulness and caring and older buddies with opportunities to act in prosocial ways. As with cooperative activities, however, it is important that buddies activities be carefully structured and be consistent with the practical tasks and general academic goals of the school. If they are not practical or academically worthwhile, teachers will not find the time to do them; if they are not carefully structured, helpfulness can turn into bossiness or belittling one-upmanship. Ideal buddies tasks either ease the management burdens for teachers or involve an academic skill, the exercise of which will benefit both children. For example, when older children read or take dictation from younger children, both children benefit in reciprocal ways. When older children attend assemblies or field trips with younger children, the teachers' need to manage or give individual attention is reduced.

Buddies activities are structured in much the same way as cooperative lessons. They begin with the teacher helping the children realize the importance of relevant prosocial values and discussing or teaching the particular skills and knowledge the children will need in order to carry out the activity. The activities are carefully monitored, and afterward, teachers help the children discuss and think about things that went well, things that were not successful, and any changes that might be needed to do better in the future.

Understanding Others and Highlighting Prosocial Values

These two components will be described together because they are both important parts of the three previous components, and because they both receive their special focus through the use of literature. The other components, for the most part, help to develop children's prosocial skills and orientations toward others in the immediate environment—classroom, school, and community. While it is important that children acquire prosocial values and learn to apply them in these settings, it is also important for them to learn to apply them in a broader range of settings and to understand and empathize with others who may differ in many ways from those encountered in the school and community. The use of literature helps us extend children's knowledge of situations and people to wider arenas.

Literature also provides teachers with opportunities to teach children the meaning and importance of fairness and caring and the way such values as truthfulness, generosity, or respect for the environment or another's property are enacted in our society. By involving children in discussions of such issues in the context of literature, teachers can help children understand how values relate to actions and why it is important to act in accord with prosocial values. These situations are vivid and concrete and often relevant to the children's everyday lives, yet no child's personal interests are at risk. Such situations should bring out the best moral reasoning of which children are capable.

Discussing values in the context of literature is different from the usual discussions about moral dilemmas in which values conflict. While some situations portrayed in literature involve conflicting values, most involve clear morally right ways for the character to behave but very human personal-interest reasons why he or she might not do so. The discussion is designed to help children see a number of possible morally right ways to behave as well as understand the reasons that might prevent such behavior. Literature is thus used as a catalyst for engaging the children in "moral discourse" (Habermas 1981, as cited by Oser 1986). This discourse is designed to deepen children's understanding of morality and broaden the sphere to which that morality applies.

Conducting such discussions is not easy, especially with a class of thirty or more students. Furthermore, most teachers have been trained to ask specific questions directed toward predetermined "right" answers, not to lead children in discussions in which varieties of opinions are possible (and desirable) and to help them gradually see that some opinions have better support than others. To help teachers conduct such lessons, we train them in discussion leading and provide both a set of "read-aloud" stories carefully selected to raise social and moral issues and examples of questions designed to help draw out general moral principles and relate them to the children's lives. For example, after reading aloud the chapter entitled "To Catch a Thief" from *Nothing's Fair in Fifth Grade* by Barthe

DeClements (1981), in which something is stolen from a student's desk at recess time, the teacher might pose one or more of the following questions:

What kinds of problems do people have when they suspect they have a thief in their midst?
Does a teacher have the right to search people's desks?
How would you feel if your desk were searched?
Why was Jenny (the story heroine) so upset when her mother asked her if she had stolen the money?

THE INTERVENTION DESIGN AND FINDINGS

Research Plan and Teacher Training

A detailed description of the CDP intervention and evaluation design may be found in Solomon and colleagues (1985). In brief, our training procedures and assessments were designed to allow us to focus on the cumulative effects of the program on children's social development. Consequently, the basic design of the project involved following a cohort of children as they progressed through the grades, beginning with kindergarten, at the three program elementary schools. A parallel cohort of children at three other schools in the same district that did not receive the program served as a comparison group. The six schools were first classified into two similar groups on the basis of socioeconomic status and degree of faculty and parent interest in the program, and one of the groups was then randomly chosen to receive the program. Before the start of the intervention the program and comparison schools were equivalent with respect to such characteristics as number of students, teacher experience, student mobility, family size, and student achievement, and a cross-sectional assessment of a large random sample of students revealed no large or consistent differences between program and comparison students with respect to a variety of social attitudes, values, skills, and behaviors.

Consistent with this design, training in the program components has been delivered primarily to teachers of the longitudinal cohort of children as they progressed through the grades. Although our training procedures have been modified on occasion during the course of the project, we generally have begun with a week-long workshop during the summer before the teachers began teaching the cohort children. During this initial workshop, teachers have been given both a general orientation to the program and detailed information about the five program components, including manuals and specific lesson plans. This workshop has then been followed up by monthly group meetings throughout the school year that provide further training in particular elements of the program, allow for more detailed discussion of individual program components, provide teachers with opportunities to discuss problems they have encountered in trying to implement the program, and include planning for future activities. Individualized training and feedback have been provided by having project training staff observe the program teachers in their classrooms and meet with them about once a week during the school year for "coaching" sessions.

Although relatively intensive training has been provided to teachers during their "program year," the extensive changes in classroom practices required of most teachers by the CDP program take considerable time and effort to implement fully and effectively, and the vast majority of our teachers have received only a single year of training. This means both that implementation was assessed during the same year that the teachers were first being trained and that most of the children in the longitudinal cohort experienced the program only from teachers who were still struggling to master it. This is an important, and perhaps unfortunate, aspect of the intervention design that should be kept in mind when considering the findings from our assessments of classroom implementation and child outcomes.

Implementation Assessments and Findings

Our assessments of program implementation have involved a number of procedures, including classroom observations, interviews with students, teacher and student questionnaires, and informal assessments by project training staff (for a detailed description of our implementation assessments and findings to date, see Solomon, Watson, Delucchi, Schaps, and Battistich, in press). In this chapter we will focus on implementation findings from the classroom observations, since these procedures yield the most complete and objective measures of implementation (i.e., they are based on approximately sixteen hours of structured observations by "blind" observers in each program and comparison classroom each year, and they provide relatively comprehensive and detailed scores for implementation of each program component, as well as a summary measure of overall implementation). It is important to note, however, that analyses of implementation measures from student interviews and teacher and student questionnaires have corroborated many of the findings from the classroom observations discussed here.

Overall, our analyses of implementation scores from the classroom observations indicate that we were generally successful in getting program teachers to implement our program, at least as compared to what has been observed in the comparison classrooms. As shown in Figure 4-2, when these data are combined across the first five years of the intervention (kindergarten through fourth grade), the scores for each component are significantly higher among program than comparison classrooms, and the effect sizes are quite large, with an overall effect size of .44 for the summary measure of overall program implementation.

Relatively speaking, then, our training procedures appear to have been successful in creating the kind of classroom environment we felt would be conducive to promoting prosocial development. However, while we clearly have produced group-level changes in classroom practice, there has been considerable variability in the quality of implementation among program teachers, indicated both in our analyses of the structured observation indices and in informal observations by project training staff. Generally, our trainers have indicated that most teachers had achieved only an "adequate" level of implementation by the spring of their program year. Only a few teachers could be considered to have mastered the program, and another small group of teachers have been unable (or unwilling) to even approach adequate levels of implementation. In addition, as will be discussed below, while our summary scores for implementation of each program component are significantly higher among program teachers, more detailed analyses of differences in particular "elements" of our two most complex components, cooperative learning and developmental discipline, indicate that we have been only partially successful in our training activities to date.

Cooperative Learning. Figure 4-3 summarizes differences between program and comparison teachers on each of five "subcomponents" of cooperative learning that, together, compose the summary component score presented in Figure 4-2. As indicated,

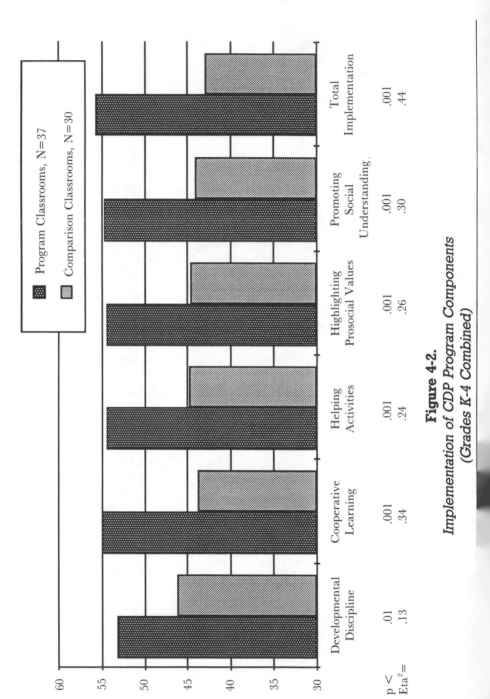

Figure 4-2.
*Implementation of CDP Program Components
(Grades K-4 Combined)*

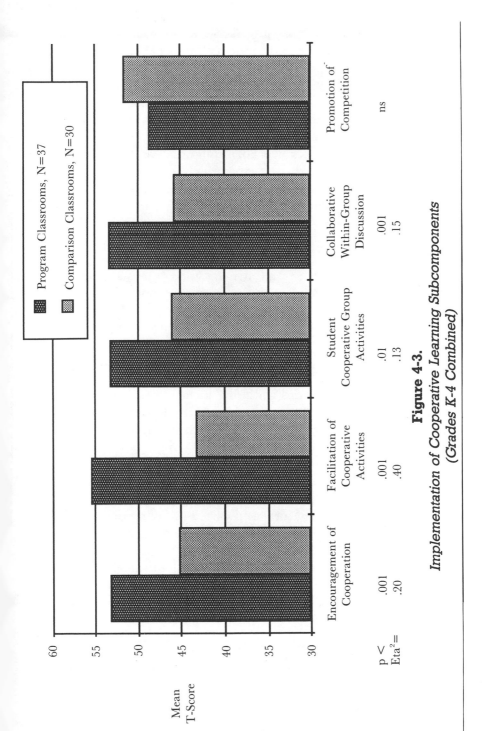

Figure 4-3.

Implementation of Cooperative Learning Subcomponents
(Grades K-4 Combined)

program teachers encouraged students to cooperate and facilitated students' cooperative interactions more than did comparison teachers (e.g., by teaching or demonstrating social skills, acknowledging group effort or products, encouraging students to work together, discussing the value of cooperative work, setting up cooperative groups), and program students were observed more often than comparison students to be working collaboratively toward a group goal (as opposed to working toward individual goals within a nominal group, as in typical ability groups for instruction in reading and mathematics). In addition, program students were observed to engage in more collaborative discussion within their groups than were comparison students (e.g., seeking out others' ideas, using reasoning, expressing support for and elaborating on others' opinions, explicitly polling opinions, and striving for consensus). It is noteworthy, however, that while there was more cooperative interaction in program classrooms, program and comparison teachers were not significantly different in their promotion of competition (although the absolute level was quite low in both program and comparison classrooms).

Overall, while not all teachers were able to learn to conduct cooperative learning lessons skillfully, most were enthusiastic about trying. They were able to see the potential benefits of helping children learn to cooperate, and they were enthusiastic about adding a new technique to their teaching repertoire.

By the spring of their year with the cohort children, most program teachers were conducting cooperative lessons reasonably frequently. However, the quality of those lessons varied considerably. Teachers often failed to achieve a natural and varied presentation style because they were following our lesson formats without making the adjustments required to bring the lessons to life for their students. Sometimes they simply stated the lesson's learning goals, without sufficiently tailoring the presentation to the understanding and interests of the particular group of children. Questions designed to encourage children to think about what they learned and how they worked together would result in pat, stereotyped responses if they were asked repeatedly or if the children's answers were not skillfully probed.

Cooperative learning is a complex instructional strategy. While our formal classroom observations showed that the program teachers conducted cooperative lessons of higher quality (e.g., involving group goals and student interdependence) and with greater frequency than comparison teachers, the cooperative lessons in program classrooms

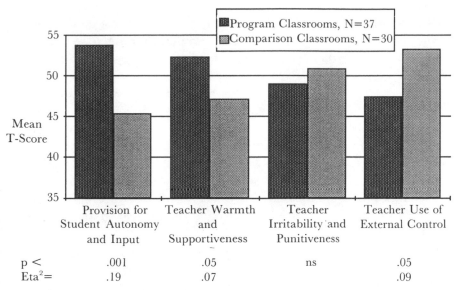

| p < | .001 | .05 | ns | .05 |
| Eta² = | .19 | .07 | | .09 |

Figure 4-4.

*Implementation of Developmental Discipline Subcomponents
(Grades K-4 Combined)*

were sometimes not done well enough to be likely to help students achieve optimal social and academic growth. Informal observations indicate that program teachers sometimes failed to challenge or pique students' interest, to organize the group work so that children would achieve high levels of productivity and cooperation, or to guide children's thinking and discussion so that they would gain useful insights into the effects of their behavior on their ability to learn and to work fairly and considerately with others. While only a few teachers succeeded in conducting frequent, high-quality cooperative lessons, we believe that with more time to experiment with this teaching strategy, most of the program teachers would be able to do so. Most of the teachers who did consistently conduct high-quality cooperative lessons were those who worked with the program for more than one year.

Developmental Discipline. Teachers generally had more difficulty achieving good implementation with developmental discipline than with the other program components. As shown in Figure 4-4, however, analyses of the classroom observational data revealed that significant differences between program and comparison teachers were achieved on three of the four subcomponents composing the summary measure of developmental discipline. Program teachers provided for more student autonomy and input by soliciting students' opinions, having them participate in classroom decision making and in other activities that allowed them a degree of choice, helping with problems by providing suggestions or choices or asking questions (rather than by providing direct solutions), and involving them in the determination of class norms and procedures and in class meetings in which classroom problems and their solutions were discussed. Program teachers were also less likely to use external means to control students' behavior in the classroom (although further analyses indicated that the difference in the "external control" subcomponent was primarily due to lesser use of punishments and threats of punishments by program teachers).

The program teachers were also warmer and more accepting and supportive of their students. Thus, program teachers were more apt to create a classroom environment in which children's needs for positive and supportive relationships and for autonomy were met and to involve their students in discussion and decision making that could help them to understand the moral or prosocial reasons behind rules or expectations.

The differences between the program and the comparison groups were not as great in this component as in the others, probably, we think, because it requires a greater shift from traditional modes of teaching. Most teachers have been trained both to use external incentives to control children's learning activities and social behavior and to maintain relatively restrictive classroom environments. Such long-term habits cannot be changed in a single year in most cases. We tried to "soften" the teachers' views of children, and we feel that some did make significant changes in their views of children's motivations and in their use of rewards and punishments in the classroom. Those who changed most substantially were among the small minority who received more than one year of training.

Helping. Most classroom teachers involve their children in classroom chores and in some form of community-wide charity. Program teachers immediately saw the value of providing opportunities for children to be helpful, and found it easy to increase these opportunities for their students both within the classrooms and at the school and community levels. When teachers had difficulty with this component, it usually involved a failure either to develop children's intrinsic motivations for helping or to show them how their individual actions fit into a complex network in which people help one another.

Understanding Others and Highlighting Prosocial Values. Teachers have been quite enthusiastic about this aspect of the program, and they have generally achieved better and broader implementation of these two program components than the others. These activities are interesting to teachers and are seen as clearly consistent with their overall academic goals. They are also consistent with guidelines recently published by the California State Department of Education, calling for the use of literature in the teaching of reading and for a focus on values and understanding of others in the literature/language arts program (California State Department of Education 1987).

A Brief Overview of Major Program Effects

Over the years, a large and comprehensive set of assessment procedures and measures has been used in the project evaluation. These include student interviews and questionnaires to assess social attitudes, values, and skills, and observations of behavior in structured small-group tasks, in the classroom, and on the playground. A description of these various assessment procedures and an overview of our entire set of findings through third grade (the fourth year of the project) may be found in Solomon, Schaps, Watson, and Battistich (1987). More detailed discussions of the major findings reported below may be found in Battistich, Solomon, Watson, Solomon, and Schaps (in press) and in Solomon and colleagues (in press).

Observations of student behavior in the classroom have consistently found that program students are more helpful and cooperative and more frequently display affection, concern, support, and encouragement toward one another than do comparison students. These differences are quite robust, and they do not seem to be attributable either to differences in teacher-initiated cooperative learning activities or to generally better organized and more efficiently managed classrooms, as they are statistically significant even when both teachers' general competence and students' participation in cooperative activities are controlled.

A second area in which we have observed large and consistent differences between program and comparison students is in cognitive social problem-solving skills and strategies. Beginning in the second program year (first grade), interview measures of these social competencies have yielded significantly higher scores for program students in perspective-taking skills, consideration of other persons' needs as well as their own in hypothetical problem situations, consequential and means-end thinking, and use of prosocial and cooperative resolution strategies (e.g., discussing the problem, explaining their position, sharing or other compromise solutions). Other analyses have shown that the interview responses to hypothetical problem situations correlate both with teacher ratings of social competence and prosocial behavior and with sociometric indices of peer acceptance, suggesting that they have some ecological validity.

Finally, questionnaires administered in third and fourth grades indicate that program children are also more committed to certain democratic values than are comparison children. In third grade, program children scored higher on a measure of assertion responsibility (the belief that one has a responsibility to state one's position even if it seems unlikely to prevail), while in fourth grade, program children had higher scores than comparison children on the same measure of assertion responsibility and also on a measure of equality of representation and participation (i.e., the belief that all members of a group have a right to participate in the group's decisions and activities).

Overall, these findings suggest that the CDP program is having a number of its anticipated effects. In particular, the findings for interpersonal problem solving and support for democratic values suggest that we may be engendering in children the tendency toward "self-other balance" in social interactions and outcomes that we believe reflects a prosocial orientation. Although we have yet to see this tendency reflected to a significant degree in children's interactions in small-group activities outside the classroom (see Solomon et al. 1987), program children clearly treat one another with more kindness, consideration, and respect in the classroom.

SUMMARY AND CONCLUSIONS

In the CDP program, teachers provide children with (a) instruction in how to be fair, caring, and responsible in the classroom; (b) opportunities to think about and discuss the meaning and importance of fundamental prosocial values; and (c) opportunities to practice these values primarily in the classroom but also in the school at large, at home, and in the community. We think this combination of instruction, practice, and reflection is a powerful way for children to learn. It is, in part, a "blending" of central aspects of both traditional and developmental approaches to values education; but our program also extends these approaches in significant ways. In particular, we stress that both establishing warm and supportive adult-child relationships and enhancing children's empathic responsiveness are important for the development of moral motivation.

Like most traditional values education programs, we emphasize that children need to be taught the moral wisdom of the culture and the specific practices the culture follows for carrying out its code of values. However, we make a clear distinction between *teaching* moral values and what might be called *indoctrinating* children into a moral code. Our teachers foster the learning of moral values by providing explanations and experiences that help children to understand more clearly the reasons behind rules, norms, and expectations. The teachers also give children time to develop gradually a personal understanding of why adherence to a particular value is important. They expect that children will question values and even experiment with conflicting ones, but also that with guidance, understanding, and experience, the children will eventually come to understand the importance of such values as fairness, kindness, and responsibility. Indoctrination, which may derive from an overzealous traditional approach, stresses telling children what they should think. Explanations may be provided, but there is no attempt to provide different viewpoints and to examine them critically. What is essential is that children know the values, know that their behavior should reflect those values, and adhere to them. The stress is on performance, not on understanding, or as one skeptical principal put it to us, "There is no need for class meetings to discuss rules and norms; children just need to be told the rules in clear, concrete terms and then be held accountable for upholding them."

The major differences between our approach to character development and that taken by most traditional character education programs derive from our assumptions about the child's motivations. Unlike most traditional programs, we think children are both intrinsically motivated to adopt the values of their social group and self-oriented. We expect children to be willing participants in their own socialization. Therefore, unlike most traditional character education programs, we do not strive to entice prosocial behavior by the promise of reward or to coerce it by the threat of punishment. We recognize that adults will need to exercise control while children are developing their cognitive and self-regulating capacities. However, because we assume that children are intrinsically motivated to acquire these capacities, we explicitly warn against the *extensive* use of external control with elementary school children. Such control, in our view, is likely to undermine the primary goal of character education: the development of an internalized commitment to a prosocial moral code.

The major differences between our approach to character development and that taken by cognitive-developmentalists derive from our view of the function of the adult-child relationship in fostering children's moral development. Cognitive-developmentalists emphasize the differences in status and power between adults and children, and view the adult-child relationship as likely to coerce the child into conforming to adult demands. They view the socialization practices of adults as leading to an authority-oriented morality rather than to a morality based on a personal commitment to principles of justice and caring. We focus on the potential of the adult-child relationship to provide warmth and care, and view a caring adult-child relationship to be of primary importance in developing children's motivation to be "good." Both our approach and the "just community" programs derived from the cognitive-developmental approach stress the importance of an adult-guided community in developing children's moral values. But the cognitive-developmentalists focus on the importance of adult provision of autonomy and justice, while we explicitly focus on the importance of adult caring as well.

We also differ from cognitive-developmentalists in our views of the role and importance of peer interaction. Cognitive-developmentalists see peer interaction to be of paramount importance for the development of autonomous morality. Although we also see peer interaction as playing an important role in child socialization, we see adult-child interaction, at least for young children, as being of primary importance. In our view, one of the most important moral tasks of young children is to learn the culture's norms and its accumulated moral wisdom. They can learn this only from adults (or older children). They must also learn that their needs will be met if they trust others and respect legitimate authority. It is adults (first parents and then teachers) who are responsible for seeing that this trust and respect are warranted. Finally, we believe that adults must monitor children's interactions to ensure that children learn the skills and value of kindness and reciprocity and not merely those of might and manipulation. Of course, not all adults perform optimally in these areas, and when, on balance, they are more coercive or neglectful than caring, it is likely that the children in their care will not develop an autonomous morality. When children approach adolescence, it seems likely to us that their peer relationships will begin to have a more independent and important role in their socialization; but for elementary school age children, we see adult-child relationships as more important than peer relationships.

In developing the CDP program, we were strongly influenced by the work and thinking of educators and psychologists working from the cognitive-developmental and the traditional socialization perspectives. Our efforts to integrate these two perspectives have led us to think in new ways about the role of both adult-child and peer relationships in children's moral development. We also believe that incorporating complementary elements from these two quite different perspectives has led us to develop a more comprehensive and effective approach to values education. We are encouraged in this view by our finding of positive program effects on children's classroom behavior, social problem-solving skills, and commitment to democratic values. On the other hand, this blend may have been a partial cause of the great variation in levels of classroom implementation that we observed. While many factors may have impeded classroom implementation of the program (e.g., shortness of training time, working with only one grade level at a time, turnover of principals, and changes in the program itself), the fact that our program is a blend of two perspectives probably made it more difficult to learn than either perspective would have been separately.

For example, the fact that we, like traditionalists, stress the teaching of values, but think of teaching in a manner similar to the cognitive-developmentalists, may cause some confusion among teachers. Teachers who take a more traditional approach to the classroom and think that their only task is to control and instruct children may believe that they are implementing our program when they take extra time to teach children about values. These teachers tend to think that teaching is "telling" and learning is "listening."

Thus, they may fail to understand the equal stress we place on helping children analyze and challenge values, because this process is not part of their notion of "teaching."

Similarly, it is possible that teachers who are child-centered might believe that they are implementing our program because they are allowing children to solve problems on their own and also allowing them autonomy and the time to develop their own thinking. These teachers might fail to understand the equal emphasis we place on exercising careful control over children and teaching them moral values, because such practices generally are not associated with child-centered education. On the basis of informal observations by CDP program staff, it appears that child-centered teachers tend to let children struggle to learn "on their own," sometimes concentrating more on fostering children's independence than on teaching or guiding them to a higher level of understanding.

In closing, we should stress that while our program has had clear positive outcomes, much is still unknown about its effectiveness. We are still analyzing our accumulated data and still collecting data in the upper elementary grades. We have developed program materials and activities for all grade levels, but next year will be the first time we will work extensively with teachers of sixth-grade children. Also, we have worked to date only in a middle- to upper-middle class suburban school district; next year we will begin working with schools in an urban district where the population is much more heterogeneous. Finally, our program has been implemented and assessed as a whole. We are not able to determine as yet which aspects of the program may be most effective. As we gain experience in working with older children and with children with different family backgrounds, and we analyze our data more deeply, we hope to develop a clearer understanding of how widely effective the program might be and some better indication of which aspects are most important in producing our effects.

REFERENCES

Akers, John. Speech to the Bay Area Council of the Business Roundtable, San Francisco, February 10, 1988.

Aronson, Elliot. *The Jigsaw Classroom.* Beverly Hills, Calif.: Sage, 1978.

Association for Supervision and Curriculum Development (ASCD). *Effective Classroom Management in the Elementary School.* Alexandria, Va.: ASCD, 1980.

Bandura, Albert. "Social Learning Theory of Identificatory Processes." In *Handbook of Socialization Theory and Research*, ed. David Goslin. Chicago: Rand McNally, 1969.

Battistich, Victor; Solomon, Daniel; Watson, Marilyn; Solomon, Judith; and Schaps, Eric. "Effects of an Elementary School Program to Enhance Prosocial Behavior on Children's Cognitive Social Problem-solving Skills and Strategies," *Journal of Applied Developmental Psychology*, in press.

Battistich, Victor; Watson, Marilyn; Solomon, Daniel; Schaps, Eric; and Solomon, Judith. "The Child Development Project: A Comprehensive Program for the Development of Prosocial Character." In *Moral Development and Behavior: Advances in Theory, Research and Application*, Vol. 1, ed. William M. Kurtines and Jacob L. Gewirtz. Hillsdale, N.J.: Erlbaum, forthcoming.

Baumrind, Diana. "Child Care Practices Anteceding 3 Patterns of Preschool Behavior," *Genetic Psychology Monographs* 75 (1967): 43–48.

Baumrind, Diana. "Current Patterns of Parental Authority," *Developmental Psychology Monograph* 4 (1971): 1, Pt. 2.

Berkowitz, Marvin W., Ed. *Peer Conflict and Psychological Growth: New Directions for Child Development*. San Francisco: Jossey-Bass, 1985.

Blatt, M. M., and Kohlberg, Lawrence. "The Effects of Classroom Moral Discussion upon Children's Level of Moral Judgment," *Journal of Moral Education* 4 (1975): 129–61.

Brown, Dyke, and Solomon, Daniel. "A Model for Prosocial Learning: An In-progress Field Study." In *The Nature of Prosocial Development*, ed. Diane L. Bridgeman. New York: Academic Press, 1983.

Bryan, James H. "Children's Cooperation and Helping Behaviors." In *Review of Child Development Research*, Vol. 5, ed. E. Mavis Hetherington. Chicago: University of Chicago Press, 1975.

Burns, Marilyn. "Groups of Four: Solving the Management Problems," *Learning* (September 1981): 46–51.

California State Department of Education. *English-Language Arts Framework for California Public Schools.* Sacramento, Calif.: The Department, 1987.

California State Department of Education. *History-Social Science Framework.* Sacramento, Calif.: The Department, 1988.

Canter, Lee. *Assertive Discipline*. Los Angeles: Lee Canter and Associates, 1976.

Chandler, Michael J. "Egocentrism and Antisocial Behavior: The Assessment and Training of Social Perspective-taking Skills," *Developmental Psychology* 11 (1973): 326-32.

Cohen, Elizabeth G. *Designing Group Work: Strategies for the Heterogeneous Classroom*. New York: Teachers College Press, 1987.

Connell, James P., and Ryan, Richard M. "A Developmental Theory of Motivation in the Classroom," *Teacher Education Quarterly* 11 (1984): 64–77.

Cook, Stuart W. "Interpersonal and Attitudinal Outcomes of Cooperating Interracial Groups," *Journal of Research and Development in Education* 12 (1978): 97–113.

Cowan, Phillip A. *Piaget with Feeling: Cognitive, Social, and Emotional Dimensions*. New York: Holt, Rinehart and Winston, 1978.

DeClements, Barthe. *Nothing's Fair in Fifth Grade*. New York: Scholastic, Inc., 1981.

Dewey, John. *Democracy and Education*. New York: Macmillan, 1916.

Doyle, Walter. "Classroom Organization and Management." In *Handbook of Research on Teaching*, 3rd ed., ed. Merlin Wittrock. New York: Macmillan, 1986

Erickson, Erik. *Childhood and Society*. New York: Norton, 1950.

Graves, Nancy B., and Graves, Theodore D. "Creating a Cooperative Learning Environment: An Ecological Approach." In *Learning to Cooperate, Cooperating to Learn*, ed. Robert Slavin, Schlomo Sharan, Spencer Kagan, R. Hertz-Lazarowitz, C. Webb, and R. Schmuck. New York: Plenum, 1985.

Grolnick, Wendy S., and Ryan, Richard M. "Autonomy in Children's Learning: An Experimental and Individual Difference Investigation," *Journal of Personality and Social Psychology* 52 (1987): 890–98.

Grusec, Joan E., and Mills, R. "The Acquisition of Self-control." In *Psychological Development in the Elementary Years*, ed. J. Worell. San Francisco: Academic Press, 1982.

Habermas, Jürgen. *Theorie des kummunikativen Handelns. Bd. 1. Handlungsrationalitat und gesellschaftliche Rationalisierung. Bd. 2. Zur Kritik der funktionalistischen Vernunft*. Frankfurt: Suhrkamp, 1981. Cited in Oser, Fritz K., "Moral Education and Values Education: The Discourse Perspective." In *Handbook of Research on Teaching*, 3rd ed., ed. Merlin Wittrock. New York: Macmillan, 1986.

Hersch, Richard H.; Paolitto, Diana P.; and Reimer, Joseph. *Promoting Moral Growth*. New York: Longmans, 1979.

Hoffman, Martin L. "Empathy: Its Development and Prosocial Implications." In *Nebraska Symposium on Motivation*, Vol. 25, ed. C. B. Keasey. Lincoln: University of Nebraska Press, 1978.

Hoffman, Martin L. "Empathy, Social Cognition, and Moral Action." In *Moral Behavior and Development: Advances in Theory, Research, and Application*, ed. William M. Kurtines and Jacob L. Gewirtz. Hillsdale, N.J.: Erlbaum, forthcoming.

Hoffman, Martin L., and Saltzstein, Herbert D. "Parent Discipline and the Child's Moral Development," *Journal of Personality and Social Psychology* 5 (1967): 45–57.

Honig, William F. *Last Chance for Our Children*. Menlo Park, Calif.: Addison-Wesley, 1985.

Johnson, David W., and Johnson, Roger T. *Learning Together and Alone: Cooperation, Competition, and Individualization*. Englewood Cliffs, N.J.: Prentice-Hall, 1975.

Jones, Fred H. "The Gentle Art of Classroom Discipline." *National Elementary Principal* 58 (1979): 26–32.

Kagan, Spencer. *Cooperative Learning Resources for Teachers*. Riverside, Calif.: Spencer Kagan, 1985.

Koestner, Richard; Ryan, Richard M.; Bernieri, Frank; and Holt, Kathleen. "Setting Limits on Children's Behavior: The Differential Effects of Controlling versus Informational Styles on Intrinsic Motivation and Creativity," *Journal of Personality* 52 (1984): 233–48.

Kohlberg, Lawrence. "State and Sequence: The Cognitive-developmental Approach to Socialization." In *Handbook of Socialization Theory and Research*, ed. David Goslin. Chicago: Rand McNally, 1969.

Kohlberg, Lawrence. "Moral Stages and Moralization: The Cognitive-developmental Approach." In *Moral Development and Behavior*, ed. Thomas Lickona. New York: Holt, Rinehart and Winston, 1976.

Kohlberg, Lawrence; Kauffman, K.; Sharf, P.; and Hickey, J. *The Just Community*

Approach to Corrections. Cambridge, Mass.: Moral Education Research Foundation, 1974.

Lepper, Mark R., and Greene, David. *The Hidden Costs of Reward.* New York: Wiley, 1978.

Lewis, Catherine C. "The Effects of Parental Firm Control: A Reinterpretation of Findings," *Psychological Bulletin* 90 (1981): 547–63.

Maccoby, Eleanor E., and Martin, John A. "Socialization in the Context of the Family: Parent-child Interaction." In *Handbook of Child Psychology*, 4th ed., Vol. 4, *Socialization, Personality, and Social Development*, ed. E. Mavis Hetherington. New York: Wiley, 1983.

Maslow, Abraham H. *Motivation and Personality*, 2d ed. New York: Harper and Row, 1970.

Minuchin, Patricia P., and Shapiro, Edna K. "The School as a Context for Social Development." In *Handbook of Child Psychology*, 4th ed., Vol. 4, *Socialization, Personality, and Social Development*. New York: Wiley, 1983.

Mussen, Paul H., and Eisenberg-Berg, Nancy. *Roots of Caring, Sharing, and Helping.* San Francisco: Freeman, 1977.

Oser, Fritz K. "Moral Education and Values Education: The Discourse Perspective." In *Handbook of Research on Teaching*, 3rd ed., ed. Merlin Wittrock. New York: Macmillan, 1986.

Piaget, Jean. *The Moral Judgment of the Child.* New York: Free Press, 1932.

Power, Clark. "The Moral Atmosphere of a Just Community High School: A Four-Year Longitudinal Study." Doct. dissertation, Harvard University, 1979.

Pulkkinen, Lea. "Self-control and Continuity from Childhood to Adolescence." In *Life-Span Development and Behavior*, Vol. 4, ed. P. B. Baltes and O. G. Brim. New York: Academic Press, 1982.

Radke-Yarrow, Marian; Zahn-Waxler, Carolyn; and Chapman, Michael. "Children's Prosocial Dispositions and Behavior." In *Handbook of Child Psychology*, 4th ed., Vol. 4, *Socialization, Personality, and Social Development*, ed. E. M. Hetherington. New York: Wiley, 1983.

Rest, James R. "Morality." In *Handbook of Child Psychology*, 4th ed., Vol. 3, *Cognitive Development*, ed. John H. Flavell and Ellen M. Markman. New York: Wiley, 1983.

Schantz, Carolyn U. "The Development of Social Cognition." In *Review of Child Development Research*, Vol. 5, ed. E. Mavis Hetherington. Chicago: University of Chicago Press, 1975.

Schmalz, Jeffrey. "Cuomo Plans Effort to Get Schools to Return to Teaching of 'Values,'" *New York Times* (29 August 1986).

Selman, Robert. "The Relation of Role-taking to the Development of Moral Judgments in Children," *Child Development* 42 (1971): 1721–34.

Sharan, Schlomo, and Sharan, Yael. *Small-group Teaching.* Englewood Cliffs, N.J.: Educational Technology Publications, 1976.

Slavin, Robert E. *Cooperative Learning.* New York: Longmans, 1983.

Solomon, Daniel and Kendall, Arthur J. "Teachers' Perceptions of, and Reactions to, 'Misbehavior' in Traditional and Open Classroom Settings," *Journal of Educational Psychology* 67 (1975): 528–30.

Solomon, Daniel; Schaps, Eric; Watson, Marilyn S.; and Battistich, Victor. "Promoting Prosocial Behavior in Schools: A Second Interim Report on a Five-year Longitudinal Project." Paper presented at the annual meeting of the American Educational Research Association, Washington, D.C., 1987.

Solomon, Daniel; Watson, Marilyn; Battistich, Victor; Schaps, Eric; Tuck, Patricia; Solomon, Judith; Cooper, Carole; and Ritchey, Wendy. "A Program to Promote Interpersonal Consideration and Cooperation in Children." In *Learning to Cooperate, Cooperating to Learn*, ed. Robert Slavin, Schlomo Sharan, Spencer Kagan, Rachel Hertz-Lazarowitz, Clark Webb, and Richard Schmuck. New York: Plenum, 1985.

Solomon, Daniel; Watson, Marilyn; Schaps, Eric; Battistich, Victor; and Solomon, Judith. "Cooperative Learning as Part of a Comprehensive Classroom Program Designed to Promote Prosocial Development." In *Current Research on Cooperative Learning*, ed. Schlomo Sharan. New York: Praeger, forthcoming.

Solomon, Daniel; Watson, Marilyn S.; Delucchi, Kevin E.; Schaps, Eric; and Battistich, Victor. "Enhancing Children's Prosocial Behavior in the Classroom," in *American Educational Research Journal*, in press.

Sroufe, L. Alan. "Infant-caregiver Attachment and Patterns of Adaptation in Preschool: The Roots of Maladaptation and Competence." In *Minnesota Symposia on Child Psychology*, Vol. 16, ed. M. Perlmutter. Hillsdale, N.J.: Erlbaum, 1983.

Staub, Ervin. "To Rear a Prosocial Child: Reasoning, Learning by Doing, and Learning by Teaching Others." In *Moral Development: Current Theory and Research*, ed. D. Depalma and J. Folley. Hillsdale, N.J.: Erlbaum, 1975.

Staub, Ervin. *Positive Social Behavior and Morality, Vol. 1: Social and Personal Influences.* New York: Academic Press, 1978.

Staub, Ervin. *Positive Social Behavior and Morality, Vol. 2: Socialization and Development.* New York: Academic Press, 1979.

Watson, Marilyn S.; Hildebrandt, Carolyn; and Solomon, Daniel. "Cooperative Learning as a Means of Promoting Prosocial Development among Kindergarten and Early Primary Grade Children," *International Journal of Social Education*, in press.

White, Robert W. "Motivation Reconsidered: The Concept of Competence," *Psychological Review* 66 (1959): 297–333.

Whiting, Beatrice B., and Whiting, John W. M. *Children of Six Cultures: A Psychocultural Analysis.* Cambridge, Mass.: Harvard University Press, 1975.

Whiting, John W. M., and Whiting, Beatrice B. "Altruistic and Egoistic Behavior in Six Cultures." In *Cultural Illness and Health: Essays in Human Adaptation* (Anthropological Studies, No. 9). Washington, D.C.: American Anthropological Association, 1973.

Youniss, James. *Parents and Peers in Social Development.* Chicago: University of Chicago Press, 1980.

Zahn-Waxler, Carolyn; Radke-Yarrow, Marian, and King, M. "Child Rearing and Children's Prosocial Initiations toward Victims of Distress," *Child Development* 50 (1979): 319–30.

Part II

The Cognitive-Developmental Approach to Moral Education

5

The Character of Moral Development

Dwight Boyd

INTRODUCTION

One of the criticisms that has often been leveled at Lawrence Kohlberg's conception of moral development is that it manifests an impoverished view of human persons, perhaps even one of warped character. Forms of this criticism can be found, either asserted or implied, in intellectually respectable critiques published by a number of our colleagues (Sullivan 1977; Gilligan and Murphy 1979; Murphy and Gilligan 1980) and in the blatantly rhetorical and not so intellectually respectable papers of former U.S. Secretary of Education William Bennett (e.g., Bennett and Delattre 1979). What motivates this chapter is the belief that although there is an important concern underlying this criticism, at least a good part of how it is developed is mistaken. What *can* be taken from the criticism is an encouragement to think more directly and explicitly about how matters of character interact with the theory of moral development as currently expressed in the writings of Kohlberg and his colleagues—which is a major part of the motivation for the dialogue in this volume. On the other hand, the mistake that seems to me quite common is to misinterpret certain aspects of the theory in such a way as to create a straw person, the character of which can then be dismissively caricatured (and along with it, the theory as a whole).

In this paper I will endeavor to articulate a more adequate understanding of Kohlberg's theory, with respect to which the straw-person nature of some lines of criticism can be more clearly seen, and within which some positive claims about character can be illuminated as an integral part of the theory. In order to do this I will cover several different kinds of ground. After I present a more focused statement of the problem, I will first synthesize what I think are some of the most fundamental philosophical assumptions underlying Kohlberg's theory, which the aforementioned criticisms often lose sight of but which must be kept clearly in mind for any full picture of the character of moral development. Then I will work dialectically from correcting some of the common but mistaken character implications of the notion of principled morality to showing what positive picture of character emerges from an appreciation of recent elaborations of the nature of stage six, in the context of the philosophical assumptions already identified. Finally, in order to accomplish the positive task I will also argue that this more adequate interpretation hinges on an understanding of objectivity in morality different from that commonly assumed.

THE PROBLEM REFINED

Using a unique blend of philosophical reflection and empirical study, Kohlberg sought to describe moral learning over the lifespan in developmental terms. As the notion of "development" carries with it not only the notion of change but also the idea of change with regard to some specified dimension *and* in some direction considered to be an improvement, he also needed to articulate his conception of the aim of that development. Kohlberg understood that one's conception of the endpoint of a hierarchically related sequence of developmental stages serves both to draw boundaries around what is to be counted as falling within the domain of this empirical study and to establish criteria by which one can order the data so found into increasing steps of greater adequacy. In addressing this aspect of his theory, Kohlberg repeatedly described a postconventional level of moral reasoning and more specifically, a "stage six" within that level, in terms of the notion of a *principled* interpretation of justice as respect for persons. He has spelled this out in a variety of ways, but a good example for my purposes here is his following description of stage six:

> *The universal-ethical-principle orientation.* Right is defined by the decision of conscience in accord with self-chosen *ethical principles* appealing to logical comprehensiveness, universality, and consistency. These principles are abstract and ethical (the Golden Rule, the categorical imperative); they are not concrete moral rules like the Ten Commandments. At heart, these are universal principles of *justice*, of the *reciprocity* and *equality* of human *rights*, and of respect for the dignity of human beings as *individual persons.* [Kohlberg 1971, p. 165]

A communicative problem arises here: such short content descriptions of complex structures of judgment can be extremely misleading. An analogy for such descriptions of content is that they are like the small, usually dirty windows on the landings of staircases through which, if you are on the outside of a building and *lucky*, you can sometimes get a vague glimpse of people and the direction they are walking on the staircase within the building. Despite Kohlberg's several efforts to articulate the form of stage six more fully, it is certain aspects of such short content descriptions, extrapolated out to their assumed full meaning, that have been generally accepted as constituting an accurate picture of stage six, at least by critics. The problem is, however, that these aspects are taken out of the context of a full understanding of the theory as a whole and the structure of stage six within it. The result is a severely warped, attenuated picture. Moreover, what is important in the context of this chapter is that what gets warped and attenuated is not only stage six as a form of moral judgment, but also, through an oddly intellectualized process of guilt by association, the *person* who might find such a form of moral judgment accommodating. By correcting these misinterpretations of stage six we can lay the groundwork for a more balanced and plausible understanding of the character of moral development implicit in Kohlberg's theory.

Before my main analysis and argument can proceed, however, two further refinements are necessary to clarify the nature of the task; both involve additional problems of communication, in this case not inherent in Kohlberg's writings but in the way the notion of character is being used here. The first is an acknowledgement of the intentional ambiguity in this chapter's title, "The Character of Moral Development." That is, what I intend here is to work *from* the "character of moral development" in the sense of the understanding we currently have about the nature of moral development and the direction it takes (according to Kohlberg's theory) *to* an articulation of the "character of moral development" in the sense of what we might then want to say about the moral character of a person, fully developed according to this view. A shorthand way of saying this is with this question: What moral aspects of the person, of character, would seem best to "fit" our current understanding of stage six in Kohlberg's theory? Having thus asked this, I want to finesse the concern that might reasonably then be raised about the nature of this project—that is to say, what *kind* of "fit" am I presupposing and seeking to uncover? The stages of moral development, as conceived by Kohlberg, are clearly not descriptions of types of persons; nor should they ever be thought of in this way. They are, instead, qualitatively different patterns of interpreting and resolving particular aspects of social interaction among human persons. They are descriptions of a psychological function that persons *engage in*, not descriptions of the moral persons themselves. It is, then, conceptually confused, and in some contexts morally pernicious, to speak in terms such as "the stage two person," or "the stage six person." Thus I want to head off, and reject, any interpretation of my project as simply translating stage descriptions into character talk. On the contrary, this move must be framed more hypothetically, indeed, more speculatively. The question is better understood as follows: If a person had the capacity for stage six moral judgment, and were to be conceived as *using* that capacity to interpret and seek resolution of moral problems, what character traits would we see, given our current understanding of stage six, as congruent with and as facilitating this capacity or use? I realize, of course, that this approach walks immediately into a barrage of conceptual questions having to do with the difference between having a capacity and using that capacity, and this distinction must, in the end, be taken seriously in any thorough consideration of mature moral character. Moreover, there are also quite a number of other empirical questions about the relationship between moral development in terms of stages of moral judgment and in terms of the manifestation of a set of (approved) character traits. I want to acknowledge that these are all crucial questions for us to explore. However, at this time I think we are necessarily at a much grosser level. What we need first, I believe, is a theoretically sound and plausible picture of the categories of concern that will be the basis for such further exploration.

The second refinement is to avoid vagueness in the use of the term "character." That is, to what do I think the notion of moral character refers? This is *not* a notion that has received much attention within mainstream moral development theory ever since Kohlberg (1970) excoriated it with the label "bag of virtues." Of course, some critics of this rejection have repeatedly argued that one cannot get rid of the term so easily (e.g., Hamm 1977; Peters 1972), and it may even be sneaking back into favor in current developmentalist work on the notion of "the moral self." But it is clear that the notion itself is not very clear in any of this; much of the argument and counterargument hinges, I suspect, on different understandings of what character encompasses. In order to avoid adding to these problems of interpretation (especially in the context of the aims of this volume), but without getting into an elaborate conceptual analysis, I will simply assert here as concisely and precisely as possible the outlines of the concept of moral character as I will be using it. In short, I will use "moral character" to mean those enduring aspects of the expression of personhood to which we are inclined to give moral evaluation across different attitudinal and behavioral contexts. Several components of this understanding need emphasizing. (1) Character is the way we express our being *as persons* via attitudinal and behavioral dispositions. (2) These expressions are not just episodic, but must be relatively consistent over time. That is why we often refer to character *traits*. (3) They raise dependable expectations from other persons, regardless of what particular behavior is evidenced—or even regardless of whether this particular behavior is a *successful* expression of the intended aspect of character. (Note that 2 and 3 together allow us to speak of "strong" or "weak" characters.) (4) Some expressions will be nonmoral character traits; others will be clearly moral; and it is possible for some to be both, depending on context. What will determine whether or not something is an instance of *moral* character will be whether it is tied in some way to a particular normative moral orientation. (5) In addition to dividing on the moral/nonmoral description, those traits that *are* moral in this category sense are open to either positive or negative evaluation from a given moral point of view. (This latter point allows us to speak of "good" or "bad" character, as well as "strong" or "weak.")

SOME BASIC STARTING POINTS

For almost thirty years Lawrence Kohlberg endeavored to describe, to measure, and to explore the educational implications of the development of moral judgment. In doing so he engaged in scores of empirical studies, using samples from the whole human age span and a wide variety of cultures. His empirical methodology is now very well known worldwide and has spawned both hundreds of studies replicating and extending his findings and a large number of critiques aiming to show that these findings are spurious in some way. His six stages of moral judgment are now as well known to psychologists as Campbell's soup is to the American cook. But equally as important as the empirical methodology and claims are the philosophical dimensions of this theory. Indeed, one of the unique aspects of Kohlberg's theory of moral development, compared to the rest of mainstream North American social psychology, is the way that it explicitly integrates into an empirical concern certain understandings of persons and morality that would normally be solidly located on the philosophical side of the renowned gap between psychology and philosophy. As I have argued elsewhere (Boyd 1985), it is this combination of kinds of claims that has led to one of Kohlberg's more radical, but still mostly misunderstood, theoretical claims about the "naturalistic fallacy." Although individually these philosophical starting points of Kohlberg's theory are undoubtedly well known, a synthesis of them is warranted here, first, because any thorough dialogue with alternative approaches to moral experience and growth will in the end revolve around these starting points, and second, because my eventual claims about the kind of character that fits stage six are necessarily tied to these starting assumptions that ground and frame developmental theory.

The following are what seem to me some of the most basic starting points of Kohlberg's theory.

1. At the most foundational level is an assumption about the human self, which is probably drawn from George Herbert Mead. The assumption is that the psychological self—the sense of "myself" that we all have—is a social construct. "Self" and "other" are not metaphysical entities, each standing alone, totally independent. They are, rather, *correlative categories*, both conceptually and developmentally. One's own self and the self's needs can be delineated only in reference to an awareness of others as selves and their needs, and vice

versa. We then give moral weight to these divisions via our notion of *person*hood, which recognizes that the welfare of oneself can be both benefited and harmed by others.

2. The second assumption, then, is that the institution of morality is a mode of regulating the interaction of persons with regard to both manners of possible effect on each other. Kohlberg shared with many contemporary philosophers an understanding of morality as a kind of social tool and an understanding of the twin functions this tool is meant to serve. For example, Thomas Nagel has articulated this assumption quite neatly: "The central problem of ethics [is] how the lives, interests, and welfare of others make claims on us and how these claims, of various forms, are to be reconciled with the aim of living our own lives" (Nagel 1986, p. 164). Moral evaluations are then judgments of the appropriateness of some act or pattern of action that might be performed by a (or any) person insofar as it affects the interests of another person or other persons. The type of effect can then be described in terms of persons' benefiting from another's help or care, in terms of their claims to forbearance of another's infringement on their projects or autonomy, or by some combination of these two directions of influence. In short, Kohlberg's psychological theory and findings must always be understood in the context of a particular view of morality; the "moral" in "moral development" has specific and explicitly recognized conceptual boundaries. To put all this in Kohlberg's own terms, let me quote from his response chapter in the recent collection, *Lawrence Kohlberg: Consensus and Controversy*:

> Some philosophic definition of the moral domain is required as a starting point for psychological or empirical study of moral development or morality becomes synonymous with all valuing. Since my thesis I have defined developing morality as involving "a moral point of view" including not only Kant's or Hare's prescriptivity, universalizability and over-ridingness and its implication of judging and acting on principles, but also including impartiality or considering the good of everyone alike and reversibility, which is not quite the same as universalizability. The "moral point of view" is somewhat broader than a concern for distributive, commutative and restorative justice, since it can center on an attitude or principle of beneficence in situations without conflicting claims between two or more others and only involving the self and one other. [Kohlberg 1985, pp. 500-1]

3. A third assumption consists of an integration of the first two; that is, it returns to a view of the person, but now in the context of the interaction of persons and their construction of the mode of mutual

regulation called morality. The assumption is that part of what it means to be a person is the effort to be a *moral* person. Kohlberg rarely acknowledged this assumption in so many words, perhaps because it was so central to his own understanding of his project of identifying stages of moral judgment that he assumed it would be obvious to anyone else. But unfortunately it has remained too much in the background of the common understanding of his theory, with the result, I would suggest, that much of the interpersonal relational flavor of the theory has been missed by both critics and supporters alike. However, it was acknowledged quite explicitly by Kohlberg in a recent reply to some critics. Arguing that he has always avoided any "emotivist" view of the stages (by which he means an interpretation of the stages in terms of different *motives*), Kohlberg points out that, instead, "I have claimed that in some sense there is a primary motivation 'to do the right thing' in the sociomoral world as Piaget assumed a primary adaptation [of] 'truth' motivation for the infant and child's actions toward the physical world" (1985, pp. 498–99). This may be a slightly misfortunate way of putting it because the notion of *doing* the right thing overshadows the notion of *figuring out* what is the right thing to do and tends to eclipse the conceptual point that the latter is necessarily *part of* "doing the right thing." Moreover, I am not sure what kind of action Kohlberg had in mind here, nor the extent to which he wanted to build a behavioral disposition into his conception of the person at this level. However, I think that at the very least—and this is all we need from this assumption—he is claiming that his conception of the human person includes a natural disposition to seek a balance actively between (to use Nagel's words again) "how the lives, interests, and welfare of others make claims on us and how these claims, of various forms, are to be reconciled with the aim of living our own lives." The self of our first assumption does get delineated not just in terms of the other (and vice versa) but *also* in terms of its active attempt to understand, respond to, and *balance* the perceived needs of both the self and others.

4. A fourth step in these starting points of Kohlberg's theory pulls these existing strands together even tighter: the intentionality of morality is assumed and integrated with the developmental nature of the moral person. I have already noted that Kohlberg shared with many contemporary philosophers a view of morality as a social tool constructed by humans to regulate certain aspects of their interaction. However, to say this in this way is to take an external view of that

function, to stand outside the institution of morality and make a descriptive theoretical claim about it. But such an external perspective can never provide more than a partial picture of that institution. The reason for this is that a moral act is an *intentional* act that is tied intrinsically to a particular kind of *reason*. It is not just a piece of behavior that when observed from the outside can be seen to serve a certain social function; instead, it must also be viewed from the inside, from the point of view of the moral agent. And from this perspective a moral act is something a person *does in order to* accomplish some goal or purpose, which is judged to be good and/or obligatory by that person, according to that person's understanding of how the needs of self and other can best be balanced. As Charles Bailey has made this point recently, "Out of the context of reflection and judgment pieces of behavior are neither moral nor immoral but mere happenings: part of the natural world but not of the world of morality" (Bailey 1985, p. 199). Kohlberg often identifies this part of this assumption by referring to his "formalist" meta-ethical position that guides his empirical enquiries. For example, "For the 'formalist' meta-ethical philosophic position I hold, a necessary part of a moral action is guidance or justification by a moral reason, that is, by a judgment of rational and autonomous obligation" (Kohlberg 1985, p. 499).

In addition, the second part of this fourth assumption is that the particular form this "judgment of rational and autonomous obligation" may take in any instance of intentional moral behavior (whether engaged in or contemplated) will depend, at least in part, on the understanding of the notions of moral persons and their interrelation that is currently operative for the person making the judgment. That is, within this theory moral agents are seen as *meaning makers*. They do not more or less successfully just passively absorb and reflect some fixed moral reality that is *a priori* and independent of their efforts; instead, they are continually engaged in the activity of *constructing* that reality through their efforts to "make sense" of their relations to others, who are perceived as like the self but *not* the self. Depending on the experiences a person has had, not the least of which are role-taking opportunities, different coherent patterns of understanding this aspect of the social environment emerge and function as a framework for communication and interaction with other persons. (In short, these are the stages of moral judgment that form the core of Kohlberg's empirical theory.)

5. Finally, a fifth assumption elaborates the interpersonal nature of

this constructive endeavor. It is true that the individual person strives to "make sense" of his or her moral relationships to others and then uses this understanding to frame intentional moral acts. But this further point consists of the recognition that the only meaning that *can* make sense, given the area of concern as defined, is *shared* meaning. This is now the full sense of the notion of morality as a social tool; in short, it is a mode of interpreting human experience that is meaningful only because it is a construction shared by more than one person. Moral concepts of this sort (e.g., trust, equality, care, respect) are the meaning tools that are our preeminent expressions of our recognition of the lived reality of others *and* our claim on their recognition of ours. Moreover, the use of these concepts in the formulation of reasons and rules meant to guide moral action is also necessarily a matter of shared construction. As we have seen from previous assumptions, morality according to this view is our way of balancing the claims arising from the interaction of lives, interests, and welfare. But these very claims are not *given*, not *static*; they emerge from the real interaction of different but connected persons. And they always necessarily have points of view built into them. Thus reasons for action aimed at balance are always essentially contestable, and can only be *aimed* at mutual acceptance. As Kohlberg puts this point, "the function of moral reasoning, judgment and argumentation is to reach agreement where claims or interests conflict, most especially where the conflict is between two or more persons." (Kohlberg 1985, p. 510). In short, moral persons "are not thought of as independent, isolated 'rule followers,' with greater or lesser direct access to moral truth, but rather as rule-followers-in-relation who must construct and continually reconstruct through public dialogue the perspective from which rules governing their interaction have validity" (Boyd 1980, p. 204).

As I have already argued, it is the kind of assumptions just outlined that describe Kohlberg's theory of moral development as much as, or *more than*, the empirical claims that are perhaps more commonly known. These assumptions, quite literally, give the empirical claims meaning; that is, they allow us to interpret what it means to say that people tend to solve moral problems by use of different stages of moral reasoning and tend to go through these stages in a sequential, invariant order, from stage one to stage six. There are probably other such general assumptions we would need to explicate if we were after a comprehensive view of Kohlberg's theory. However, I would argue that any such comprehensive view would have to include, and be anchored in, the assumptions I just articulated. Moreover, I believe they are all we need for my purpose in this chapter, which is to explore the character of moral development in the way I have suggested.

SOME WAYS OF GOING WRONG IN INTERPRETATION OF STAGE SIX (AND THE CHARACTER OF THAT INTERPRETATION)

Given an acceptance of these basic assumptions as philosophical starting points of Kohlberg's theory, I think it is easier to see why some common interpretations of stage six are surely mistakes, mistakes with character implications that are thus avoidable. In identifying some of these mistakes, then, I have the aim of not only correcting them but also illuminating the direction of a more insightful understanding of the character traits that should be thought of as intrinsic to (or at least required by) Kohlberg's theory.

Probably at the bottom of this line of interpretation that I want to deflect is a narrow view of reason that gets exaggerated to the point of caricature by the time stage six is considered. That is, Kohlberg's theory is often characterized as describing increasingly adequate stages of moral *reasoning*. But then, so this misinterpretation goes, if each stage is a stage of reasoning, the lower stages are lower because they have just a little reasoning. As you go up the sequence, you get more reasoning. And this increases until you reach the end, stage six, which is "pure reason," that is, stage six is thought to be *nothing but* reason. But then, a critic will say, what an inhumane notion of moral maturity! Instead of a notion of moral goodness described in human terms of flesh and blood, aspirations and their perversion, affect, will, and strength of character, we get a cold, bloodless, calculating machine, or at least a rigid template for making calculations.

Because this problem raises large issues about theories of rationality and the emotions and about the relationship between the two, I cannot deal completely with it here. However, I believe it is sufficient to avoid this absurd conclusion to point out that it rests on a confusion of the conceptual point about what constitutes a moral act, with the normative criterion that must be appealed to for any "developmental" claim with regard to the increasing adequacy of the stages. As we have already seen, one of Kohlberg's starting points *is* the intentionality of morality, which simply means that (to use Bailey's words again) " to be viewed in a moral dimension at all, a situation and its attendant feelings must always be rationally appraised" (Bailey 1985, p. 203). What counts as appropriate and thorough rational appraisal cannot come from this conceptual point alone. Magnifying the rational side of "rational appraisal" to the image of "cold and calculating" rests on exactly this confusion. That image of stage six begins to lose its influence on us when we realize it depends on this confusion.

It loses even more influence when we realize that to say that something is conceptually tied to rational appraisal is simply to say, at the most basic level, that it is something about which one can or should "stop and think," and without this input (at least in principle), one is engaged in something other than morality, such as anxiety reduction. Finally, it begins to look downright silly when we realize that, contrary to the image of a calculating machine that can only manipulate *a priori* assumptions, any developed form of rational appraisal such as stage six will necessarily be imbued with strong powers of *imagination*. What I mean here can perhaps best be expressed with the words of the Canadian novelist Robertson Davies (via the Oxford lawyer, Pargetter, speaking to Davey Staunton): "When I say imagination I mean capacity to see all sides of a subject and weight all possibilities; I don't mean fantasy and poetry and moonshine; imagination is a good horse to carry you over the ground, not a flying carpet to set you free from probability" (Davies 1972, p. 227).

In this case, the "ground" that needs to be covered has already been formally staked out in the other starting assumptions of Kohlberg's theory identified above. Seeing all sides of a subject and weighting all possibilities is clearly *required* in any mature form of our constructive activity of "making sense" of our social environment— and especially the conflicts within it arising from the different points of view inherent in different persons—in service of balancing the claims arising from the lives, interests, and welfare of both others and self. To reduce this to any narrow sense of calculative reason is simply to miss the rich theoretical context within which the stages exist.

A second characteristic of this line of interpretation that I want to expose and reject probably originates from a shallow understanding of the notion of a moral principle, which, according to the quoted short description of stage six, will be a mainstay of the appropriate rational appraisal. According to this mistaken view, principles are abstract moral rules, "out there," external to but discoverable by human consciousness. They are seen as rigid, inflexible stopping points to our moral deliberation and justification. They are thought to be *sufficient* to dictate answers to concrete moral problems, with the additional power to determine unique answers in all cases. They are, supposedly, by virtue of being blind to context and situational particularities, the way in which we establish consistency in our moral response, even when (especially when?) that consistency is at the expense of perceived complexity and remaining problems. When the notion of moral principles is interpreted in this rigid way, the mind that must find them congenial is to some large extent *closed* (especially in complex moral conflictual situations of the sort stage six is supposed to be able to handle). Further, the character this suggests approaches the caricature of a martinet "goody two-shoes."[1]

Again, I think an adequate response to this view can be made without elaborating a thorough analysis of the nature and role of moral principles in moral deliberation or justification. What we need to see is that the notion of being principled picks out a kind of consistency, but it is not the kind identified by the view at hand; and it can be seen as a kind of virtue, though for entirely the opposite reason from what this mistaken view suggests. In short, we need to keep in mind that principles are not directly related to particular concrete acts, as are moral rules (as in "Do not steal"), but rather serve to compare and evaluate different acts falling under different, often conflicting direct rules. They are, in Dewey's words, "a method and scheme for judging" (1960, p. 136), which exist because we construct them. They are not, then, final stopping points of deliberation or justification but rather flexible attempts to integrate solutions to difficult problems into coherent patterns. A sense of consistency *is* part of the principled picture, but it is consistency in consideration of relevant perspectives, not sameness of answer. When this characteristic of consistency is extended from a logical property of principles to an aspect of personhood, it must then be properly qualified by the quality of *openmindedness*. Principled judgment is dynamic, not static; it is not evidence of a closed mind achieving consistency by ignoring

---

1. A careful synthesis of the implied interpretation of Kohlberg against which Gilligan and Murphy (1979) (and Murphy and Gilligan 1980) offer their critique will adequately support the claim that this is *not* a case of fighting a straw person with another straw person.

things but rather the way in which we strive to keep our minds open in order to *seek* consistency of evaluation.

A third commonly implied, but I think mistaken, characteristic of principled moral judgment could perhaps be developed as part of the second just discussed; however, I believe it is enough of an extension of this mistaken view of principles, and of sufficient importance, to warrant separate treatment. What I have in mind here is what happens when this mistaken view of the logical and functional properties of principles gets extended to more psychological process claims about how principles are thought of as being *used* in moral judgment. Here we run into the common notion of a "principled person" as one who is in a sense flexible in the context of adherence to chosen principles, as one who does not countenance doubt or slippage when it is a case of, or opportunity for, "sticking to one's principles." This is the sense of principle-in-use that is captured by the colloquial notions of "standing on principles" and not budging from a claim with regard to what one sees as "the principle of the matter." There is, of course, an important truth in this view. This truth is that a universalizability requirement is built into our notion of "principle" and the particularly stringent test case for meeting this requirement with regard to some principle that one is claiming to use occurs if one still maintains the principle even when dropping it would somehow favor one's own interests.

However, this truth is only part of the whole picture; it is a serious misrepresentation when taken as all of the picture. What we need to balance it and complete the picture of how principles function might be captured by the notion of a *sense of irony*. That is, it is the flexible perspective on judging, which principled consideration can provide, that gives one room to acknowledge and appreciate incongruities between rule-dictated expectations and what one senses ought to be the case. It is this openness to irony in the face of moral imperatives that provides the superior adaptability of principled judgment and is a necessary antidote to blind persistence of commitment. It is, in short, an essential aspect of attitude for a view that, as we have seen earlier, conceives of moral principles as *interpersonal constructions* of meaning.

This line of argument could be continued for some time, all of it suggesting ways in which we need to be careful in how we conceptualize principled moral judgment. However, I think we already have in front of us enough to facilitate a more direct analysis of what might be at issue between the two views. It should be remembered that my purpose in exposing and correcting these mistaken interpretations is ultimately to approach the question of what kind of character best "fits" our understanding of the stage-six form of moral judgment. What I have done so far, then, is to synthesize one common view that I think takes us in the wrong direction in answering this question, and to suggest what needs to be added in order to correct the view. To summarize, I have noted how the mistaken view tries to paint a picture of a person who is "purely rational," disposed simply to casuistically manipulate known factors; who seeks a sense of consistency through appeal to external abstract rules that simply lay down answers for us; and who has a strong sense of stick-to-it-ive-ness whenever a situation calls a rule into question. I have, then, sought to repaint this picture by noting how appropriate use of reason requires a strong, active imagination, how principles really require consistency of perspective seeking that entails an openmindedness, and how proper *use* of principles promotes ironic adaptability more than inflexibility.

THE STAGE SIX MORAL POINT OF VIEW, OBJECTIVELY SPEAKING

Now these characteristics of persons, as extrapolated from the two different interpretations of stage six, are aspects of personality that could at least in some contexts be considered aspects of character. But, as they stand so far they are what we would have to call nonmoral character traits; neither interpretation is as yet a picture of *moral* character, because all the components of both interpretations can be manifested in clearly nonmoral contexts. As was noted above, such traits can be described as *moral* character traits only when they are manifested in service of a normative moral orientation. The question I want to turn to now is: What are the moral orientations that could convert these two pictures into pictures of *moral* character? I want to show how only the second of the two pictures will be congruent with, and can be seen as traits in service of, the particular moral point of view expressed by stage six. Further, this point of view can be operationally expressed in such a way as to uncover and illuminate heretofore unsuspected dimensions of character that would seem to be required by stage six.

To answer the question of what moral point of view could utilize the two pictures, we have to return to the "starting points" of Kohlberg's theory that I articulated at the outset of this chapter. I have pointed out that Kohlberg's theory starts from a view of morality as a social construction aimed at mutually acceptable regulation of the interaction of persons in terms of how they might benefit from, and avoid harm in, that interaction. Or, as Nagel puts it, morality is the institution that organizes our attempts to solve the problem of "how the lives, interests, and welfare of others make claims on us and how these claims, of various forms, are to be reconciled with the aim of living our own lives" (1986, p. 164). Since the whole point of morality, according to this view, is the achievement of this regulation in some sort of reasonable balance, it cannot be done from solely within the point of view of any particular person's life, interest, and welfare. Instead, it necessitates the construction of an external perspective (one that is "out there") relative to any and all such particular points of view, while at the same time maintaining an appreciation of exactly that particularity in its every instance. But note that what I have just said identifies the concept of *objectivity* as intrinsically connected to the moral project so understood: objectivity is exactly that characteristic of our judgment that somehow is congruent with something "out there" such that error in judgment can be picked out with some confidence and with intersubjective recognition. The "moral point of view" that Kohlberg often refers to (as quoted earlier) is then that point of view within human judgment about acts involving the claims arising from the lives, interests, and welfare of more than one person that *lays claim to objectivity*. What is needed is a better understanding of how a particular view of objectivity shapes the moral point of view at the heart of Kohlberg's theory.

First of all, we need to see that an inadequate view of objectivity permeates the mistaken interpretation of stage six that I have been at pains to avoid. In short, I think that the characteristics I identified as part of the common but mistaken interpretation could be seen as moral character traits *only* by their being conjoined with the interpretation of objectivity inherent in what Kohlberg has described as a "conventional" understanding of morality. That is, on this interpretation what suffices to establish objectivity about moral claims is not any direct reference to the lives, interests, and welfare of persons involved, but rather an appeal to whatever set of abstract role expectations or rules of conduct constitute a particular social system.

It is the existence (or *positing* of the existence) of these role expectations and systemic rules that provides the "out there" perspective
relative to the claims inherent within any particular person's point of
view. And it is in reference to this conception of morality that the
person with a casuistical sense of reason, seeking consistency via clear
appeal to rigid rules and simple solutions, not wavering from the task
of maintaining allegiance to the rule, is thought to have moral
character.

Now if this *were* the interpretation of objectivity inherent in Kohlberg's ideal of stage six principled morality, then we *would* have good
reason to express concern, along with the critics, about the concomi-
tant picture of character. But I would argue that this view of objectivity is at fault for leaving the subjectivity of persons—both that of the
moral judge and that of the others whose claims need considering—
out of the picture, in a way that stage six cannot do. It is a kind of
reification of the "out there" that is more appropriately identified, as
Max Deutscher (1983) does, as "objecti*vism*": "Objectivism is the
view that would have us forget that it is a view; the objectivist is a
subject who would forget and have others forget that he is a subject.
There is only what is viewed; the viewing of it is passed over" (p. 29).
When objectivity is understood in this way it spawns a legitimate
complaint that the particularities of real persons and their interaction
are eclipsed and seen as secondary in importance to the "objectivity"
of impersonal and abstract "principles." That this complaint *cannot* be
justifiably directed at Kohlberg can be shown by combining a fuller
understanding of the normative core of stage six with the more
dynamic sense of objectivity that this stage requires. In the process of
doing this, I will also illuminate the essential dimensions of the
character of stage six.

First of all, as I have argued elsewhere (Boyd 1980), the normative
core of Kohlberg's moral orientation is properly located in the notion
of *respect for persons*, not in any narrow view of "justice." It is true that
justice has usually been explicitly identified as his focus of attention;
and in a few places he has even seemed to equate all of morality with
justice. However, this has always turned out to be a very broad notion
of justice, one grounded in and seeking to express (in his words)
"respect for the dignity of human beings as *individual persons*" (1971,
p. 165). Given the conception of persons articulated earlier as one of
Kohlberg's basic starting points (that is, persons are relationally
defined social selves who have claims on each other both in their need

for positive help in fulfilling interests and in their requests for equal consideration of those interests as an expression of autonomy), *respect* for persons does necessitate justice as one dimension. But it is important to keep in mind that this dimension is always contextualized by a more general and diffuse dimension of furthering the other's welfare *as one's own*, that is, of benevolence.

An active, reflexive dealing with these different dimensions of moral experience is now quite clearly articulated by Kohlberg as a necessary aspect of our understanding of stage six. I quote from a recent paper entitled "The Return of Stage 6," coauthored by Kohlberg, myself, and Charles Levine:

> From a Stage 6 standpoint the autonomous moral actor has to consciously coordinate the two attitudes of justice and benevolence in dealing with real moral problems in order to maintain respect for persons. The way of regarding the other which we are calling benevolence views the other and human interaction through the lens of intending to promote good and prevent harm to the other. It is an attitude which presupposes and expresses one's identification and empathic connection with others. . . . Thus, as a mode of interaction between self and others which manifests a Stage 6 conception of respect for persons, benevolence is logically and psychologically prior to what we are calling justice. On the other hand, justice views the other and human interaction through the lens of intending to adjudicate interests, that is, of intending to resolve conflicts of differing and incompatible claims among individuals. Given this adjudicatory lens, justice presupposes a momentary separation of individual wills and cognitively organizes this separation in the service of achieving a fair adjudication through a recognition of equality and reciprocal role-taking. Thus, these two attitudes of benevolence and justice may be experienced in potential tension with each other. . . . We wish to emphasize that although these two attitudes are in tension with each other, they are at the same time mutually supportive and coordinated within a Stage 6 conception of respect for persons. This coordination can be summarized thus: benevolence constrains the momentary concern for justice to remain consistent with the promotion of good for all, while justice constrains benevolence not to be inconsistent with promoting respect for the rights of individuals conceived as autonomous agents. In other words, the aim of the autonomous Stage 6 moral agent is to seek resolution of moral problems in such a way that promoting good for some does not fail to respect the rights of others, and respecting the rights of individuals does not fail to seek promotion of the best for all. As Baier (1965) has succinctly put it, the moral point of view must evaluate "for the good of everyone alike." We think this coordination is what makes the golden rule so compelling and timeless. That is, in its positive interpretation, "Do unto others as you would have them do unto you," it expresses the attitude of benevolence as elaborated in the Christian maxim of "Love thy neighbor as thyself." On the other hand, in its proscriptive interpretation, "Do not do unto others as you would not wish others to do unto you," it expresses the attitude of justice as respecting and not

interfering with the rights and autonomy of others. [Kohlberg, Boyd, and Levine forthcoming]

It is this understanding of respect for persons that must be kept in mind in any analysis of the normative orientation underlying Kohlberg's conception of moral maturity, and thus his whole theory of moral development. Clearly, a thorough exposition of the claims made with regard to this orientation, and particularly how it gets operationalized in terms of psychological processes, is beyond the scope of this chapter. (See Kohlberg, Boyd, and Levine, forthcoming, for further discussion.) However, we already have enough here for us to proceed with the question at hand. The essential point is that the disposition to treat others with *respect* in this general sense will necessarily be at the core of the view of moral character congruent with stage six. The different aspects of the view are then as follows.

Although it is often overlooked, the first point is quite straightforward: both "dimensions" of moral experience—one might even say "poles"—found within the aim of maintaining respect for persons can be expressed in character terms. The attitudes of benevolence and justice are "ways of regarding" others in view of the claims their lives, interests, and welfare make on us. Each of these ways of regarding others can be expressed as a principle of action, resulting in analysis of moral problems from the perspective of principles of justice and beneficence. But in addition, both can also find expression as a disposition state of being, *qua person*. That is, both benevolence and justice can be understood as fundamental moral character traits. Indeed, Frankena (1973) argues, and I agree, that these two are the *only* instances of what he calls "cardinal virtues." What he means by this is that "(1) they cannot be derived from one another and (2) all other moral virtues can be derived from or shown to be forms of them" (p. 64). In short, a character formed primarily of the cardinal virtues of benevolence and justice is clearly congruent with stage six.

Another aspect of this view is the way respect for persons is seen as organizing benevolence and justice in stage six. Frankena also recognizes the potential tension or conflict between the two dimensions or poles (benevolence and justice), but he does not actively deal with it beyond expressing the "hope" that they "are in some sense ultimately consistent" (1973, p. 53). What I want to say about stage six, however, is that it is a form of moral judgment that entails the *active seeking* of the *coordination* of the attitudes of benevolence and justice via the attitude of respect for persons. Stage six does not just view some situations as matters of benevolence and others as matters of justice; rather, it realizes that approaching a situation with either concern may have implications for the other concern. And it is the placing of oneself within the process of coordinating the different pulls of moral action that the active sense of respecting persons captures. Further, what this means for our central question in this chapter is that there must also be aspects of character congruent with this attitude of respectful seeking of coordination of moral response, in an enduring expression of moral personhood.

OBJECTIVITY RECYCLED AND THE CHARACTER TO MAKE IT WORK

Here we have to return to the issue of the nature of objectivity in morality raised earlier. I want to argue that this requirement of conscious coordination of benevolence and justice is inherently tied to a particular, dynamic understanding of objectivity in morality. In the end I want to show that it is through a view of objectivity in moral judgment as "essentially performative" that the centrality of persons to stage six is firmly established and the full nature of respect for persons is operationally captured. Through this analysis we will also see how certain further character traits are not superfluous additions but rather necessary ingredients of a stage-six sense of respect for persons.

I have already noted, very roughly, how the concept of objectivity links the possibility of error in judgment with both some kind of external perspective and the aim of intersubjective agreement. And I have also rejected the particular interpretation of this linkage, found in the common, mistaken view of principled morality, that sees a shared acceptance of a set of definitive, abstract, inflexible moral rules from which any person can derive "*the* correct" answers to moral questions. I have labeled this view "objectiv*ism*" because it consists of a reification of moral truth in such a way as to leave the subjective activity of persons constructing that perspective impossible to see. In contrast, to put it more positively, I think we should be looking for a much more constructive understanding of moral truth and error. This has been argued by a number of contemporary philosophers of various persuasions, from Henry David Aiken (1965) to John Rawls

(1980) to J. L. Mackie (1977); and most recently it is the position Thomas Nagel comes to in *The View from Nowhere* (1986), even though he considers himself to be a thoroughgoing realist. Pointing out that "realism about values is different from realism about empirical facts," Nagel argues that the difference amounts to the fact that in the case of morality, "It is not a question of bringing the mind into correspondence with an external reality which acts causally on it, but of reordering the mind itself in accordance with the demands of its own external view of itself" (p. 148).

With this revision of our aim in mind, what we need is some account of *how* objectivity can be understood as providing an external perspective for identifying error, *in such a way that does not lead us into objectivism*. The essentials of such an account are as follows. First of all, I think objectivity needs to be seen as identifying a certain kind of perspective on judgment, when "judgment" is taken in its activity sense, as something that one does or performs. Then, second, this perspective can be loosely expressed as a kind of *detaching* or *decentering*. That is, the objective perspective is in the direction of recognizing, and seeking some kind of reflexive or "reconsiderative" distance on, some aspects of our present understandings or claims. The essential functional point about objectivity, then, is that it consists of whatever kind of *detaching* or decentering best facilitates reflexivity on our own claims—*and* in such a way as to keep open the possibility of the continuation of this reflexive detaching. I think Nagel has captured all the constituent parts of this understanding very precisely in his general interpretation of objectivity.

> Objectivity is a method of understanding. It is belief and attitudes that are objective in the primary sense. Only derivatively do we call objective the truths that can be arrived at in this way. To acquire a more objective understanding of some aspect of life or the world, we step back from our initial view of it and form a new conception which has that view and its relation to the world as its object. In other words, we place ourselves in the world that is to be understood. The old view then comes to be regarded as an appearance, more subjective than the new view, and correctable or confirmable by reference to it. The process can be repeated, yielding a still more objective conception. [Nagel 1986, p. 4]

I need to emphasize several points of this interpretation before exploring what it means in the context of the moral point of view of stage six. The first point that is crucial to keep in mind is that objectivity is primarily connected to inquiry, not answers. Thus in the passage just quoted, Nagel identifies objectivity as a "method of understanding" and notes that only derivatively do we call objective the truths that can be arrived at in this way. What we should be focusing on is not some kind of results or products of understanding, for example, as determined by rigid rules deductively applied, but rather the way or manner in which they are pursued. (In the context of a concern about objectivity in moral *judgment*, it is important to keep in mind that the term "judgment" is often ambiguous: it can refer either to a way or mode of making decisions—a *process*—or to the *result* of particular efforts at decision making—a product. The point here is that the focus of our attention, when we are concerned about objectivity, is properly judgment-as-process rather than judgment-as-product). *Active language* is the appropriate mode of description, as is accurately reflected in Nagel's further description in this passage: "To acquire" it "we step back," "place ourselves," in a "process" that "can be repeated."

The second point I want to emphasize here is a corollary of understanding objectivity as a method of understanding; interpreted in this way, objectivity must always be tied, in some way, to an intentional subject. It is something that *one does*, not something that happens or a state of affairs. The reflexivity that properly modifies the detaching aim of objective thinking can exist *only* if there is a human subject still within the thinking to refer back to, a fact that must be held consciously even when in tension with that direction. As Deutscher (1983) says, "Objectivity is a form, a style, an employment of our subjectivity . . . not its antithesis" (p. 41), and "We can speak of a 'point of view' and say that objectivity is possible only within a point of view and is thus a quality of one's subjectivity" (p. 42). Only an intentional, thinking *subject* can be said to *have* a point of view, and objectivity is the aiming at a particular kind of point of view—one that includes some aspect of that subject or its thinking as part of its object.

The final point important for my purposes here consists of a recognition of the *necessarily* paradoxical flavor of this conception. As Nagel (1986) so clearly sees, the puzzle is that for any pursuit of objectivity,

> its aim is naturally described in terms that, taken literally, are unintelligible: we must get outside of ourselves, and view the world from nowhere within it. Since it is impossible to leave one's own point of view behind entirely without ceasing to exist, the metaphor of getting outside ourselves must have another meaning. We

are to rely less and less on certain individual aspects of our point of view, and more and more on something else, less individual, which is also part of us. [P. 67]

Since we can't literally escape ourselves, any improvement in our beliefs has to result from some kind of self-transformation. And the thing we can do which comes closest to getting outside ourselves is to form a detached idea of the world that includes us, and includes our possession of that conception as part of what it enables us to understand about ourselves. We are then outside ourselves in the sense that we appear inside a conception of the world that we ourselves possess, but that is not tied to our particular point of view. [Pp. 69–70]

Now if we work with *this* notion of objectivity, as opposed to the one I have suggested is inadequate, what then can we say about what this means for our understanding of the stage-six moral point of view? As I have already suggested, and will now try to show, I think this conception of objectivity is what locates persons at the center of the stage-six notion of principled moral judgment, both as intentional moral agents and as objects and subjects of respect. To see this clearly, we must again refer back to Kohlberg's philosophical starting points, which I briefly elaborated at the beginning of this chapter. It will be remembered that the conception of morality underlying Kohlberg's theory is grounded in a view of social selves correlatively defined and then is elaborated as persons trying to "make sense" of their interaction, through their shared endeavor of striving to balance the claims that the lives, interests, and welfare of each make on each other. Then when we take this understanding as the arena within which objectivity, in the sense just articulated, is understood, what we immediately see more clearly is that the plural form ("we") in Nagel's discussion of the basic metaphor of objectivity—"we must get outside ourselves"—cannot always be interpreted as referring to a "royal we" or as referring to all of us, but as referring to persons individually and separately. Within the moral point of view of stage six, however, the "we" that must "get outside ourselves" is truly and necessarily *plural*.[2] Objectivity in *morality* is a method of understanding that simply cannot, in the end, be engaged in by one person alone. On the contrary, it entails two people (or more) aiming at reflexive detaching

---

2. The claim I am making here is my own, not Nagel's. Certainly there is a monological flavor to much of his discussion, at least when he is outlining his *general* conception of objectivity. It is unclear to me whether he would agree with me that this will not do for morality.

or decentering *together*, with respect to each other and self, often at the same time. In regard to this mutual effort, in the context of claims of both benevolence and justice arising from the lived reality of each (or all), the earlier noted characteristics of imagination, openmindedness, and a sense of irony are subordinate moral character traits.

However, other, more central aspects of character also only now become clearly visible. The first of these puts to rest, once and for all, the criticism of stage six as cold and impersonal: an essential aspect of moral objectivity must be the enduring expression and presentation of oneself to the other as *sympathetic*! Mutual decentering hinges directly on this disposition to try to see and feel as the other sees and feels within his or her lived context and understanding of that context. As Frankena puts it, "we must somehow attain and develop an ability to be aware of others as persons, as important to themselves as we are to ourselves, and to have a lively and sympathetic representation in imagination of their interests and of the effects of our actions on their lives" (1973, p. 69). He points out how the need for this has been stressed by Josiah Royce and William James:

> Both men point out how we usually go our own busy and self-concerned ways, with only an external awareness of the presence of others, much as if they were things, and without any realization of their inner and peculiar worlds of personal experience; and both emphasize the need and the possibility of a "higher vision of inner significance" which pierces this "certain blindness in human beings" and enables us to realize the existence of others in a wholly different way, as we do our own. [P. 69]

As James says, "we ought, all of us, to realize each other in this intense, pathetic, and important way" (quoted by Frankena 1973, p. 70). What it requires, as a character expression of moral objectivity, is the enduring disposition to seek an integration of one's understanding and affective appreciation of what the other is *really* like and what the other is *really* feeling, as much as possible independent from both one's own phenomenological situation and one's preconceived understanding and appreciation of the other.

Then, in addition to resting on this kind of basic, mutual sympathetic connection, the kind of objectivity that a stage-six respect for persons seeks also entails a *mutual* reflexivity on understandings and claims. And this requirement has additional, distinct character implications. To see this we must first recall not only that objectivity requires a kind of detaching or decentering (which we have just seen to involve sympathy in the case of moral judgment), but also that this is to be sought in such a way as to facilitate reflexive reconsideration of some present understanding or claim. But, as we have also seen, in morality there is by definition a plurality of points of view from which such understandings and claims arise. Thus there is also a plurality of both subjects and objects of such reflexivity required by objectivity. In short, to put this together, stage-six moral objectivity is expressive of respect for persons through its necessitating a disposition of persons to engage others *performatively* with regard to moral interactions, both those involving benevolence and those involving justice, and especially those requiring an integration of the two attitudes. What this performative engagement requires is, quite simply, the dispositional realization that an individual's understandings of either benevolence or justice claims are potentially (and likely) limited by that individual's particular subjective point of view and that offering these understandings to others with the expectation of their agreement or disagreement, supported by their counterunderstanding from their points of view, is a necessary condition of determining the best understanding. In short, complete reflexivity in matters of moral understandings can be achieved only through *dialogue*.

The additional character implications of this full picture are then, finally, as follows. First of all, as we saw earlier, all of the traditional subordinate character traits, such as courage, patience, loyalty, and the like, should be thought of as derivatives of (or sometimes expressions of) the two cardinal virtues of benevolence and justice. That is, they can be considered *moral* character traits only insofar as they are put into context by the moral point of view framed by benevolence and justice. The connection most commonly seen here is that sometimes in order to *act* benevolently or justly one does need to *be* courageous, patient, loyal, and so on. Undoubtedly this is true. But our understanding of objectivity adds that, in addition and perhaps at a more fundamental level, these other traits are matters of moral character insofar as they make possible and facilitate our performative engagement of each other about what *constitutes* the benevolent or just act.

A more important point is that we can now identify two additional higher-level character traits that seem to be required by our understanding of how a particular view of objectivity interacts with the normative dimensions of stage six. Both of these are on a par with the manifestation of sympathetic connection discussed earlier. The first is *humility*, which is perhaps surprising in the context of the self-righteous flavor often attributed to stage six. One's performative engagement of the other involves making claims of validity for one's current understandings, but it simply cannot function without the conscious realization, expressed in both attitude and behavior, that "*I could be wrong*" about those understandings. Only through *being humble* can a person allow room for other persons and their alternative understandings to be heard and to be considered reflexively by all. Whereas being sympathetic, in the sense outlined above, provides the substantive concerns around which moral judgment revolves—and thus objectivity in moral judgment must accommodate—viewing the validity of one's moral claims and the appropriateness of one's moral actions with humility is required to show respect *for other persons'* sympathetic interpretations and subsequent claims to objectivity in judgment and action.

The other high-level character trait that we can also now see as required by an operative notion of stage-six principled morality consists of a dispositional expression of a *sense of responsibility* for maintaining the conditions of dialogue through which performative engagement can function, and thus objectivity can be sought. As being sympathetic is needed for identifying moral concerns, and being humble is needed to facilitate their common interpretation, being responsible undergirds the whole activity through time. Responsibility is called for in at least two senses. First, one needs to be responsible in the sense of being ready and willing to *respond to* the other. It is not enough merely to be sympathetic and humble; unless one is also prepared and inclined to respond to others' differing perspectives and judgments, one is simply not respecting them as equals in the performative engagement. Second, and in conjunction with this first sense, one also needs to be responsible in the sense of doing everything one can to ensure that the material preconditions of dialogue are in place and maintained adequately. Here we cycle back to our starting point of what morality is all about in the first place. That is, any number of different, concrete acts may be called for by this sense of responsibility—not only because one thinks them to be morally required, but *also* because performing them enhances the possibility that their obligatoriness or worthwhileness will become matters of universal intersubjective agreement. At another level this sense of responsibility may also call for forms of "praxis"—in particular, reflective action aimed at breaking down political barriers of unequal distribution of power and economic barriers of unequal distribution of resources and wealth. Finally, also at this level, being responsible in this sense means taking the next generation seriously enough to educate them. Dialogue with the following generations is an essential aspect of the development of our shared humanity. With this concern in mind, one can then see that "moral education" is a precondition of that particular dialogue if it is to express respect among equals. In short, moral education is an activity of responsible character, located at the intersection of respect for persons and a dynamic search for objectivity in morality.

A CONCLUDING NOTE

It is one thing to call for people of good character and for the education to help them nurture it. It is quite another thing still to do so in a way that goes beyond cliché to a conceptually clear, coherent picture that is theoretically grounded. Kohlberg's theory of moral development is not primarily a theory of moral character. It is a theory about how humans learn to make moral judgments in a psychologically mature way, and it is at the same time a theory that is philosophically rich compared to much of the rest of North American mainstream social psychology. As a *developmental* theory, however, it also necessarily includes a vision of maturity that is not morally neutral. Starting with a different way of focusing its attention, such a theory will naturally see things somewhat differently from those perspectives that view the moral arena primarily in character terms. But in this chapter I have tried to show how an adequate understanding of the moral point of view of stage six, combined with the sense of objectivity that makes this point of view viable, goes some distance toward requiring a vision of good character in addition to a preferred form of moral judgment. It still remains to be worked out how people attain (develop?) such aspects of moral character, how educational efforts might enhance the likelihood of success in this endeavor, and how the aim might need modification to accommodate matters of additional, and perhaps competing, concern with regard to character. From my argument here, however, I hope it is at least clear that there is sufficient ground of common concern and an intersection of kinds of claims to make these tasks worth pursuing.

REFERENCES

Aiken, Henry David. "The Concept of Moral Objectivity." In *Morality and the Language of Conduct*, ed. Hector-Neri Castaneda and George Nakhnikian. Detroit: Wayne State University, 1965.

Baier, Kurt. *The Moral Point of View: A Rational Basis of Ethics*. New York: Random House, 1965.

Bailey, Charles. "Kohlberg on Morality and Feeling." In *Lawrence Kohlberg: Consensus and Controversy*, ed. Sohan Modgil and Celia Modgil. Philadelphia: Falmer Press, 1985.

Bennett, William J., and Delattre, Edwin J. "A Moral Education: Some Thoughts on How Best to Achieve It," *American Educator* 3 (1979): 6–9.

Boyd, Dwight. "The Rawls Connection." In *Moral Development, Moral Education, and Kohlberg: Basic Issues in Philosophy, Psychology, Religion, and Education*, ed. Brenda Munsey. Birmingham, Ala.: Religious Education Press, 1980.

Boyd, Dwight. "The Oughts of Is: Kohlberg at the Interface between Moral Philosophy and Developmental Psychology." In *Lawrence Kohlberg: Consensus and Controversy*, ed. Sohan Modgil and Celia Modgil. Philadelphia: Falmer Press, 1985.

Davies, Robertson. *The Manticore*. New York: Penguin Books, 1972.

Deutscher, Max. *Subjecting and Objecting*. St. Lucia, Queensland, Australia: University of Queensland Press, 1983.

Dewey, John. *Theory of the Moral Life*, 3d ed. New York: Holt, Rinehart and Winston, 1960.

Frankena, William. *Ethics*. Englewood Cliffs, N. J.: Prentice-Hall, 1973.

Gilligan, Carol, and Murphy, John Michael. "Moral Development in Late Adolescence and Adulthood: The Philosopher and the Dilemma of the Fact." In *Intellectual Development beyond Childhood*, ed. D. Kuhn. San Francisco: Jossey-Bass, 1979.

Hamm, Cornel. "The Content of Moral Education, or In Defense of the Bag of Virtues," *School Review* 85 (1977): 219–28.

Kohlberg, Lawrence. "Education for Justice: A Modern Statement of the Platonic View." In *Moral Education*, ed. Nancy F. Sizer and Theodore R. Sizer. Cambridge, Mass.: Harvard University Press, 1970.

Kohlberg, Lawrence. "From Is to Ought: How to Commit the Naturalistic Fallacy and Get Away with It in the Study of Moral Development." In *Cognitive Development and Epistemology*, ed. Theodore Mischel. New York: Academic Press, 1971.

Kohlberg, Lawrence. "A Current Statement on Some Theoretical Issues." In *Lawrence Kohlberg: Consensus and Controversy*, ed. Sohan Modgil and Celia Modgil. Philadelphia: Falmer Press, 1985.

Kohlberg, Lawrence; Boyd, Dwight; and Levine, Charles. "The Return of Stage 6: Its Principle and Moral Point of View." In *The Moral Domain*, ed. Tom Wren. Cambridge, Mass.: MIT Press, forthcoming. Previously published in German as "Wie Wiederkehr der sechsten Stufe: Gerechtigkeit, Wohlwolen und der Standpunkt der Moral." In *Zur Bestimmung der Moral: Philosophische und Sozialwissen-*

schaftliche Beiträge zur Moralforschung, ed. Wolfgang Edelstein and Gertrud Nunner-Winkler. Frankfurt am Main: Suhrkamp, 1986.

Mackie, John Leslie. *Ethics: Inventing Right and Wrong*. New York: Penguin Books, 1977.

Murphy, John Michael, and Gilligan, Carol. "Moral Development in Late Adolescence and Adulthood: A Critique and Reconstruction of Kohlberg's Theory," *Human Development* 23 (1980): 77–104.

Nagel, Thomas. *The View from Nowhere*. New York: Oxford University Press, 1986.

Peters, Richard S. "Moral Development: A Plea for Pluralism." In *Cognitive Development and Epistemology*, ed. Theodore Mischel. New York: Academic Press, 1972.

Rawls, John. "Kantian Constructivism in Moral Theory," *Journal of Philosophy* 77: 9 (1980): 515–72.

Sullivan, Edmund. *Kohlberg's Structuralism: A Critical Appraisal*, Monograph Series #115. Toronto: Ontario Institute for Studies in Education, 1977.

6

The Habit of the Common Life: Building Character Through Democratic Community Schools

Clark Power, Ann Higgins, and Lawrence Kohlberg

The habit of the common life in the class and attachment to the class and even to the school constitute an altogether natural preparation for the more elevated sentiments we wish to develop in the child. We have a precious instrument, which is used all too little and which can be of the greatest service.

Emile Durkheim
Moral Education

In the last few years, public discussion about moral education has taken a decidedly Aristotelian turn. Developing moral reasoning and clarifying values are out; inculcating habits and forming character are in. Former Secretary of Education William Bennett (1985), one of the most outspoken of the neo-Aristotelians, has criticized educators for "intellectualizing moral values," and proposed that they develop virtues through habituation:

In recent years although we have not overintellectualized the curriculum, ironically we have tried to intellectualize moral development. . . . Aristotle knew and psychologists confirm today, that it is habit which develops virtues, habit shaped not only by precept but by example itself. [P. 7].

His own program for character education consists of three practical steps. First, teachers and administrators have to be willing "to communicate their own moral convictions" and to give "good examples." Second, the school's physical environment must reflect pride and care. Finally, the school must be run with discipline and order.

Although we do not deny that Bennett's proposals may be sanguine, they appear rather vague and weak in comparison to our own "just community" approach, which aims at building character through participation in a democratic community. Bennett would probably agree with us that the growth of students' character depends on the character or culture of the school. However, his suggestions for improving the ethos of the school go in a different direction. He emphasizes shaping behavior through authority and discipline, while we advocate promoting moral reasoning and responsibility through democracy.

Bennett's charge that we may be overintellectualizing moral education echoes the one raised by Aristotle against Socrates. However, we also recognize the limitations of the Socratic model, as is evident in the shift in our approach from a focus on moral discussions to the creation of democratic communities. Kohlberg acknowledged the implications of that shift by substituting "Socratic" for "Platonic" in the subtitle of the 1984 reprinting of his essay "Education for Justice: A Modern Statement of the Platonic View." He explained that he had come to see his later work in moral education as more closely related to Plato's vision in *The Republic* than one attributed to Socrates in *The Meno*. Just as Plato's *Republic* serves as a bridge from Socrates to Aristotle, so we hope to show that the just community approach to moral education can serve as a bridge between cognitivist and character approaches. In so doing, we argue that a proper understanding of Aristotelian character education demands a far greater appreciation of the role of cognition than many of its current proponents generally admit.

HARTSHORNE AND MAY'S STUDIES OF CHARACTER AND
CONDUCT

Contemporary advocates of character education tend to overlook the fact that character education enjoyed its heyday in America during the first four decades of this century. Judging by entries in the educational periodical indices, interest in character education peaked in the early 1930s and then declined at a precipitous rate (see Figure 6–1). A similar pattern appears in the periodical indices of psychology. By 1970 the entry "character" had disappeared altogether; "personality," a morally neutral construct, had taken its place.

From a research perspective the death blow to character education was delivered by Hartshorne and May's (1928–1930) famous research on character, consisting of studies of deception, self-control, and service conducted in the late 1920s. Their research had as its aim the betterment of character education efforts, but its effect was to debunk the very notion of character itself, thereby pulling the rug out from under the educators. Hartshorne and May hypothesized that the constructs of character and virtue presupposed a certain integration of moral functioning, such that a sample exposed to a variety of situations involving temptation would exhibit a U-shaped distribution of conduct scores: individuals would tend to demonstrate either virtue in all situations or vice in all. After research with over 8,000 students they found the opposite: conduct scores fell into a bell-shaped normal curve, indicating that most children cheated, were selfish, and lacked self-control a fair amount of the time. Hartshorne and May (1930) concluded from these results that there were no character traits *per se* but "specific habits learned in relationship to specific situations which have made one or the other mode of response successful" (p. 372).

In discussing the implications of their findings for character education, Hartshorne and May (1930) claimed that the standard approaches of moral instruction through didactic teaching, exhortation, example, and practice were ineffective and possibly harmful: "Prevailing ways of teaching ideals and standards probably do little good and may do harm when the ideals set before the pupils contradict the practical demands of the very institutions in which the ideals are taught" (p. 377). Contemporary character educators who ignore the research by Hartshorne and May seem doomed to repeat the mistakes of their predecessors. If habituation is to play a role in contemporary

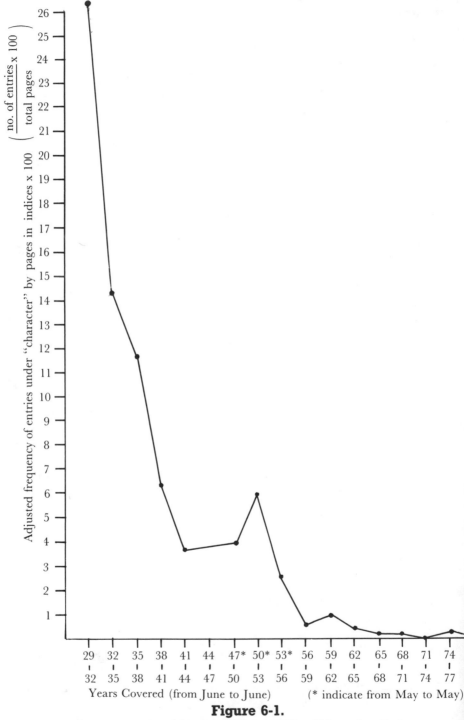

Figure 6-1.
Entries under "Character" from The Education Index
(1929 to 1979)

moral education, then perhaps we can retrieve a more viable notion of the process from Aristotle himself.

THE ARISTOTELIAN CONCEPT OF HABITUATION

In his earlier work, Kohlberg, drawing on Hartshorne and May's studies as well as subsequent research, including his own, associated Aristotle's character education model with the popular bag of virtues approach and made the following criticisms:

1. Virtues and vices are labels by which people award praise and blame to others, and are not traits of character.
2. Virtues can come into conflict, and thus depend upon a principle such as justice for their ordering and application to concrete situations.
3. By defining virtues in terms of the consensual values of a society, the critical dimension of moral reasoning is lost.
4. The inclusion of virtues in any particular scheme appears arbitrary and relativistic. [Kohlberg 1970, pp. 95–98]

In place of the virtues, we identify stages of moral development. The stages take into account the way persons organize virtues, rules, and norms in making an integrated moral choice. Our research on the stability of the stage of moral reasoning across a wide variety of moral dilemmas demonstrates, contrary to Hartshorne and May's findings, that there is an empirical basis for the construct of character as an internally organized disposition to moral action.

Although we stand by our critique of the bag-of-virtues approach, we admit that it oversimplifies Aristotle's understanding of virtue and the process of character education. In his more recent writing, Kohlberg (1985) credited Aristotle with the recognition that justice is the master principle that integrates the virtues and accounts for their moral or other-regarding worth. Furthermore, our research on just community programs in Cambridge and Scarsdale, and most recently in the Bronx, has led us to see similarities between the emphasis we give to building collective norms and Aristotle's process of habituation.

In Kohlberg's early references to Aristotle, he focused on the following well-known passage in the *Nicomachean Ethics* in which Aristotle distinguishes between the intellectual and moral virtues and states that teaching is necessary for the former and habit for the latter:

> Virtue, then, is of two sorts, virtue of thought and virtue of character. Virtue of thought arises and grows mostly of teaching, and hence needs experience and time. Virtue of character [i.e., of *ethos*] results from habit [ethos]; hence its name "ethical," slightly varied from "*ethos*." [1103a14–18]

Taken alone, this passage implies that moral virtues can be acquired through habit as opposed to reason. While Kohlberg found this to be inimical to his own position, Bennett refers to it approvingly to support his criticism of the cognitivistic approach to character education.

A more balanced understanding of the Aristotelian position, which integrates habituation and intellectual development, has been put forth by a number of commentators, such as Burnyeat (1980), Irwin (1985), Nicgorski and Ellrod (1986), R. S. Peters (1963), and Sorabji (1980). Peters (1963) argues that habituation must be understood as the first of a two-phase process of education: "[Young children] can and must enter the palace of reason through the courtyard of habit and tradition" (pp. 54, 55). We typically think of habits as stereotypical behaviors acquired through imitation, repetition, and reinforcement. Yet as Peters points out, certain types of habits can be regarded as more complex activities in which deliberation and adaptability are required. For example, sportscasters repeatedly refer to the way Michael Jordan plays basketball as both "creative" and "fundamentally sound" because of his intelligent application of highly refined skills of passing, shooting, and rebounding. Years of practice or habituation have not routinized his play into predictable patterns but have increased his ability to react with flexibility and novelty. Clearly Aristotle must have had this enlarged sense of habit in mind; otherwise he would have advocated an educational process that would have undermined his ultimate educational aim: the development of a person guided by practical wisdom.

A second problem posed by the notion of habituation has to do with the role of feelings. Habits are typically viewed as mechanical responses, performed without emotion. For example, William James (1912/1985) referred to their function as "the effortless custody of automatism" (p. 12). Aristotle sees habituation as a means of cultivating a love for what is fine and noble and a hate for what is base and ignoble: "Hence we need to have the appropriate upbringing—right from early youth as Plato says—to make us find enjoyment or pain in the right things; for this is the correct education" (1104b11–13). Believing that young persons "live in feeling," he thinks it crucial that their feelings be refined so that they are attracted to what is good and just. The idea of cultivating feelings through practice is familiar to any parent or teacher who has tried to introduce children to good literature, music, or cuisine. Although we can describe how much we appreciate such delights and can encourage others to partake of them, no one can acquire a taste for them without direct and repeated experience.

Habituation presents a third problem in that it connotes a solitary activity. For example, William James offers the following maxims for acquiring or breaking habits:

1. Launch yourself with as strong and decided an initiative as possible.
2. Never suffer an exception to occur till the new habit is rooted securely in your life.
3. Seize the very first opportunity to act on every resolution you make, and on every emotional prompting you may experience in the direction of the habits you aspire to gain.
4. Keep the faculty of effort alive in you by a little gratuitous exercise every day. [1912/1985, pp. 12–16]

In elaborating on these maxims, James, borrowing on Bain's treatment, likens habituation to walking "on the straight and narrow path, . . . looking neither to the right nor to the left" (p. 13). This picture of the resolute individual absorbed in the task of self-improvement and oblivious to others is far different from the one Aristotle offers. Aristotle thinks of the ideal moral educator as the community and the habituation process as profoundly social. As does Plato, he identifies moral education with citizenship education; and his selection of virtues, such as courage and generosity, manifests a concern for the common good.

While Aristotle does not mandate a communitarian setting for ethical education, as does Plato in the *Republic*, he emphasizes that character education is a social endeavor. He understands persons as social and political by nature and points out that friendship is thus not only a virtue in itself but also a condition for the development of the virtuous life as a whole. Furthermore he describes friendship as a civic virtue, noting that it "seems to hold cities together" and that legislators should be "more concerned about it than justice" (1155a24–25). MacIntyre comments that the whistleblower's dilemma of choosing between loyalty to one's friends or loyalty to one's community cannot arise in a genuine Aristotelian community:

In an Aristotelian perspective anyone who can formulate such a contrast . . . has no polis; he is a citizen of nowhere, an internal exile wherever he lives. . . . [He possesses] at best that inferior form of friendship which is founded on mutual advantage. [1981, p. 147]

For Aristotle, education in a community ideally requires "correct laws and practices" not only for young people, who need to learn to limit their desires, but also for adults, "who must continue the same practices and be habituated to them" (1179b35–11811a1–5). Aristotle's emphasis on correct laws and practices becomes clearer in his argument that legislation based on reason is a far more effective means of instruction than the command of authority:

> A father's instructions lack this influence and compelling power; and so in general do the instructions of an individual man. . . . Law, however, has power that compels; and law is reason that proceeds from a sort of intelligence and understanding. Besides, people become hostile to an individual human being who opposes their impulses even if he is correct in opposing them; whereas a law's prescription of what is decent is not burdensome. . . . It is best then if the community attends to upbringing and attends correctly. [1180b20–24, 29–30]

No doubt Aristotle would have questioned the educational wisdom of the "get tough" approach to discipline epitomized on the cover of *Time* by Principal Joe Clark brandishing a baseball bat while patrolling the corridors of his school. In advocating that educational authority be based on the legislation of a community, Aristotle anticipated what would become a major theme in the sociology of education from Durkheim to the present: that the role of the school is to act as an intermediary between the personal authority of the home and the impersonal authority of the society.

ARISTOTLE'S SCHEME OF ETHICAL DEVELOPMENT

Thus far we have described Aristotle's view of habituation as an educational process involving reason, the emotions, and community. We now turn to his understanding of habituation in relationship to childhood and adolescent development. It is clear from the *Nicomachean Ethics* that Aristotle intends to promote the development of his students to a level in which they can lead their lives in accord with a self-constructed, rational conception of the good life. Yet he recognizes that they are born ignorant and at the mercy of their own impulses. As a lecturer on ethics, who acknowledged that he was less than 100 percent successful in helping students to advance to full ethical maturity, he has a clear opinion on the developmental prerequisites for "success" in his course:

Arguments and teaching surely do not influence everyone, but the soul of the student needs to have been prepared by habits for enjoying finely and hating finely, like ground that is to nourish seed. For someone whose life follows his feelings would not even listen to an argument turning him away, or comprehend it [if he did listen]; and in that state how could he be persuaded to change? And in general feelings seem to yield to force and not to argument. [1179b24–29]

In the above passage Aristotle treats habituation and teaching through rational argumentation as different but developmentally related phases of education. Habituation is not teaching per se, but it is necessary in early life to prepare the soul so that the teaching process can be effective.

Burnyeat (1980) differentiates the three levels of ethical development in Aristotle's *Nicomachean Ethics*, with each level having distinctive cognitive and motivational characteristics. These levels correspond to the three parts of the soul, the appetites, spirit, and reason, which, as Plato notes in the *Republic*, must be educated sequentially. In the *Politics*, Aristotle states that the irrational parts of the soul (the appetites and spirit) are operative in children from birth, unlike the rational part, which develops later. He concludes from this that the training of the irrational part must come first, but cautions "nonetheless, our care of it [the appetitive part] must be for the sake of reason" (1334b22–25).

As Table 6–1 illustrates, Aristotle's levels bear a striking resemblance to the preconventional, conventional, and postconventional levels of moral development in our own work. On the first level, individuals are motivated by concrete pleasures and pains and by fear of punishment rather than by shame or a desire to be virtuous for its own sake:

For the many naturally obey out of fear, not shame; they avoid what is base out of penalties, not because it is disgraceful. For since they live by their feelings they pursue their proper pleasures and the sources of them, and avoid the opposed pains, and have not even a notion of what is fine and [hence] truly pleasant, since they have no taste of it. [1179b11–16]

Because such persons are ruled by their passions and lack a sense of honor, Aristotle calls them "slavish."

On the second level, children and adolescents act out of an intrinsic desire to practice virtue and to avoid vice, which leads to shame. They develop an understanding of what the virtues demand, although they do not grasp their relationship to each other and to the underlying principles that provide their justification:

Table 6-1
Aristotle's Levels of Ethical Development and Kohlberg's Levels of Moral Judgment

	Aristotle	*Kohlberg**
Level 1	*Ethics of Fear*	*Heteronomous Morality*
	The passions rule, and fear of punishment constrains.	Concrete individual perspective from which rules and social expectations are seen as something external to the self.
Level 2	*Ethics of Shame*	*Conventional Morality*
	The desire for honor leads to good behavior; but feelings are not under full rational control.	Member-of-society perspective from which the self is identified with or has internalized the rules and expectations of others, especially the authorities.
Level 3	*Ethics of Practical Wisdom*	*Postconventional or Principled Morality*
	Reason and desire are interpreted in the pursuit of a freely chosen life plan.	Prior-to-society perspective from which the self defines moral values in terms of self-chosen principles.

*Adapted from Colby and Kohlberg 1987, p. 17.

> This is why we need to have been brought up in fine habits if we are to be adequate students of what is fine and just and of political questions generally. For the origin we begin with something that is true, and if this is apparent enough to use, we will not, at this stage, need the reason why it is true in addition. [1195b6–8]

In his *Rhetoric*, Aristotle comments that at this level young persons are "shy," accepting the rules of society in which they have been trained but not yet believing in any other standard of honor (1389a29–30). They depend on the moral wisdom of significant adults, who help them acquire correct beliefs about virtue. These correct beliefs are necessary for complete development and in this sense are the "origin" for that further stage. Only at the third level are individuals capable of being able to think for themselves. Thus Aristotle quotes Hesiod with approval: "He who understands everything himself is best of all; he is noble also who listens to one who has spoken well; but he who neither understands it himself nor takes it from another is a useless man" (1195b11–14). Although children at the first level also depend on others for ethical guidance, they do not really take it to heart or appreciate it. Therefore threats of punishment are needed. Children at the second level do not depend on such sanctions because they have acquired a "taste" or love for virtue itself (1179b31).

Indicative of having attained the second level is the feeling of *aidos*, commonly translated as shame. *Aidos* is actually a broader term than shame; it refers to antecedent as well as consequent states of consciousness of one's social obligations. Persons with *aidos* are conscientious about acting properly and experience shame when they do not (Irwin 1985, p. 425). Aristotle commends those who obey *aidos* rather than fear of punishment, which is why Burnyeat (1980) describes *aidos* as the "semi-virtue of the learner" (p. 78). Nevertheless, Aristotle describes *aidos* as a "feeling," not a virtue, belonging to a transitional developmental level:

> For the feeling of shame is suitable for youth, not for every time of life. For we think it right for young people to be prone to shame, since they live by their feelings and hence go astray, but are restrained by shame. No one, by contrast, would praise an older person for readiness to feel disgrace since we think it is wrong for him to do anything that causes a feeling of disgrace. [1128b15–20]

Aidos is not a characteristic of individuals at level three for at least two reasons. First and most obviously, persons at the third level live no longer by their feelings but by reason. This is not to say that they have eradicated their passions but that their passions are subordinated to reason. In contrast, youth at the second level struggle with incontinence or *akrasia* (Burnyeat 1980). They typically experience temptations in which their feelings come into conflict with their reasoning or in which they impetuously act on a desire to do what is good without evaluating what the situation requires. A second limitation of *aidos* is that it motivates extrinsically. Aristotle defines it as a "sort of fear," not of punishment as at level one, but of disrepute. In his discussion of bravery Aristotle makes it clear that acting out of a fear of disgrace (citizen's bravery) is better than being compelled by threats of punishment; but it is not as good as acting out of a concern for what is fine or right for its own sake (1116a11–29).

Aristotle's notion of *aidos* sheds light on the relationship between the development of the self and moral reasoning. Contemporary moral philosophers, such as Rawls and Frankena, distinguish between judgments about the moral worth of actions and that of agents. This distinction is also relevant from a psychological point of view, since individuals may vary in the extent to which they blame themselves for moral failure. As Blasi (1984) explains, persons may develop their moral reasoning without making moral integrity a central aspect of their identity or sense of self. Research by Damon (1984) suggests that the self and moral judgment may develop as two independent systems until early adolescence. For example, Damon finds that prior to early adolescence children typically describe themselves in terms of physical characteristics ("I'm tall") or activity-related abilities ("I'm fast"). They rarely refer to their moral attributes, although they can articulate them in another context. However, adolescents typically describe themselves in terms of social and psychological characteristics ("I'm friendly"; "I'm shy"), which includes moral attributes ("I'm not mean"; "I'm not unthankful"). Damon concludes from such data that adolescents have acquired the capacity to integrate evaluations into self-understanding.

The habituation process may thus be understood as a way of forming a moral identity during adolescence. Just as one becomes a musician through practicing music, so too, as habituation theory maintains, does one become a virtuous person through the practice of virtue. In becoming an artist or a virtuous person, the standards of worth that are applied to one's productions or one's activities are applied to one's self. Thus, one feels ashamed of failure and determined to improve. It follows from this that the moral education of adolescents might profitably focus not only on their moral reasoning but also on their moral actions and self-evaluations.

Aristotle's developmental scheme culminates with the development of practical wisdom or *phronesis*. Practical wisdom involves proper deliberation about the good life and what promotes such a life. Aristotle seems to believe that the truly virtuous person must be in some sense autonomous. As Sorabji (1980) notes, Aristotle, in his *Politics*, characterizes the virtue of slaves, women, and children as inferior to that of rulers, because only rulers have the full power of deliberation.

At the level of practical wisdom the feelings are governed by intelligence, and the tension experienced at the earlier level between reason and desire is no longer present. Aristotle contrasts the practically wise with the clever in noting that only the latter can be incontinent:

> Nor can the same person be at once both intelligent and incontinent. For we have shown that an intelligent person must also at the same time be excellent in character [and the incontinent person is not]. However, a clever person may well be incontinent. . . . Moreover, someone is not intelligent simply by knowing; he must also act on his knowledge. But the incontinent person does not. [1152a8–10]

The conflict between reason and desire, which is so prominent in Kant's ethics, is not found in Aristotle's, because the habituation process harmonizes the desires to accord with one's rational conception of the good life. Thus in Aristotle's view even continent persons, who manage to make their passions conform to reason, are lacking in the development of virtue: "In the continent person it [the irrational part of the soul] obeys reason; and in the temperate and brave person it presumably listens still better to reason, since there it agrees with reason in everything"(1102b26–28).

A DURKHEIMIAN PERSPECTIVE

In discussing Aristotle's view of habituation and levels of ethical development, we did not specify the virtues that we thought ought to be acquired. As an alternative to prescribing particular virtues, we propose the Durkheimian notion of developing *the* habit of the common life. Such a move would be in keeping with the idea found in Aristotle and more fully developed in Aquinas (1966) that the virtues are united and that through habit we develop a "second nature."

Contrary to the "bag of virtues approach" to habituation, the Durkheimian approach requires the development of general dispositions of moral functioning:

> To influence the child morally is not to nurture in him a particular virtue, followed by another and still another; it is to develop and eventually to constitute completely, by appropriate methods, those general dispositions that, once treated, adapt themselves readily to the particular circumstances of human life. . . . To operate effectively one must have an *idée fixe*, or a small number of ideas that serve as lodestar. [1973, p. 21]

Durkheim identifies three basic moral dispositions or "elements of morality": discipline, altruism, and rational autonomy. His great contribution to moral education lies in showing that the common life of the classroom and school is a "precious" but too often neglected instrument for promoting moral development. We will illustrate how this instrument can be used by discussing our just community approach to moral education, which we have derived in part from Durkheim's theory.

THE JUST COMMUNITY APPROACH

The just community approach to moral education has evolved out of experimental secondary school programs in Cambridge, Scarsdale, and the Bronx. The programs have been relatively small, involving from sixty to ninety students and four to eight staff members. They function as schools within schools, providing a core curriculum and homeroom or adviser group while allowing students to take courses in the large school. The central institution is the community meeting in which issues related to life and discipline in the school are discussed and democratically decided, with all students and teachers having an equal vote.

These just community programs have as their aim the development of the basic elements of morality, as described by Durkheim; and in a broad sense employ an Aristotelian habituation process. All of the rules and norms decided in the just community programs express a concern for fairness and community. From our point of view, the particular rules made in a school are less important than the basic values that they symbolize. Although a case could be made that rules lead to the acquisition of particular virtues (e.g., a rule on cheating leads to honesty and a rule regarding stealing, to respect for private property), we would prefer to stress the relationship of rules in general to the formation of a habit of common life. Nevertheless, certain "master virtues of community" seem indispensable for the common life and are advocated in all just community programs: caring, trust, collective responsibility, and participation. Sometimes these master virtues are embodied in particular rules; for example, rules concerning attendance and drugs focus on participation. Other times the master virtues are promoted through informal or even tacit agreement. For example, no rules are usually made obligating members of the same community to help each other, but caring is regarded as a duty just as is following the formal rule to attend class.

Democracy helps students to take school rules and norms for prosocial behavior seriously. Typically schools foster student irresponsibility by placing the entire burden of enforcing the rules on the adults. When discipline breaks down, the students blame the staff for not being tough enough. Meanwhile the students refuse to "snitch" or "narc" on a peer. In the just community programs, disciplinary infractions are presented as problems for the group as a whole to resolve democratically. We have found that although students may initially be somewhat reluctant to make and enforce rules, they do rise to the occasion after several community meeting discussions (Power, Higgins, and Kohlberg, forthcoming).

Democracy is more than a means of developing the master virtues of the common life; it is itself a master virtue, a subtype of the more general virtue of participation. As a virtue, democratic participation may be understood as a disposition to bring problems before the appropriate forum for public discussion and democratic resolution. Although we have no hard data to indicate whether students in the just community programs acquire this virtue so that they practice it outside school or after they graduate, we have some positive anecdotal evidence of students requesting family meetings and of graduates making efforts to democratize their college dorms and workplaces.

According to Durkheim (1973) the development of a spirit of discipline through master virtues, such as democratic participation, depends on the development of a corresponding spirit of altruism, based on attachment to the group:

> Basically it consists in the attachment to a social group. If a man is to be a moral being, he must be devoted to something other than himself; he must feel at one with society, however lowly it may be. . . . The school has, above all, the function of linking the child to this society. [P. 79]

According to Aristotle, cultivating a "love" for virtue is a vital part of the habituation process. In our just community approach we endeavor to cultivate a love of the common life by building a strong sense of community through participatory democracy and by advocating the master virtues of the common life. As Durkheim noted, the most crucial of these master virtues for developing community solidarity is collective responsibility:

There is such a thing as a general atmosphere of moral health, which contributes to the development of good students although they themselves do not personally deserve the entire credit. Everybody contributes to the whole. . . . What [but collective sanctions] is the most powerful means to instill in children the feeling of solidarity that binds them to their companions, a sense of sharing in the common life? . . . There is no better way of instilling the feeling that we are not self-sufficient, but a part of the whole that envelops, penetrates, and supports us. [1973, p. 245]

Our experience confirms the wisdom of Durkheim's stress on collective responsibility. In two of the just community programs, stealing virtually ended when members decided the community would make restitution for thefts. The decision that everyone should chip in to repay the victim was based on an acknowledgment that each person should be responsible for the other and for the group as a whole.

In addition to the norm of collective responsibility, the norms of helping, trust, integration, and participation serve to both create and express a sense of community. One common feature of these norms is that they are ordinarily viewed as supererogatory; that is, they are viewed as requiring more than justice strictly obligates. A second is that they reflect a concern not only for individual welfare or fairness but also for the quality of relationships among individuals and within the group itself. By adopting these norms as shared expectations, groups transform from being pragmatic associations to communities; that is, their members not only pursue personal educational goals but value their common life as an end in itself. We can illustrate the distinction between schools that are pragmatic associations and those that are communities by contrasting the ways in which the problem of skipping class is approached in each. In Table 6-2 we present data comparing samples of students from two just community programs with peers in the same high schools but not in the program. The students were asked to rate, on a five-point scale from -2 to $+2$, reasons for why skipping class without an excuse would be wrong. On item 3, "because you will not learn as much," the means of the just community programs are similar to those of the comparison groups. Item 3 reflects a nonmoral self-oriented or personal concern. In contrast, item 2, "because it hurts the spirit of the class," reflects a concern for the effects of skipping class on the community. Here we see significant differences between the means of the responses of students in the just community program and those in the conventional high schools.

Table 6-2
Reasons for Not Skipping Class, Assessed by Norm Content

	Just Community Group A	Comparison Group A	Just Community Group B	Comparison Group B
Skipping class without an excuse is wrong . . .				
1. because the teachers will feel let down. (Conventional)	0.6	−0.8**	0.7	−0.1*
2. because it hurts the spirit of the class. (Community)	0.5	−0.4***	1.0	0.0***
3. because you will not learn as much. (Personal)	0.9	1.0	3.6	3.9
4. because it is unfair to those who try to follow the rule. (Fairness)	1.2	0.5**	0.2	0.2
5. because you might get caught and punished. (Personal or low-stage moral)	0.6	0.7	0.4	0.5

*p .1
** p .05
*** p .01

In focusing on the way students think about disciplinary actions, we are led to consider the third of Durkheim's elements, the spirit of autonomy. If the just community programs were not democratic, they would be guilty of indoctrination and would undermine their moral purpose. Democracy entails rational persuasion and respect for the freedom of others. Involving students in discussion about matters of concern and empowering them to make decisions is an ideal educational method for stimulating students to reason about moral concerns. This is not to say that high school students should be left alone to make decisions as they see fit. We think that faculty members have a vital leadership role to play in advocating norms, rules, and policies that embody developmentally elevated concern for justice and community. In a sense, the faculty must initiate students into the common life; and yet this initiation must involve a concern for developing the students as morally autonomous persons.

CONCLUSION

In our view, cognitive developmentalists and neo-Aristotelians may find that the just community approach provides a point of departure for future dialogue on the ends and methods of moral education. Just as Aristotle's treatment of habituation served as a corrective for the Socratic dialogic method of moral education, so too do we see our own just community approach as a corrective to the moral discussion approach. Acknowledging the centrality of the cognitive dimension of moral education, we also recognize the importance of cultivating feelings of social attachment and concern as well as basic dispositions or habits of common living. In response to the charge that we have overintellectualized moral education, we have tried to show that Aristotle never lost sight of the cognitive dimension of moral education, even as he distinguished habituation from teaching.

As a developmental educator, Aristotle accommodated to the demands of different ethical levels, keeping in mind his ultimate aim of promoting practical wisdom. We think that the just community approach represents an extension of his vision, and we encourage the continued discussion of Aristotle's enduring contribution to moral education.

REFERENCES

Aquinas, Thomas. *Treatise on the Virtues*, trans. J. A. Oesterle. Englewood Cliffs, N.J.: Prentice-Hall, 1966.

Aristotle. *Nichomachean Ethics*, trans. Terence Irwin. Indianapolis: Hackett, 1985.

Bennett, William. Address to the National Press Club. Washington, D.C., 27 March 1985.

Blasi, Augusto. "Moral Identity: Its Role in Moral Functioning." In *Morality, Moral Behavior, and Moral Development*, ed. William M. Kurtines and Jacob Gewirtz. New York: Wiley, 1984.

Burnyeat, M. F. "Aristotle on Learning to Be Good." In *Essays on Aristotle*, ed. Amelie O. Rorty. Berkeley: University of California Press, 1980.

Colby, Anne, and Kohlberg, Lawrence. *The Measurement of Moral Judgment*, Vol. I. Cambridge, Mass.: Cambridge University Press, 1987.

Damon, William W. "Self-understanding and Moral Development from Childhood to Adolescence." In *Morality, Moral Behavior, and Moral Development*, ed. William M. Kurtines and Jacob Gewirtz. New York: Wiley, 1984.

Durkheim, Emile. *Moral Education: A Study in the Theory and Practice of the Sociology of Education*. New York: Free Press, 1973.

Hartshorne, Hugh, and May, Mark A. *Studies in the Nature of Character*. Vol. 1: *Studies in Deceit* (1928); Vol. 2: *Studies in Service and Self-Control* (1929); Vol. 3: *Studies in Organization of Character* (1930). New York: Macmillan, 1928–1930.

Irwin, Terence. *Notes and Annotated Glossary to Aristotle, Nicomachean Ethics*. Indianapolis: Hackett, 1985.

James, William. *Psychology, the Briefer Course*. Notre Dame, Ind.: University of Notre Dame Press, 1912/1985.

Kohlberg, Lawrence. "Education for Justice: A Modern Statement of the Platonic View." In *Moral Education: Five Lectures*, ed. Theodore Sizer. Cambridge, Mass.: Harvard University Press, 1970.

Kohlberg, Lawrence. "A Just Community Approach to Moral Education in Theory and Practice." In *Moral Education: Theory and Application*, ed. M. W. Berkowitz and F. Oser. Hillsdale, N.J.: Erlbaum, 1985.

MacIntyre, Alasdair C. *After Virtue*. Notre Dame, Ind.: University of Notre Dame Press, 1981.

Nicgorski, Walter, and Ellrod, Frederick E. "Moral Character." In *Act and Agent: Philosophical Foundations for Moral Education and Character Development*, ed. George F. McLean, Frederick E. Ellrod, David L. Schindler, and Jesse A. Mann. Lanham, Md.: University Press of America, 1986.

Peters, R. S. "Reason and Habit: The Paradox of Moral Education." In *Moral Education in a Changing Society*, ed. W. R. Niblet. London: Faber, 1963.

Power, Clark; Higgins, Ann; and Kohlberg, Lawrence. *Lawrence Kohlberg's Approach to Moral Education*. New York: Columbia University Press, forthcoming.

Sorabji, Richard R. "Aristotle on the Role of Intellect in Virtue." In *Essays on Aristotle*, ed. Amelie O. Rorty. Berkeley: University of California Press, 1980.

7

Seeing and Resolving Moral Conflict: Students' Approaches to Learning and Making Choices

Nona Lyons

"What does morality mean to you?" We asked two high school students this question in an interview; each gave different definitions and elaborated on their thinking about morality and responsibility. Roni, a sophomore, said:

> Morality? Wow. If I just use the noun "morals," I guess . . . I guess just a code of beliefs, you know, a code of honor, that one person would follow that's not necessarily anyone else's beliefs. I think morality maybe is a level or the level of personal integrity someone has. . . . Personal integrity I think is also a level of following rules. It is a level of following rules, abiding by rules so that you can function, because if I had no personal integrity . . . I would be amoral. . . . So I think also a level of personal integrity also establishes a basis for judging whether something is right or wrong.

Beth, a freshman, replied:

> I see a moral question as like, say: Is it better to drop a bomb? Would that save more lives than it would to fight? Moral questions are like that, they have drastic effects on life, I think. . . . Should I go out and fight along with my friends or

I want to thank the students of Emma Willard School, their teachers, Robert Parker, Trudy Hanmer, and the Geraldine R. Dodge Foundation who with us, a group of researchers, made this work possible.

should I go to Canada and watch my friends die? Or something like that. . . . I'm
not totally sure that [this situation] is a question of morality. It is a question of
responsibility, I think. . . . [What does responsibility mean to you?] Something
that if I don't do other people will suffer. . . . My homework is my responsibility
because I should, I have to, do it because if I don't, that will bog other people
down and then the class has to go over it again and I wouldn't be helping people
and I don't want to hinder people. I don't think that is right.

For Roni, morality is a code of beliefs, a measure of personal
integrity tied to abiding by rules, which can in turn become the basis
for judging whether something is right or wrong. Her code is personal,
not necessarily anyone else's. For Beth, morality has to do with
questions that can have drastic effects on life, like the dropping of a
bomb. Yet, she also ties morality to ideas about responsibility that
have to do with everyday things, like failing to do one's homework,
because that might bog other people down and would not be helping
them. For Roni, morality has to do with following one's code; for
Beth, it has to do with helping people, being sure to do something so
that others will not be hurt or hindered. Thus, two different definitions of morality are revealed.

While at first glance the contrast between these two responses may
not appear striking, they suggest that different kinds of issues can
become moral concerns. The responses have implications not only for
revealing how a girl constructs the meaning of morality but also for
understanding how she might act. Thus we want to ask here: What
does become a moral problem for each of these young women? And
why?

In this chapter I consider these issues of moral conflict and choice
and the logic of choice in the thinking of one group of adolescent high
school girls at Emma Willard School, a private high school for girls in
Troy, New York. Through an examination of some of the typical
conflicts the girls report, I first identify two orientations to morality: a
morality of justice and a morality of care (Gilligan 1977, 1982; Lyons
1982, 1983). I then explore a set of ideas related to the logic of each
orientation. Finally, I discuss the implications of these approaches to
construing and resolving moral problems, especially the applicability
of these approaches to the ways high school students see and approach problem solving in general. In particular, I present implications of this work as seen by teachers at Emma Willard. Although I
make use of data gathered at this school as part of a larger study—

The Emma Willard School Study Project—I will not report here the findings of that study. Instead, my purpose is to present a set of ideas and to discuss their implications for thinking about the education and learning of adolescent girls.

THE CONTEXT

The Emma Willard School Study Project was initiated in 1981, when the new headmaster, Robert Parker, turned to psychological research to find out what was known about adolescent girls' ways of knowing and learning that might inform school practices and might suggest how girls should be educated in the 1980s. Puzzled by some of his observations of how girls at the school made choices (frequently, he believed, on the basis of their personal relationships to others), Parker and his associate, Trudy Hanmer, wanted to see what research might suggest. They found very little research about adolescent girls or their approaches to learning. Psychologist Joseph Adelson made a similar discovery while putting together the *Handbook of Adolescent Psychology*. He tried to commission a chapter that would summarize recent research on adolescent girls' development. When he discovered that there was not enough research to warrant a single chapter, he concluded that adolescent girls had not been much studied. He believed that the inattention to girls and to the processes of feminine development in adolescence "has meant undue attention to such problems as impulse control, rebelliousness, superego struggles, ideology and achievement, along with a corresponding neglect of such issues as intimacy, nurturance, and affiliation" (Adelson 1980, p. 114). It was not just that adolescent girls had not been studied but that the important categories of analysis and explanation used to interpret behavior had been derived from boys' experiences. New descriptive studies were needed so that categories derived from girls' experiences could be constructed to help explain their adolescent behavior.

Parker and Hanmer then asked Carol Gilligan, a developmental psychologist at Harvard University, to help them think through their concerns about educating young women. Gilligan's research had focused on women and girls, and she had specifically examined choice and particularly moral choice. She had recently challenged the field of moral psychology to expand its domain beyond the traditional conception of morality as justice and had done so in part through the study of women's moral concerns.

Listening to people, mostly women, talk about the moral conflicts in their lives, Gilligan thought she recognized a set of considerations not predicted by the dominant model of moral development (Gilligan 1977, 1982). That model, largely based on the work of Lawrence Kohlberg (1969, 1984), suggests that moral conflicts arise from the conflicting claims between people and are resolved using objective procedures, considering such principles of justice as fairness. But in addition to justice and rights, Gilligan detected a set of different considerations: moral conflicts that arose from concerns about the fractures in the relationships between people or from concerns that someone was excluded or not cared for. Such conflicts were resolved by considering situations in their contexts and through the restoration of relationships or attention to needs. Gilligan called this a "morality of care or response" and suggested that the domain of morality had to include both justice and care.

My own research, the first testing of Gilligan's hypotheses, identified both considerations—justice and care—in people's thinking (Lyons 1981, 1982, 1983). I found justice and care considerations in the thinking of both men and women but different patterns in their use of these considerations. Men more frequently focused on considerations of justice, whereas women focused predominantly on care considerations. This discovery of patterns of use of justice and care considerations in one's thinking, especially the phenomenon of focus (i.e., that one consideration, or orientation, predominates in an individual's thinking when he or she uses both orientations) shifted my interest to the logic of each moral orientation. For example, this work called attention to different conceptions of the relationships between people embedded within justice and care: a morality of justice implied relationships of equality; a morality of care or response implied relationships of interdependence. The Harvard researchers recognized that the Emma Willard School's call for help in thinking about how girls made choices would be a special opportunity to examine firsthand how adolescent girls might define and characterize relationships in their lives and in the conflicts they construed as having moral dimensions.

That this study would be an important study of adolescent girls and that theory from moral psychology could inform an understanding of girls' behavior were ideas that intrigued the Emma Willard staff. They became eager participants in the research. Discussion between faculty and researchers in formal workshops and informal conversations took place over the four years of the project. These conversations shaped new questions to be added to the study and raised issues concerning how the staff interpreted the behavior of their students as well as how they might modify their own practices. Through open-ended interviews, the primary method of the study, Emma Willard girls shared their ideas about themselves, their life in school, their understanding of relationships, the moral conflicts they saw and dealt with in their lives, and how they envisioned their futures.

Roni and Beth's statements exemplify the predominant use of either justice or care reasoning found in the thinking of Emma Willard students who took part in this study (Gilligan and Lyons 1985). By examining the moral conflicts they report, we can identify and explore the two moral orientations and the logic of a set of related ideas. We present these two students as representatives of a larger sample of both males and females, who have similarly been found to use either justice or care as the predominant orientation in making moral choices (Lyons 1982, 1983; Gilligan et al. 1982; Johnston 1985). Although a third pattern in the use of the justice and care considerations has been identified (that is, an equal use of both justice and care considerations), we discuss only justice and care here for purposes of contrast.

A MORALITY OF JUSTICE AND A MORALITY OF CARE OR RESPONSE

For Roni, who defines morality as a code that gives her a way of judging what to do, moral conflict emerged when she was trying to determine whether or not she should follow school rules. The situation occurred when she herself was sitting as an active member of a school disciplinary committee, the Faculty-Student Judiciary Committee (FSJ), which determined how to deal with students who broke school rules:

> I remember when I was confronted with a situation where I could go out and get drunk with some friends who were on the FSJ (Faculty-Student Judiciary

Committee). . . . This was at the time when I was saying, "Well, if this rule really isn't ethical or moral, then to hell with it," and "They don't really expect us to follow these rules, they just don't want us to get caught," but a little voice in me was yelling, "It's wrong, it's wrong." And I think of all those people whose cases I sat on, where people were caught drinking . . . (but) I think I turned the girl down more from an extreme fear of getting caught, it wasn't any great moral realization. . . . I thought about it and we are not dealing with, "Oh, come back to me in an hour." This was minutes, seconds. I said, "No, thanks. I've got to go." But through my mind in those few seconds flashed, you know, stuff that I was breaking a rule.

Out of that, I think . . . it forced me, I said . . . it's wrong to break a rule and if you go here, you abide by the rules. . . . If you don't like them, leave. So this is another one of my great theories.

In recounting this situation, Roni reveals a complex and changing way of thinking about rules and why she will obey them. Forced to respond to the friend who invites her to break a rule, she judges that it is wrong and suggests the grounds on which she makes that judgment. Thinking first of all of the cases she herself has witnessed and judged as a member of the FSJ, she goes on to acknowledge that it was really no great moral realization but a fear of getting caught that made her say "No." The implications of not obeying rules have consequences. Realizing that she would be breaking a rule if she went out drinking, she simultaneously reasons that if you go to school here, you abide by school rules. Thus, she mediates and judges her own behavior with a standard she uses for others as well. Applied universally across situations, rules mediate her relationships and moral decision making in this instance.

For Beth, who is concerned not to hinder others, moral conflict arises from a situation in her relationship with her mother:

I was in a situation where my parents are divorced and I wanted to go to boarding school because I didn't want to live with my parents at that point. And my mother didn't want me to go. I have a younger sister by her second marriage and she said that I should stay home with my sister and take care of my sister and help the family in that sense. . . .

So I thought about it (and) decided to come back. . . . I guess I took an objective viewpoint . . . and decided that I love my sister and I love my mother but staying there and doing what she wanted me to do wasn't healthy for our relationship. . . . I did have a responsibility toward my family but that was not to take care of my sister but to make myself a person that wasn't going to be dependent on my family constantly and the only way to do that was to go (here) and . . . make something of myself. And then I could help my family.

In a dilemma caused by the special request of her mother, to come home from school to take care of a younger sister, Beth considers both what is healthy for their relationship and how she can help her family. Asked to comment on whether or not she thought her decision was the right thing to do, she goes on to say:

> I felt very guilty. I almost changed my mind . . . but I walked away and tried to think about what I was doing and I realized that I was right and for me, I was right. I don't think you could be totally right in that situation because there are different parts, different amounts of being right and you could have done one thing and I could have stayed with my mother and that would have been partially right or I could have come here and that would have been partially right, but each way I am cheating someone. But I have to work for myself. I have to do things for myself because if I can't do them now, how will I be able to do them when I become an adult and am supposed to?

Concerned, then, that "each way I am cheating someone," Beth sees no one right way—only different amounts of right. She resolves her conflict by deciding that "making something of myself" is necessary in order to be able sometime to "help my family." From a way of thinking about morality that is constructed as not hindering others, to a definition, resolution, and evolution of a moral problem, a logic is revealed in this young woman's thinking: Individuals in relation must each be considered in their own contexts and needs.

Similarly, Roni, also responding to the question "Do you think it was the right thing to do?" says:

> Definitely. . . . I think it is not fair for this school to ask you to live under some sort of rule, and to break those rules and then sit in on a case where you are judging someone else for doing the very same thing that you did. That is why it seemed like a contradiction to me because you are creating the wrongness the FSJ deals with and I don't think (it is fair) for someone to sit there and talk about punishing someone else if they had been drinking themselves last night.

Embedded in the two kinds of conflict these students present are what may be called two kinds of logic, two different ways of thinking about the relationships between people that give rise to different moral considerations. For Roni, relationships are construed as if through some kind of contract with an underlying conception of fairness and equality between individuals. All individuals should be and are considered in fairness.

Beth looks at the situation from the point of view of each person, including herself, not in strict equality but in each person's terms and contexts. She acts to do what is right for herself and her family, while considering their long-term relationship. Here the underlying value is interdependence and responsiveness, responsiveness implying an acknowledgment of the reality of the situation as well as an understanding of each person's particularity and needs.

From perspectives of fairness and reciprocity or of response and interdependence, these young women see and seek to resolve conflicts they term moral conflicts. I present here other examples from the experiences of Emma Willard students; they similarly report moral conflicts they have encountered, conflicts that include justice and care considerations.

> I didn't get my math homework done. . . . We had to hand in computer tapes and my friend had an extra computer tape and I knew that the teacher was absolutely going to freak out and scream at me and I would get into trouble if I didn't hand in a tape, and my friend had an extra one she was offering me, but I couldn't do it. I couldn't take it. . . . Sort of like the principle, damn it, I didn't do the computer tape. . . . I couldn't hand it in when I didn't do it. It would have been like cheating.

• • •

> I don't go to chapel any more because I find that offensive and I guess that's moral. We have required chapel once a week and I don't like the idea of being required to go, of being forced into religion. I go to church on my own sometimes. I think that's enough for me and I don't feel that I need to go to these required services. It was a big decision.

• • •

> I lied to my parents about my grades. I told them that my biology grade was going to be marvelous and it is not going to be marvelous. . . . Suddenly, my sister who has always been National Honor Society and all those wonderful things, has gotten horrible grades this past month and (my parents) called me up and told me this and then wanted to know how mine were. . . . Knowing my parents, they would go to the ends of the earth if they knew both their children were doing horribly in school. My parents are educational fanatics, and so I've told them that my grades are fine and there was almost a sigh of relief from my father and I think that outweighed the idea that I was lying to them. . . . I couldn't bring myself on the phone to say, "Well, Dad, you are looking at two academic failures for the term," and I think that's a moral dilemma.

• • •

> When my father decided to get remarried, it was really a hard decision on my part as to whether and when to tell my mother that, because on the one hand, I knew that it was really going to really kill her to find that out, and on the other hand, I

thought I had an obligation to tell her. . . . I was really happy for my father, because I loved who he was getting married to and I thought it was going to be really good for him, but it was really difficult to decide whether to tell my mom, because I knew that it was going to tear her apart.

In these examples it is apparent that different issues can become salient moral conflicts for students, and that the same issue can be given different meanings. Lying is an example. The student who talks about lying to her parents about her grades is seeing a problem different from that of the student who cannot lie about computer tapes. For the girl concerned about the tapes, to hand in her friend's homework as her own would have been cheating, and would have involved for her the violation of some principle of fairness. "I didn't do the tape. . . . I couldn't hand it in." But a different kind of issue concerns the student who lies to her parents about her grades, namely, the direct effect on her parents of the bad news of her failing grades. As she says, knowing how intensely her parents value their children's education makes her tell them that her grades will be good when they will not be. In an instant she not only can call up the values of her parents but can enter into their world, and act to prevent their disappointment for however short a period of time. In these two constructions, different considerations frame and shape conflict, conflicts both girls label as "moral." We describe one set of considerations as a "justice" orientation and the other as a "care" orientation.

Similarly, it is possible to examine the underlying perspectives of different conflicts the girls present and thus see a similar logic at work across different situations. For instance, the girl who found a moral conflict in deciding not to go to required chapel acts out of her principles and standards in much the same way as Roni, who decided it was wrong to break the school rule when she was sitting on the school Judiciary Committee. Both act from a set of standards they hold about what is the right thing to do. The underlying values are fairness to themselves, to their standards, or to others. This way of thinking about real-life moral conflict is here termed a "morality of justice."

The girl who does not know whether to tell her mother that her father is to be remarried acts in response to need in much the same way as the girl who does not tell her parents she will have a failing grade. The logic that shapes their behavior is a logic that acts in response to need, considering the situation of the individuals involved.

This way of thinking about moral conflict is termed here a "morality of response or care." And while it is clear that girls can act out of either of these two moral orientations—and usually the conflicts they report have elements of both—girls can also present both modes equally in their thinking. It is important to emphasize that while girls present moral conflicts that include both justice and care (response) considerations, here we have been considering either "justice" or "response" to illuminate the characteristic features in a girl's thinking if one kind of moral consideration predominates.

Table 7-1 presents a summary of the central moral issues and logic of the two moral orientations. This construction of morality as justice and response (care) expands the traditional construction of morality described in the dominant model of moral psychology, most notably in the work of Kohlberg (1969, 1984). In Kohlberg's model, morality is defined as justice, and moral problems are seen to emerge from the conflicting claims of individuals and are resolved through the application of principles of justice as fairness. Fair treatment and broadly contractual rules and individual rights provide a set of related ideas within this orientation to morality. But a second construction, previously identified but revealed here as well in the thinking of adolescent girls, suggests that there is another definition of morality, that is, morality as responsiveness to another. This ethic, called the ethic of care or response, was first identified by Gilligan; I present here my conceptualization of it with its logic, along with the ethic of justice.

Table 7-2 summarizes the logic of the two moral orientations with a set of related ideas. These ideas are conceptualized as forming the logic of each orientation. In particular, I draw attention to the features of knowing and thinking evident in each orientation. It is this set of ideas, especially the characteristic features of the two approaches to problem posing and problem solving, that I believe have larger implications for learning and learning environments.

The experience of teachers at Emma Willard School tells us that this research, especially the identification of the two moral orientations in the thinking of Emma Willard girls and the phenomenon of a focus or predominance in girls' thinking, is useful to teachers in a number of ways. First, it can help to account for and explain girls' behavior. For example, girls who value the maintenance of relationships and the welfare of their friends could be expected to act accordingly in their day-to-day life in school, whereas those who value fairness could be expected to act in a manner consistent with that value.

Table 7-1

Overview of the Central Moral Issues and the Logic of Care and Justice in the Construction of, Resolution of, and Evaluation of the Resolution of Moral Dilemmas

A MORALITY OF CARE (RESPONSE)	*A MORALITY OF JUSTICE*
A. In What Becomes a Moral Problem	A. In What Becomes a Moral Problem
A morality of care rests on an understanding of relationships that entails response to others in their terms and contexts. Therefore, what becomes a moral problem has to do with relationships or the activities of care. The conflicts of relationships are raised as issues surrounding the potential fractures between people, that is, not with breaking trusts or obligations but with severing ties between people; or conversely, with restoring or maintaining relationships.	A morality of justice as fairness rests on an understanding of relationships as reciprocity between separate individuals. Therefore, what becomes a moral problem has to do either with mediating issues of conflicting claims in the relationships between people or with how one is to decide conflicts or how one can justify one's decision and actions, considering fairness as a goal between individuals.
The conflicts surrounding the activities of care have to do with response itself, that is, how to respond (or the capacity or ability to respond) to another within the particular situation one encounters; how to promote the welfare or well-being of another; or to relieve their burdens, hurt, or suffering, either physical or psychological.	The moral dilemmas of conflicting claims have to do with the conflicts of obligation, duty, or commitment stemming from different role relationships one may have between oneself and others, between oneself and society, or to one's own values and principles. The conflicts with respect to how one is to decide come from the need to have some impartial, objective measure of choice that ensures fairness in arriving at a decision.
B. In the Resolution of Moral Conflict	B. In the Resolution of Moral Conflict
In a morality of care, resolutions to moral conflict are sought (1) in restoring relationships or the connections between people and (2) in carrying through the activities of care, ensuring that good will come to others or that hurt or suffering will be stopped.	In a morality of justice, resolutions to moral conflicts are sought considering (1) meeting one's obligations or commitments or performing one's duties or (2) holding to or not violating one's standards or principles, especially fairness.
C. In the Evaluation of the Resolution	C. In the Evaluation of the Resolution
In a morality of care, the evaluation of moral choice is made considering (1) whether relationships were restored or maintained; (2) how things worked out or will work out; and in some instances	In a morality of justice, the evaluation of moral choice is made considering (1) how the decision was justified or thought about or (2) whether values, standards, or principles

there is only the acknowledgment that there is no way to know or to evaluate resolution. Whether relationships were restored can be measured in several ways: simply if everyone is happy, if people talk to one another, or if everyone is comfortable with the solution. If people talk and everyone agrees with the solution, one knows relationships are maintained.

How things work out is a measure of resolution in that in seeing what happens to people over time, one then knows if the resolution worked. This marker also carries the notion that only over time can one know results, that is, know in the sense of seeing what actually happens.

were maintained, especially fairness.

How the decision was justified or thought about is an important measure to make of living up to one's obligations (duty or commitments) or of fairness; whether values, standards, or principles were maintained is a measure both of ability to live up to one's obligations or principles and of the standards used in decision making.

Source: Extracted from Nona Lyons, *A Manual for Coding Real-Life Dilemmas*, 1982.

One faculty advisor who was also a house parent in a dorm relates how he found a new way to think about girls who did not obey a "lights out" command and were found visiting friends. Whereas in the past he believed that a girl's argument that she needed to visit a friend was but an excuse for breaking a rule (and a poor one at that), the teacher now realizes that the student might indeed be acting on a logic other than obedience to rules, that is, she was acting from genuine concern for another.

Second, when teachers see the two moral orientations as embodying two logics, they can look at behaviors in a new way. They recognize, for example, that girls may want to be involved in the school's judicial procedures for very different reasons—reasons that will shape their behaviors. Some may wish to help prevent student troubles; others may want to have a chance to be in charge of procedures that will guarantee fairness in deliberations. These views may be compatible, but they are subtly different, suggesting different values that in turn lead to different ways of interacting with others.

Third, probably of most significance to teachers are the ways teachers now think about the education of girls. Not only did the Emma Willard faculty review and "balance" their curriculum to guarantee that women were included in it (e.g., in the novels assigned

Table 7-2

The Logic of Two Moral Perspectives: A Set of Related Ideas

	The Perspective of Response in Relationships	The Perspective of Rights in Relationships
Perspective towards others	See others in their own terms and context; enter into their situation	See others as one would like to be seen (through self's lens); in equality and reciprocity. Step back from situation for objectivity
Conception of self in relation to others	Inderdependent in relation to others	Autonomous, equal, independent in relation to others
Ideas and images of relationships	Attachment as given, interdependence of people; concern with responsiveness, isolation of people; relationships as webs	Attachment through roles; obligation, duty; concern with equality and fairness in relationships; relationships as hierarchies
Mode of thinking and knowing	Particularistic; contextual; question posing; suspended judgment; use of dialogue, discussion; goal is understanding; thinking and feeling held together	Objective; generalizing; abstract, rule-seeking; goal is to critique; analyze; to answer question; to prove; thinking and feeling seen as needing to be separated
Interpersonal ideas and processes	Interdependent; emphasis on discussion; listening; in order to understand others in their own contexts	Objective; role-related; in order to maintain fairness and equality in dealing with others

in reading, or in the examination in history classes of the social aspects of people's lives as well as the political aspects), but teachers became more aware of their practices in support of student learning. They report listening to questions students ask and reflecting on their own responses as well as trying out diverse approaches to learning, such as cooperative learning, in sports and mathematics classes. Table 7-3 presents a hypothetical model of characteristic features of two approaches to learning implied in the two moral orientations (the justice and care modes with their related self-conceptions): the self as autonomous or separate and the self as interdependent. I identify here autonomous or interdependent knowers and learners. This model is based on the work of Belenky and colleagues (1986), Bruner (1986),

Table 7-3
Learners and Learning Contexts: The Relationship of Mode of Self to a Learner's Interests, Goals, and Mode of Thinking

Mode of Self	Learner's Interests and Goals	Learner as Thinker and Knower
Autonomous (separate in relation to others)	To question; to prove; to find answers to questions; to solve problems	Analytical; procedural; truth seeking; rule seeking and using
	To convince by argument; logic	Test for truth: consistency; logic; reasoned hypothesis
	Know how to know truth	Transcend time and space and particulars; imagination; to see before proving; thought and feeling held apart
Interdependent (connected in relation to others)	To question; to find understanding of situations, people, and their contexts; narrative seeking; to convince by motives, particulars of lives	Tentative and questioning; judgment suspended; fact gathering; synthesizer
		Test for truth; believability; concern for understanding of human motivation; intention
		Imagination used to enter into situations, contexts; locate in time and place
		Thought and feeling held together

Source: Adapted from Belenky et al. 1986, Brúner 1986, Gilligan 1982, Lyons, 1982, 1985

and Gilligan (1977, 1982) as well as on my own work (1981, 1983, 1987); and its emphasis is on different features of the learner's goals and interests that reflect different approaches to learning.

Because the two approaches to learning are thought of as clearly complementary although significantly different, understanding and articulating these differences is an important agenda for the future. Most schools tend to foster rule-oriented, rational, abstract thinking, whether in mathematics and science or in history and social studies. Less attention is given to the features we identify here as associated with an interdependent learner. Emma Willard teachers, for example, found themselves thinking about student hesitancy and questioning in a new way once they had some familiarity with the two orientations. One new Emma Willard teacher of history, for example, shared an incident with colleagues that he had at first found perplexing. He was nearing the end of a class in which he had been emphasizing how the American political system worked in one presidential election in which a deal was struck between northern and southern Democrats and Republicans. One girl raised her hand to ask what ground the people involved had for trusting one another. The teacher, feeling as if the question had nothing to do with a systems approach he was emphasizing, was puzzled at his failure to be clear. But in sharing this situation with colleagues, he was offered a different interpretation. That is, the girl was more interested as a learner in understanding the motives of those involved. She heard the event as a narrative, a story of an encounter in the relationships between individuals. The logic she sought was not the logic of a system. Rather, she sought the logic of understanding, what Bruner (1986) calls "believability." Unlike the teacher who sought to transcend time, she was rooted in it, in the particulars of the situation and in the narrative of the relationships between people. It is this approach to learning with its different concerns and interests that educators need to understand better and listen for. They also need to make opportunities for this voice to be expressed and heard. If this is a mode of learning more frequently found in the thinking of girls—although we know both sexes use it—educators need to be attentive to it. Emma Willard girls remind us of the centrality of Piaget's (1965) insight that "apart from our relations to other people, there can be no moral necessity," and they show us how morality, mind, self, and relationships are intricately linked in everyday ways of knowing and learning. They offer an invitation to others to help elaborate these ideas.

REFERENCES

Adelson, Joseph, ed. *Handbook of Adolescent Psychology*. New York: John Wiley & Sons, 1980.

Belenky, Mary R.; Clinchy, Blythe; Goldberger, Nancy; and Tarule, Jill. *Women's Ways of Knowing*. New York: Basic Books, 1986.

Bruner, Jerome S. *Actual Minds, Possible Worlds*. Cambridge, Mass.: Harvard University Press, 1986.

Gilligan, Carol. "In a Different Voice: Women's Conceptions of Self and Morality." *Harvard Educational Review* 47 (1977): 481–517.

Gilligan, Carol. *In a Different Voice: Psychological Theory and Women's Development.* Cambridge, Mass.: Harvard University Press, 1982.

Gilligan, Carol; Langdale, Sharry; Lyons, Nona; and Murphy, J. Michael. *The Contribution of Women's Thinking to Developmental Theory.* Final Report to the National Institute of Education. Cambridge, Mass.: Harvard University, 1982.

Gilligan, Carol, and Lyons, Nona. "Listening to Voices We Have Not Heard." Report to the New York State Department of Education on the Emma Willard School Study, 1985.

Johnston, Donna Kay. "Two Moral Orientations—Two Problem-solving Strategies: Adolescents' Solutions to Dilemmas in Fables." Doct. dissertation, Harvard Graduate School of Education, 1985.

Kohlberg, Lawrence. "Stage and Sequence: The Cognitive Developmental Approach to Socialization." In *Handbook of Socialization Theory and Research,* ed. David A. Goslin. Chicago: Rand McNally, 1969.

Kohlberg, Lawrence. *The Psychology of Moral Development.* San Francisco: Harper and Row, 1984.

Lyons, Nona. "Manual for Coding Responses to the Question: How Would You Describe Yourself to Yourself?" Unpublished manuscript, Harvard University, 1981.

Lyons, Nona. "Conceptions of Self and Morality and Modes of Moral Choice." Doct. dissertation, Harvard University, 1982.

Lyons, Nona. "Two Perspectives: On Self, Relationships, and Morality." *Harvard Educational Review* 53 (1983): 125–45.

Lyons, Nona. "Visions and Competencies: Men and Women as Decision Makers and Conflict Negotiators." Paper presented at the Annual Meeting of the American Educational Research Association, Boston, 1985.

Lyons, Nona. "Ways of Knowing, Learning, and Making Moral Choices." *Journal of Moral Education* 16 (1987): 226–39.

Piaget, Jean. *The Moral Judgment of the Child.* New York: Free Press, 1965.

8

Multifaceted Social Reasoning and Educating for Character, Culture, and Development

Elliot Turiel

A striking characteristic of the contemporary scene in the social sciences is that controversies are rampant. Whatever the reasons, there are still sufficient fundamental differences in basic assumptions to generate a great deal of disagreement among schools of thought. Some of the most acrimonious debates in social scientific controversies are over explanations of morality. Indeed, bitter disputes and biting commentaries often come from scholars of the moral aspects of human relations. As might be expected in light of this situation in the social scientific analyses of morality, controversy and acrimony are at least equally evident in discussions about the practice of moral education. However, in one significant respect the nature of debates regarding the implementation of programs of moral education in the schools is of a different order from debates over theory and research on moral reasoning and action. Whereas it is rarely claimed that proponents of alternative viewpoints should refrain from engaging in a line of research, it is frequently asserted that others ought not engage in certain types of programs of moral education.

It seems that applying psychological explanations and research findings to moral education in the schools can be risky business—especially for those taking nontraditional approaches. It opens them up to accusations of corrupting youth and even of contributing to moral decay in the society. As an example, Christina Sommers, a philosopher from Clark University, recently asserted that the advent of new programs of moral education (i.e., values clarification and those based on developmental concepts) have contributed to a moral decline in the nation (Sommers 1984). Sommers claims to have encountered a symptom of this moral decline in the attitudes of contemporary undergraduates who come to college showing the negative effects of, as she put it, "an educational system that has kept its distance from the traditional virtues" (p. 386). Although Sommers dismisses as romanticism the Rousseauian idea that society can corrupt the innocent child, she believes that some who engage in moral education are corrupters of contemporary youth. Sommers's view—that this decline of morality in the land is in some way associated with how children are being morally educated (actually miseducated)—is a common theme in other commentaries by proponents of character education (Bennett 1980a, 1980b; Bennett and Delattre 1978, 1979; Delattre and Bennett 1979; Wynne 1979, 1986), and reflects a world view of society, morality, and education that sees virtue in the past and places blame for presumed contemporary problems on modern or secular influences.

Examples of this world view abound in periodic recommendations for how to impart morality to children in educational settings. A typical recommendation was made in 1969 by an advisory committee to the California State Superintendent of Schools. The Committee's recommendations for moral instruction in the public schools were based on the presumption that "a moral crisis is sweeping the land"—a crisis which is reflected "in the increased use of drugs at colleges as well as [in higher rates] of sexual promiscuity, of illegitimate births, and . . . [of] crimes of violence." Blame for this situation was placed on a number of then current social and educational trends, especially what the committee referred to as the creeping cult of secular humanism. (John Dewey was named as high priest of the cult, and others mentioned as members of the "faith" were Margaret Mead and Ashley Montague.) To alleviate the problem it was recommended that moral education return to traditional and nonsecular forms of instruction. Their specific recommendations were to pattern education after the moral training programs of the Navy and Marine Corps, to rely on teachings in the Bible and traditional textbooks, and to provide examples of good role models, such as George Washington, Thomas Jefferson, Abraham Lincoln, J. Edgar Hoover, and William Buckley, Jr.

This perspective places the ideas and propositions of scholars of education and social science on the same plane as religious propositions as well as generally accepted cultural traditions and customs. Sometimes this is done with the argument that religious propositions are a form of science and, more often, it is done with the argument that scholarly and scientific propositions are a form of religious belief (as implied in naming John Dewey the high priest of secular humanism). The former argument is seen in disputes over the teaching of evolutionary theory. It has been asserted that creationism as an explanation of the origin of life represents a legitimate scientific rival to the theory of evolution. This contention has been the basis, for instance, of assertions that schools should not teach evolution as the only credible theory of the origin of life. Several states have laws mandating that creationism be taught alongside evolutionary theory. In California, where no such law exists, it was recently argued in court that creationism should be taught as an alternative scientific explanation, and conversely that teaching only the theory of evolution indoctrinates students into a dogma that essentially constitutes a religion of secular humanism (see Siegel 1981 for a discussion of the issues and the court case). In recent years the issue has been politicized by groups like Jerry Falwell's Moral Majority through the explicit argument that there exists a religion of secular humanism based on values derived by persons or groups rather than on values given by a deity.

DISCONTENT WITH MORAL EDUCATION AND DEVELOPMENTAL CONCEPTS

The equation of secular and nonsecular propositions also has adherents among educators and social scientists who believe this country is undergoing a moral crisis and who have been critical of recent applications to moral education based on developmental explanations of morality (e.g., those of Kohlberg 1966; Piaget 1932). These views are shared by the previously mentioned proponents of character education and others proposing that all forms of knowledge are "social constructions" (e.g., Hogan 1975; Sampson 1977, 1978, 1981; Shweder 1986). The proponents of character education, who stress the importance of educating for virtues and traditions, have asserted that secular humanism represents an ideological bias in the theories of certain social scientists. For the most part, they have contrasted secular humanism not so much with religion as with their view of morality as adherence to cultural traditions and acts of virtue. Their discontent is often with those applying developmental concepts to moral education (e.g., Blatt and Kohlberg 1975, Kohlberg 1966), whom they regard as attempting to transmit positions biased toward libertarianism and communitarian ideologies (Bennett 1980b). From their perspective, the concepts of developmentalists reflect an undesirable relativism that promotes too much tolerance and contributes to moral decay in the society. Indeed, for Sommers (1984) the moral decline symptomatic in the attitudes of contemporary college students is characterized by "... a ragbag of another stripe whose contents may be roughly itemized as follows: psychological egoism (the belief that the primary motive for action is selfishness), moral relativism (the doctrine that what is praiseworthy or contemptible is a matter of cultural conditioning), and radical tolerance (the doctrine that to be culturally and socially aware is to understand and excuse the putative wrongdoer).... The half-baked relativism of the college student tends to undermine his common sense" (p. 386).

The proponents of social construction, who stress the importance of cultural determinants in morals acquisition, have asserted that there are ideological and cultural biases in many Western social scientific explanations; some social constructionists maintain that those biases contribute to moral decay in the society (Hogan 1975) or impede moral progress (Sampson 1977). In contrast with the proponents of character education, social constructionists claim that the concepts of developmentalists represent an undesirable moral absolutism that fails to show tolerance for cultural variations. This intriguing discrepancy between social constructionists and the proponents of character education in their respective characterizations of developmental approaches stems, on the one hand, from the emphasis social constructionists place on the cultural determinants of morality and, on the other hand, from the emphasis proponents of character education place on the role of tradition and virtue in this culture. Nevertheless, the two approaches express similar disagreements with the ways developmentalists stress children's judgments and understandings of social and moral issues and levels of development as a basis for facilitating further development. Moreover, there are striking similarities in the ways each approach defines morality and its acquisition, as well as in their views of moral crises. These commonalities (and some differences) in the two approaches raise a series of interesting issues regarding character, tradition, decision making, ideological or cultural bias, and the role of culture in moral development as they bear on moral education.

From the perspective of character education, encouraging students to discuss and think about moral decisions as a means of educating for moral development contributes to the moral crisis in this society because it fails to strengthen necessary traditions and virtues. Proponents of character education believe that adequate moral training of children requires that teachers and parents impart through inculcation, and even indoctrination, the society's traditions, respect for authority, and a sense of duty. In their view, morality is not fostered by reflection, critical thought, or understandings formed by individuals. Morality is, instead, nonrational everyday conduct guided by traits of character and virtues like "sacrifice, altruism, love, courage, honor, and compassion" (Bennett and Delattre 1978, p. 97). In turn, morality needs to be transmitted to (and, when necessary, even imposed upon) children through their daily, commonplace activities in settings like schools. Programs of moral education that focus on children's judgments, decision making, and difficult conceptual problems are regarded as individualistic and, thereby, contrary to the traditions of this society: "The emphasis on collective life contrasts sharply with the individualism that pervades contemporary education, and which is often mistaken for 'humanism'" (Wynne 1986, p. 7).

Character education is based on two general notions that social constructionists also believe. The first is that morality is defined by the values held by societies. As put by Wynne (1986, p. 4), "the term 'moral values' . . . signifies the specific values that particular cultures generally hold in regard." Those values represent uncontroversial norms that are integral to the society and reflect its traditions. An emphasis is placed on the individual's subordination to the group, to its hierarchy and authority. The second notion is that children learn to behave in the appropriate moral ways through the transmission of cultural values from society's appropriate adult representatives insofar as these adults use adequate means of education or training. It is, of course, this idea that morality is acquired through direct transmission from adults that leads proponents of character education to regard educational methods stressing the development of reasoning as at best ineffective and, worse, miseducative and corruptive.

Although proponents of social construction also bemoan the moral decay of this society, they have manifested little interest in the issue of moral education. They have not advised how morality ought to be transmitted to children but have focused on examining cultural influences on children and evaluating cultural orientations. Social constructionists characterize the presumed moral decay in broad, sweeping views of societies. One example is Hogan's (1975) dual assertions that contemporary Western society is characterized by individualism—"the view that societies are composed of aggregates of separate individuals, each following his or her own enlightened self-interest, and that social institutions substantially restrict individual freedom" (p. 533) —and that individualism has resulted in a collapse of social institutions, alienation, alcoholism, drug addiction, delinquency, and suicide, among other ills. Hogan sees a moral degeneration sufficiently serious to lead him to worry that "our individualism may ultimately be, in a very real sense, the ruin of us all" (p. 536). Hogan seems to be a social constructionist with a foot in the character education camp. He regards individualism as anarchistic and antipathic toward culture, tradition, and custom.

Mainstream social constructionists concentrate on contrasts between generalized cultural orientations. A major postulate is the contrast between individualistic and collectivistic cultures. Along with Hogan, others have characterized Western society as individualistic. In Shweder's (1986) view this society is characterized by individualism and a liberal, rights-based morality—which can be contrasted with the interdependent, hierarchical structure of other societies (e.g., Hinduism in India) and their duty-based morality. In Sampson's (1977) view, Western society is characterized by an ethos of "self-contained individualism"—which is contrasted with interdependence and collectivism. In a version of the theme of moral crisis, individualism is identified as inadequate for the survival of society and detrimental to optimizing human welfare (Sampson 1977, 1981). A vision of progress for society and humankind is promulgated that requires shifting from a cultural ethos of individualism to one of collectivism.

It is unclear why educators and social scientists viewing morals acquisition as cultural learning have so often asserted that society is in moral crisis and that *their* recommendations for educational and cultural changes would alleviate the problem. Perhaps it is simply that moral problems always exist and there is a tendency both to generalize them to broad societal problems and to particularize them to one's time. Alternatively, it may be due to a disposition to proselytize, requiring the assumption that a moral crisis exists. The need for crisis seems to exist whether proselytizing against change and a return to the past (character education) or for change to a different cultural orientation (social construction).

In any event, these assertions of moral crises seem to be linked with accusations that the explanations of other scholars and social scientists are ideologically or culturally biased and contribute to the crises. Along with proponents of character education, social constructionists claim that developmental approaches to morality are biased by the theorists' individualistic, liberal, and humanistic ideology. Hogan (1975), for instance, claimed that many contemporary psychological explanations, because of their ideological bias toward individualism and against culture, tradition, and custom, contribute to selfishness and exacerbate the moral crisis and degeneration occurring in this society. Like the California educational advisory committee mentioned earlier, Hogan identifies John Dewey as a major influence on individualism.

Figure 8-1 provides a telling illustration of the ubiquitous charge of the secular bias in educational material. This political cartoon was a commentary on a recent court case in which a group of fundamentalist Christian parents challenged the constitutionality of exposing their children to certain textbooks in public schools on the grounds that the books promoted an alternative secular philosophy (the objectionable plays, books, and stories included *Macbeth*, "Cinderella," *The Wizard of Oz*, Hans Christian Anderson fairy tales, and the *Diary of Anne Frank*). Equating secular and nonsecular propositions, a federal judge in Tennessee ruled in favor of the fundamentalist parents. In a more far-reaching case, a federal judge in Alabama ordered a large number of books completely banned from public schools. He based his ruling on the contention that the books promoted a "religion" of secular humanism and that, therefore, their use is a violation of the First Amendment of the U.S. Constitution.

Social constructionists equate scholarly and scientific propositions with nonsecular or any other types of secular propositions by virtue of cultural determinism. In this regard, sweeping claims are made about the influence of the historical and cultural contexts on the thought of social scientists (Hogan 1975; Sampson 1977; Shweder 1986). It has been asserted, for instance, that in most areas of psychology—cognitive, personality, and, especially, moral psychology—our explanations reflect an individualistic cultural bias because, to use Sampson's terms, we are blinded by our cultural heritage.

Claims of even greater sweep serve to equate all types of ideas and

Figure 8.1

systems of knowledge. Culturally biased individualism is presumably the dominant perspective of all academicians, who, in addition to social scientists, would include those in the humanities and the physical sciences (Sampson 1978). Moreover, it is asserted that all forms of knowledge are ideological and to some extent represent cultural myths that are beyond reason or evidence. Accordingly, Shweder (1986) argues that evidence cannot be used to decide between the validity of creationism and evolutionary theory as explanations of the origins of life. With regard to morality, Shweder's claim is that fundamental differences in the moral orientations of cultures (e.g., the rights-based American morality and the duty-based Indian morality) go unrecognized in the culturally biased explanations of developmental theorists like Piaget (1932) and Kohlberg (1969, 1971). As will be discussed shortly, there is an important and telling difference between the social construction and character education approaches. However, they are alike in their view that developmentalists' theories are biased by a liberal, secular humanistic ideology.

It seems that while character education and social construction proponents presume that most scholars are blinded by ideologies or cultural heritage such that their theories contain unrecognized biases, they believe that they themselves are able to see beyond the otherwise all-enveloping ideological and cultural blinders to provide truthful and objectively valid ideas.[1] All too often they support the relative truth of their own positions primarily by accusing the alternative positions of cultural bias. Unfortunately, accusations of such bias[2] too easily replace detailed critical analyses of the merits and evidence bearing on different points of view. It appears that character education and social construction proponents find it difficult to resist the temptation to replace the intellectual and scientific tasks of criticism and refutation with accusations of bias and with equating all types of ideas.[3]

THE CONSTRUCTION OF SOCIAL ORIENTATIONS

As noted earlier, the character education and social construction approaches have similar conceptions of morals acquisition that underlie their various perceptions of moral decay and assertions of ideological or cultural biases. Both approaches give little credence to reflectivity, critical thought, or moral understandings and propose that morals acquisition comes about through a top-down social communication process of adults conveying the morality of the culture to children. The cultural emphasis of this view is evident in Shweder's

---

1. The implicit assumption of the social constructionists that their position is not subject to ideological and cultural bias poses some serious contradictions for them. Since the general claim is that one's culture strongly influences the positions taken by social scientists, then it follows that their own positions are equally influenced by their culture. In that case, it could not be maintained that the social construction view is any more objectively valid than any other position. Alternatively, if social constructionists were to claim that their position transcends cultural influences, they would be subject to the criticism of individualism that they level at other theorists.

2. Along with accusations of bias there is sometimes a labeling of others' viewpoints that also serves to displace critical analyses. For instance, Hogan dismisses Dewey's position by referring to it as romantic individualism and Freud's position by referring to it as egoistic individualism.

3. If it were the case that culture blindly determines all ideas, then there would be no basis for making evaluations of comparative adequacy. Such a situation, however, would present a vicious cycle in which the idea that thought is culturally determined is itself culturally determined and no more valid than any other idea regarding the sources of thought.

(1986) anthropological metaphor for the idea that children learn from adults when he says that children acquire moral codes from the "local guardians of the moral order."

As a consequence of their emphasis on schooling, character education proponents stress the need for deliberate, and often difficult, efforts on the part of adults to impart morality successfully through the use of praise and blame, reward and punishment, and consistent modeling. As a consequence of their emphasis on the force of culture, some social constructionists propose that morals acquisition usually comes about smoothly. It occurs at an early age, since moral codes are packaged in coherent cultural systems of symbols and traditions that children readily assimilate (Shweder 1986; Shweder, Mahapatra, and Miller forthcoming). Given a consistent, integrated, and homogeneous cultural packaging, however, it is likely that proponents of character education would also expect children's moral learning to occur smoothly (Bennett 1980a).

In spite of their similar positions regarding the process of morals acquisition, the substantive character education and social construction positions yield a curious and contradictory state of affairs regarding the specific moral systems attributed to our own and other cultures. First, consider the claim of social constructionists that developmental conceptions are culturally biased in that their explanations reflect the morality of this culture. Individualistic, liberal, and secular humanistic morality, they say, is in accord with Western culture and different from cultures with traditional, collectivistic, and duty-based morality. For instance, this is at the heart of Shweder's (1986; Shweder, Mahapatra, and Miller, forthcoming) contrast between secular, rights-based Western morality and traditional, hierarchical, duty-based Hindu morality. Whereas Western morality is concerned with individual rights and freedoms, Hindu morality is concerned with fulfilling duties and upholding traditions. In contrast, character education proponents claim that the individualistic, liberal, and secular humanistic views represent a bias that is *not* the dominant orientation of Western society. The dominant morality of this society, they say, is, instead, reflected by traditions, duties, and virtues. It turns out, then, that one group of Western scholars (the social constructionists) believes that individualism, liberalism, and concerns with rights characterize their society's morality, whereas another group of scholars from Western society (the character education proponents) does not. Moreover, the morality that proponents of character education attribute to Western society is strikingly similar to the morality social constructionists attribute to other societies.

This paradoxical situation naturally leads one to question whether the moral orientations proposed by the two approaches are cultural constructions or mainly social constructions developed by the theorists. In certain respects the moral orientations are cultural (and individual) constructions, but in other respects they are theorists' constructions. The sense in which they are the theorists' constructions is exemplified by the contradictory portrayals of the culture's ethos and moral codes. The essence of these constructions is the proposition that cultures and individuals can be characterized through one type of social orientation (e.g., individualistic *or* collectivistic) and one form of moral concern (rights *or* duties). I believe, however, that the two proposed moral orientations are both part of our culture; not just one orientation is relevant to the concerns of society and its individual members. Social orientations at the individual and cultural levels are heterogeneous, entailing concerns with individualism and collectivism, independence and interdependence, duties and rights.

The limitations of characterizing societies in terms of one general orientation were pointed out a number of years ago by the anthropologist Malinowski (1926). On the basis of research in New Guinea, Malinowski came to the view that "the savage is neither an extreme 'collectivist' nor an intransigent 'individualist'—he is, like man in general, a mixture of both" (p. 56). Malinowski maintained, in contradiction to the prevailing views of the time, that people in so-called primitive societies are not dominated by the collectivity and do not simply have a deep reverence for tradition and custom. He maintained that the research failed to support "the idea of an inert, solid crust or cake of custom rigidly pressing from outside upon the whole surface of tribal life." Instead, individuals in those societies make sense of their social world and deal with social, moral, and legal conflicts.

Portraying societies in terms of one type of social orientation and one form of moral concern entails a stereotyping of societies and their individual members. It is stereotyping because of the one-dimensional characterizations that fail to account for the coexistence of different types of social orientations, social regulations, and moral concerns. Recent court decisions and public statements in the United States and India illustrate the coexistence of different social orientations. First, consider two recent U.S. Supreme Court rulings regarding sexual preference and freedom of speech rights. In one case (*Bowers v. Hardwick*, U.S. 85–140, 1986), the Supreme Court upheld the constitutionality of a Georgia statute forbidding private, consensual acts of homosexuality. The case was brought to the Supreme Court by a man who had been arrested for engaging in a homosexual act in the bedroom of his own home. In upholding the statute, it was ruled that homosexuality is not a fundamental right and is different from other rights to privacy affirmed by the Supreme Court (e.g., in family relationships, marriage, procreation). In the other case (*Bethel School District v. Fraser*, U.S. 84–1667, 1986), the court ruled in favor of a high school that had disciplined a student for making a public speech containing sexual innuendos. This case was brought by a high school student who was suspended for violating a rule prohibiting the use of obscene language. The student had used obscenities at an assembly in a speech to nominate a fellow student for elective office. The following statement from the Court opinion speaks to the issue of freedom of speech:

> The undoubted freedom to advocate unpopular and controversial views in schools and classrooms must be balanced against the society's countervailing interest in teaching students the boundaries of socially appropriate behavior. Even the most heated political discourse in a democratic society requires consideration for the personal sensibilities of the other participants and audiences.

Of course, the right to freedom of speech is valued in this society and has been upheld in other Supreme Court decisions. As these examples demonstrate, however, rights are not the only bases for social judgments in this society.

Now consider the following statement in a public speech by Rajiv Gandhi, the prime minister of India: "Women are the most disadvantaged and discriminated in this society. It is a shame and a sign of backwardness in our own thinking and mentality." Many of the "duties" presented by social constructionists as examples of the Indian moral code bear on the status and treatment of women (see Shweder 1986; Shweder and Miller 1985). However, Gandhi's speech is an indication that the civil rights of women are now a major concern in India and that Indians are not solely concerned with duties.

These examples are simply meant to show that at the level of public discourse and leadership, societies are not readily characterized by one-dimensional social orientations. The examples, of course, do not serve to characterize in general the nature of social orientations and moral judgments of the members of the societies; but they are in accord with the portrayal of mixed social concerns in Western society that emerges from juxtaposing the characterizations given by proponents of character education and of social construction. Documentation for this proposition comes from research evidence bearing on the social attitudes of individuals representing a wide spectrum of the population.

A recent book by McClosky and Brill (1983), *Dimensions of Tolerance: What Americans Believe about Civil Liberties*, reports the results of large-scale surveys of the attitudes of a cross-section of the general adult population (approximately three thousand persons responded to survey questionnaires of about three hundred items). The focus of these surveys on civil liberties is particularly relevant for a consideration of the purported individualistic orientation and rights-based morality of this society. In fact, one of the reasons McClosky and Brill chose to survey these particular attitudes was because of the often made assumption that this society is oriented toward individual freedom and rights. The results of these surveys, conducted in the 1970s, are especially informative because they are consistent with a number of other surveys dating back to the 1930s and because they dramatically contradict the idea that there is an ethos of individualism in this culture. Malinowski would not have been surprised by McClosky and Brill's results, since they demonstrate that individual Americans do not have one general social orientation but instead display a mixture of social concerns and moral attitudes.

McClosky and Brill were able to provide a nonstereotypical portrayal of the variety of social attitudes held by Americans because their questions covered many issues and because they tapped attitudes both toward freedoms and rights and toward the application of freedoms and rights in particular situations. The issues represented in the surveys included freedom of speech, press, assembly, and religion. The surveys also tapped attitudes toward academic freedom, dissent, privacy, and life-style. Two types of findings emerged that correspond to the distinction just mentioned between attitudes toward freedoms or rights and their application. When posed with general questions the majority of respondents endorsed freedoms and rights. Some items, for instance, inquired as to whether the respondent believed in "free speech for all no matter what their views might be," or for those "who hate our way of life," or that freedom of worship should be granted to "all religious groups, regardless of how extreme their beliefs." There were high levels of endorsement of generally stated items regarding freedom of speech and religion as well as other types of freedoms and rights included in the surveys.

The inquiries into the application of freedoms and rights essentially placed these issues in conflict with other social and moral concerns by asking about freedoms and rights in situations or contexts that include other issues, such as preventing violence or crime, the maintenance of social order, the political system, governmental procedures, and community standards. The following are examples of how the contextualized items were put to respondents: "Should a group be allowed to use a public building to hold a meeting denouncing the government? Do teachers have the right to express their opinions in class if they go against the community's standards? Is censoring books necessary to protect community standards?"

The surveys included many items of this kind dealing with a variety of issues. In the vast majority of those cases, the respondents gave relatively low endorsement to freedoms and civil liberties in certain situations. This was true for granting freedom of speech to those intolerant of the opinions of others and to foreigners who dislike the government, and for permitting the use of public buildings by certain groups (e.g., the American Nazi party). Similarly, under some conditions (such as to prevent or reduce crime) the majority did not uphold academic freedom, freedom of the press, religion, or privacy. It is clear that the respondents regarded certain rights in certain contexts to be in conflict with upholding the traditional culture. The large majority of respondents, for instance, believed that a public facility, like a civic auditorium, should not be made available for nontraditional groups (e.g., homosexuals, atheists, and political dissidents) to express their views. Moreover, there is a general expectation of conformity evidenced by their lack of endorsement of conscience-based civil disobedience in favor of upholding the collective legal system and in their disapproval of alternative life-styles in sexual and family matters.

It would take us too far afield to consider the many other issues, social concerns, and values addressed in the surveys. The main point is that the survey results show that the attitudes of Americans do not reflect an ethos of "self-contained individualism." It would be a mistake, however, simply to assume that Americans are generally inconsistent or confused about rights and freedoms. While members of this society are concerned with rights and freedoms, they are also concerned with preventing harm, reducing crime, upholding traditions, and promoting a sense of community. In many situations these concerns override the commitment to individual rights.

The mixture of individuals' social concerns and efforts at reconciling social problems is likely due to their attempts to make sense of a diversified social world. Social diversity does not solely exist in broader and more complexly organized societies, such as ours. Diversity is inherent in the nature of social interactions and is not only reflective of the relative size, scope, or variety of groups in societies. This is what Malinowski had in mind in rejecting the idea that a solid crust or cake of custom presses rigidly upon tribal life. Social interactions, in themselves, entail a diverse set of functions and goals. To name a few, social interactions include concerns with the nature and efficiency of coordinating different viewpoints, systems of social organization, politics, economics, legal regulation, and moral prescriptions. Within the social realm, there are concerns with rights, justice and fairness, promoting welfare, and preventing harm. Each of these can take the form of interpersonal and group concerns.

Many of these aspects of social interaction have been extensively examined in research on children's social thinking. The research shows that social thought is coherent and develops systematically with regard to interpersonal relationships (Damon 1977; Selman 1980), peer interactions and friendships (Selman 1981; Youniss and Volpe 1978), authority relations (Damon 1977, 1980; Laupa and Turiel 1986), politics and law (Furth 1980; Torney-Purta 1983), and morality (Kohlberg 1969, 1971; Nucci 1982).

Surveys like those conducted by McClosky and Brill tell us about attitudes or conclusions individuals come to (since only agreement or disagreement with items is measured) but do not directly assess how individuals reason. However, the research into the development of reasoning is consistent with those findings. For instance, Kohlberg has shown that in situations of conflict individuals often give lower priority to rights or freedoms than to other moral or social considerations. The reasoning of the majority of adolescents and adults about such conflicts has been characterized as oriented to duty, respect for authority, and maintenance of the existing social order.

Directly relevant to the issue of the mixture of social orientations within the society is Nucci's discussion (in this volume) of the research on moral and social-conventional reasoning. A large number of studies show that at an early age children begin to develop moral judgments pertaining to harm, justice, and rights, as well as judgments about social conventions, which are uniformities that coordinate social interactions and are part of specific systems of social organization. The analyses and research findings considered by Nucci underscore that children form understandings of different aspects of social interactions. Children develop understandings of social organization and collectivity, with its customs, traditions, and conventions. Children also develop understandings of moral interdependence, as reflected in their concerns with welfare, justice, and rights. The coexistence of these different kinds of social judgments and concerns means that individuals' social orientations cannot be adequately characterized in general, unitary terms. For instance, in some situations children's judgments are closely tied to dictates of authority, while in other situations their judgments show an independence from authority. Children accept social hierarchies and inequalities for certain purposes and value equality for other purposes. Correspondingly, some judgments are rooted in the culture or society, while other judgments may not be based on existing societal arrangements. These polarities indicate that children make a set of discriminations and distinctions that stem from their reasoning and critical thinking about matters of a social nature. To complicate matters further, research has shown that moral and social orientations are related to information about persons and assumptions about reality. An additional factor contributing to social decisions is the type of assumptions held, for example, about the natural, biological, and psychological.

SOCIAL REASONING, DEVELOPMENT, AND EDUCATION

The coexistence of different social orientations has particular relevance to the practice of moral education because it is so often thought that children must be taught the virtues, values, and traditions of the culture in a direct, simple, and straightforward way. As has been stressed here, a straightforward and one-dimensional rendition of the cultural orientation is a stereotypical view of the social elements of culture. We should not, of course, transmit stereotypes to children. Furthermore, transmitting such simple one-dimensional characterizations of morality and culture is likely to be discrepant with children's differentiated conception of the social world.

Efforts at social education with children and especially with adolescents can be beneficially more narrow in certain respects and more broad in other respects than most existing approaches. It would be useful to refine broad, general notions of morality as reflecting culture and its traditions into more narrowly defined moral judgments that do not encompass all societal and cultural considerations. A significant goal of narrowing notions of morality for purposes of moral education is to help students focus on issues of welfare, justice, and rights and on how such issues differ from, and relate to, nonmoral aspects of their social lives. In the context of narrowing the focus of morality, social education can be broadened to include concerns with the traditions, conventions, functions, and forms of societies and cultures (see Nucci 1982). These propositions are predicated on the extensive body of research showing that children and adolescents do indeed make distinctions and differentiations among different aspects of their social relationships. Given that children and adults make such differentiations and often recognize social conflicts and competing claims in social goals, it would appear that educational practice needs to deal with children's social reasoning.

Proponents of character education have vociferously rejected those aspects of programs of moral education that are actually most closely linked to fostering processes of reasoning. In the first place, character education proponents have argued that morality should not be treated as a process of deliberate decision making (Bennett 1980a, Wynne 1986). They contend that since morality stems from good habits and character, an emphasis on rationality and cognition "can lead to a serious error in a child's understanding of in what a moral life consists" (Bennett 1980a, p. 30). Character education proponents argue that the emphasis of moral education should be to influence behavior and not "states of mind" (Wynne 1986). It follows, then, that they also object to the presentation of moral conflicts or dilemmas, as is sometimes done, to encourage discussion and, thereby, stimulate thinking about moral issues (Delattre and Bennett 1979, Sommers 1984). Moral conflicts and dilemmas, they maintain, over-play the problematic aspects at the expense of the noncontroversial and nonproblematic aspects of daily moral life. They believe that the noncontroversial socially "inherited norms" should be emphasized in educating children, and, moreover, that the goal of influencing children's behavior regarding straightforward, nonproblematic moral habits should be achieved not through separate courses dealing specifically and exclusively with morality but as limited aspects of all courses. Separate courses on morality presumably convey the implicit message that morality is to be compartmentalized from the rest of life.

The message from character education proponents seems to be that in this realm the examined life is corrupting. It is a curious state of affairs in which many of the features usually regarded as part of good education—analysis, intellectual scrutiny, informed self-correction, criticism, reflection—are considered miseducative. The source of this curious state of affairs, of course, is in the assumption that morality is the individual's adherence to societal or cultural values and out of the realm of judgment or understanding. This assumption is linked to a reification of culture. For character education proponents it is not any cultural system that is reified, but the embodiment of this culture in its past. Indeed, they assert that those features of contemporary culture that emphasize critical thinking require modification.

The true objection, then, is not to moral education practices that include separate courses on morality focusing on the problematic or controversial. For if moral education were practiced with attention to behavior in relation to nonproblematic issues in the context of the regular curriculum with the aim of stimulating the development of children's thinking about morality and society, character education proponents would still object vociferously. Their primary objection is to judgment, decision making, and critical thinking with regard to moral and social issues. Reifying culture as the source of the morality of individuals leaves little room for the type of reasoning that might be involved in reflecting upon cultural or individual moral practices.

Influencing behavior, teaching about noncontroversial aspects of morality, and raising moral issues in courses other than those devoted to discussion about morality does not preclude teaching about moral conflicts or take away from the value of separate courses on the ethical. As a matter of fact, it is a general psychological principle of developmental approaches that children's thinking is significantly formed out of their everyday practices and that social judgments do not stand in isolation from the many topics normally covered in the regular curriculum (Piaget 1932, 1970, Werner 1957). Programs of moral education aimed at stimulating children's judgments should include concern with behavior in school contexts other than separate courses and should deal with noncontroversial issues—as has been done in the programs discussed by Power, Higgins, and Kohlberg in chapter 6 in this volume.

It is, however, equally important to address the place of critical thinking and reflection in children's social lives. In the moral education curriculum, separate courses and discussions about social conflicts serve not to displace the other aspects of moral education but to augment them with deliberate reflection on everyday social interactions and the nature of the moral realm. Therefore, study of children's reflective thinking is important because it provides information that can be applied to the practice of moral education. However, the rejection of reflective social thought by the character education approach coincides with recent trends in social science research (including the social construction approach) that de-emphasize reflection in the study of social reasoning. Although their reasons differ from those of the character education proponents, some social scientists have been critical of the study of children's moral development in contexts outside of ongoing supposedly naturalistic situations.

With regard to research, these social scientists have asserted that study of children's judgments about situations or issues not directly related to their actual activities is unrepresentative of how children form moral values or act upon them. For instance, they claim that the presentation to children of moral conflicts in hypothetical contexts is invalid because it is not the study of children's judgments as they are actually engaging in moral practices. Leaving aside the potential behavioristic bias, such a position gives an unjustified exclusivity to behavior and nonconflicted decisions over analysis, intellectual scrutiny, and reflection. It is as unfortunate for researchers to fail to provide educators with explanations of children's reflective thought processes as it is for educators to fail to foster analysis and reflection. If we do not rely on stereotypical portrayals of cultures as one-dimensional and recognize the relevance of the types of commonplace social conflicts grappled with by the respondents to the McClosky and Brill surveys, then trends away from reflectivity in moral development research and the practice of moral education must be seen as failing to deal with important aspects of moral judgment and conduct.

The argument for eliminating educational concerns with children's understandings and reflection regarding social and moral issues is consistent with the equation of all forms of thought or knowledge that comes from the assertions that scholarly or scientific propositions have the same status as religious propositions or that so-called secular humanism is a type of religious doctrine. The educational implications of such assertions are to eliminate important distinctions in ways of deriving knowledge and to downplay the role of reason and evidence in evaluating alternative positions. In placing all forms of knowledge on the same plane, the de-emphasis of critical analysis and intellectual scrutiny goes well beyond the moral realm. For instance, theory building, the use of evidence, and verifiability are all ignored by those who maintain that creationism is just as much scientific explanation as is evolutionary theory, and contend that evolution is just another type of religious dogma. The consequences of these contentions for science education can be profound (Siegel 1981). Banning textbooks and restricting literature on the grounds that they promote a religion of secular humanism also serve to mask intellectual traditions and important scholarly distinctions.

There may be a pattern here of deprecating reasoning, in general, when it is asserted that morality is adherence to cultural values that does not entail judgment and should not be subject to reflection, that there are no epistemological distinctions to be drawn among forms of thinking, and that scholarly and scientific explanations can be dismissed on the grounds that their proponents are ideologically or culturally biased. This focus on accusing social scientists of bias has made it possible to ignore the scientific validity of their explanations of children's moral development. However, careful evaluation of explanations of the process of development is crucial for decisions regarding ways of conducting moral education. If development is most adequately explained as the incorporation of traits, virtues, and habits of behavior, then inculcation and indoctrination may be the best educational method. If development is, in contrast, best explained as a process of constructing judgments and understandings about social relationships, society, and culture, then inculcation or indoctrination simply would be the wrong way to engage in moral education.

REFERENCES

Bennett, William J. "The Teacher, the Curriculum, and Values Education Development," *New Directions for Higher Education* 31 (1980): 27–34. (a)

Bennett, William J. "What Value Is Values Education?" *American Educator* 4 (1980): 31–32. (b)

Bennett, William J., and Delattre, Edwin J. "Moral Education in the Schools," *Public Interest* 50 (1978): 81–98.

Bennett, William J., and Delattre, Edwin J. "A Moral Education: Some Thoughts on How Best to Achieve It," *American Educator* 3 (1979): 6–9.

Blatt, Moshe M., and Kohlberg, Lawrence. "The Effects of Moral Discussion upon Children's Level of Moral Judgment," *Journal of Moral Education* 4 (1975): 129–61.

Damon, William. *The Social World of the Child*. San Francisco: Jossey-Bass, 1977.

Damon, William. "Patterns of Change in Children's Reasoning: A Two-Year Longitudinal Study," *Child Development* 51 (1980): 1010–17.

Delattre, Edwin J., and Bennett, William J. "Where the Values Movement Goes Wrong," *Change* 11 (1979): 38–43.

Furth, Hans. *The World of Grown-Ups: Children's Conceptions of Society*. New York: Elsevier, 1980.

Hogan, Robert. "Theoretical Egocentricism and the Problem of Compliance," *American Psychologist* 30 (1975): 533–39.

Kohlberg, Lawrence. "Moral Education in the Schools: A Developmental View," *School Review* 74 (1966): 1–30.

Kohlberg, Lawrence. "Stage and Sequence: The Cognitive-Developmental Approach to Socialization." In *Handbook of Socialization Theory and Research*, ed. D. A. Goslin. Chicago: Rand McNally, 1969.

Kohlberg, Lawrence. "From Is to Ought: How to Commit the Naturalistic Fallacy and Get Away with It in the Study of Moral Development." In *Psychology and Genetic Epistemology,* ed. Theodore Mischel. New York: Academic Press, 1971.

Laupa, Marta, and Turiel, Elliot. "Children's Conceptions of Adult and Peer Authority," *Child Development* 57 (1986): 405–12.

Malinowski, Branislaw. *Crime and Custom in Savage Society*. Totowa, N.J.: Littlefield, Adams, and Co., 1976. Originally published in 1926.

McClosky, Herbert, and Brill, Alida. *Dimensions of Tolerance: What Americans Believe about Civil Liberties*. New York: Russell Sage Foundation, 1983.

Nucci, Larry P. "Conceptual Development in the Moral and Conventional Domains: Implications for Values Education," *Review of Educational Research* 52 (1982): 93–122.

Piaget, Jean. *The Moral Judgment of the Child*. London: Routledge and Kegan Paul, 1932.

Piaget, Jean. *Psychology and Epistemology*. New York: Viking Press, 1970.

Sampson, Edward E. "Psychology and the American Ideal," *Journal of Personality and Social Psychology* 35 (1977): 767–82.

Sampson, Edward E. "Scientific Paradigms and Social Values: Wanted—A Scientific Revolution," *Journal of Personality and Social Psychology* 36 (1978): 1332–43.

Sampson, Edward E. "Cognitive Psychology as Ideology," *American Psychologist* 36 (1981): 730–42.

Selman, Robert L. *The Growth of Interpersonal Understanding: Developmental and Clinical Analyses*. New York: Academic Press, 1980.

Selman, Robert L. "The Child as a Friendship Philosopher." In *The Development of Children's Friendships*, ed. S. R. Asher and J. M. Gottman. Cambridge, Mass.: Cambridge University Press, 1981.

Shweder, Richard A. "Divergent Rationalities." In *Metatheory in Social Science: Pluralisms and Subjectivities*, ed. Donald W. Fiske and Richard A. Shweder. Chicago: University of Chicago Press, 1986.

Shweder, Richard A.; Mahapatra, M.; and Miller, J. G. "Culture and Moral Development." In *The Emergence of Morality in Young Children*, ed. J. Kagan and S. Lamb. Chicago: University of Chicago Press, forthcoming.

Shweder, Richard A., and Miller, J. G. "The Social Construction of the Person: How Is It Possible?" In *The Social Construction of the Person*, ed. Kenneth J. Gergen and

Keith Davis. New York: Springer-Verlag, 1985.

Siegel, Harvey. "Creationism, Evolution, and Education: The California Fiasco," *Phi Delta Kappan* 63 (1981): 95–101.

Sommers, Christina H. "Ethics without Virtue: Moral Education in America," *American Scholar* 53 (1984): 381–89.

Torney-Purta, Judith. "The Development of Views about the Role of Social Institutions in Redressing Inequality and Promoting Human Rights." In *The Child's Construction of Social Inequality*, ed. Robert Leahy. New York: Academic Press, 1983.

Werner, Heinz. *Comparative Psychology of Mental Development*. New York: International Universities Press, 1957.

Wynne, Edward A. "The Declining Character of American Youth," *American Educator* 3 (1979): 29–32.

Wynne, Edward A. "The Great Tradition in Education: Transmitting Moral Values," *Educational Leadership* 43 (1986): 4–9.

Youniss, James and Volpe, J. A. "A Relational Analysis of Children's Friendship." In *New Directions for Child Development*, Vol. 1: *Social Cognition*, ed. William Damon. San Francisco: Jossey-Bass, 1978.

9

Challenging Conventional Wisdom About Morality: The Domain Approach to Values Education

Larry P. Nucci

The current public emphasis on the need for values education is the most recent manifestation of what opinion polls have been reporting for years. The overwhelming majority of parents expects public schools to contribute to children's moral development (Gallup 1976). There is, however, considerable confusion and discord among people about what morality means. In such a context schools and teachers who want to respond to requests for moral education have difficulty even deciding what to teach, let alone how best to teach it. One aim of this chapter is to help clarify what constitutes the moral domain. Recent research indicates that the apparent public disagreement about morality is not about what is moral, but about what is "proper." There is great consistency in the ways in which children and adults identify matters of morality. This overall agreement can be shown by differentiating morality from matters of societal convention.

The arguments presented in this chapter extend an earlier discussion of "domain appropriate" values education (Nucci 1982). That review laid out the basic principles of an approach to values education based on the distinction between morality and societal convention, but the arguments could be advanced only speculatively because there were no data at the time to support directly the extension of findings from developmental psychology to educational practice. In the interim several of the suggestions for educational practice have been studied. In this chapter I present findings from those investigations and review the research on the relationship between religious rules and children's moral concepts. I will argue that public schools may address children's moral development without violating constitutional provisions regarding the separation of church and state.

THE DISTINCTION BETWEEN MORALITY AND CONVENTION

Children in any society need to learn to conform to a number of social rules if they are to become participants in the culture, a point made by Ryan in chapter 1 in this volume. In our society, children learn that certain classes of adults (such as teachers and doctors) are addressed by titles, that males and females use separate public restroom facilities, and so forth. These are examples of social conventions. Conventions are the agreed-upon uniformities in social behavior determined by the social system in which they are formed (Turiel 1983). Conventions are arbitrary because there is nothing inherently right or wrong about the actions they define; for example, children could just as easily refer to their teachers by first names as by titles of Mr. or Mrs. Through accepted usage, however, these standards serve to coordinate the interactions of individuals within social systems by providing them with a set of expectations regarding appropriate behavior. In turn, the matrix of social conventions and customs is an element in the structuring and maintenance of the general social order. Thus, concepts about social conventions are structured by underlying conceptions of social organization.

The moral domain refers to concepts of justice, human welfare, and derivative rights. In contrast with conventions, moral considerations are not arbitrary but stem from factors intrinsic to actions: consequences such as harm to others. Although moral prescriptions (i.e., "It is wrong to hurt others") are an aspect of social organization, they are determined by factors inherent in social relationships as opposed to a particular form of social, cultural, or religious structure (Nucci 1985; Turiel 1983; Turiel, Nucci, and Smetana 1988).

Research on the Moral-Conventional Distinction

This distinction between morality and convention is not generally made in values education. Traditional values educators, such as Ryan (chapter 1, this volume) and Wynne (chapter 2, this volume), hold that moral values are established by society. That is, they treat all values including morality as matters of custom and convention to be inculcated in children as a part of what they refer to as character education. The kind of distinction drawn in this chapter is also at variance with accounts that have had the greatest impact on developmental approaches to moral education (Piaget 1932; Kohlberg 1984). Those earlier views hold that only at the higher stages of moral development can morality (justice) be differentiated from and displace convention as the basis for moral judgments. Over the past fifteen years, however, over thirty published accounts have reported research demonstrating that morality and convention are differentiated at very early ages and constitute distinct conceptual and developmental domains. These studies are summarized in Turiel (1983) and in Turiel, Killen, and Helwig (1987). In brief, these studies have found the following:

1. Moral transgressions (e.g., hitting and hurting, stealing personal property, slander) are viewed as wrong irrespective of the presence of governing rules, while conventional acts (addressing teachers by first names, women wearing pants, premarital sex between adults) are viewed as wrong only if they are in violation of an existing standard.
2. Individuals view conventional standards as culturally relative and alterable, while moral prescriptions are viewed as universal and unchangeable.
3. Individuals tend to view moral transgressions as more serious than violations of convention, and as deserving of more severe punishment.
4. Prosocial moral acts tend to be viewed as better or more positive than adherence to conventions.
5. The forms of social interaction in the context of moral events differ qualitatively from interactions in the context of conventions. Specifically, it was found that children's and adults' responses to events in the moral domain focus on features intrinsic to the acts (e.g., harm, justice), while responses in the

context of conventions focus on aspects of the social order (e.g., rules, regulations, normative expectations).

The general pattern of results has been obtained for subjects ranging in age from three to twenty-five years, sustaining the claim that morality and convention emerge as distinct domains early in childhood. In addition, several studies have replicated the basic findings with subjects in other cultures (Hong Kong—Song, Smetana, and Kim 1987; Indonesia—Carey and Ford 1983; Nigeria—Hollos, Leis, and Turiel 1986; U.S. Virgin Islands—Nucci, Turiel, and Encarnacion-Gawrych 1983).

Development in the Moral and Conventional Domains

Studies examining age-related changes within domains have revealed that the development of justice concepts and social conventional concepts follows distinct patterns. Unfortunately, with respect to the moral domain, systematic research of justice concepts *independent* of conventional concepts has been conducted with young children only. The sequence of changes observed in children's distributive and retributive justice reasoning shows that as they develop, children form increased understandings of benevolence, equality, and reciprocity (Damon 1977, 1980; Enright, Franklin, and Manheim 1980; Irwin and Moore 1971; Lapsley 1982). With respect to sharing, for example, the four-year-old's premise (whoever wants the most should get it) is replaced by the idea that distributive decisions should be based on strict equality or reciprocity (everybody should get the same). This strict reciprocity is replaced in turn by a recognition that there can be multiple valid claims to justice by different individuals and that persons with special needs, such as the poor or the handicapped, deserve special consideration (Damon 1977, 1980; Enright, Franklin, and Manheim 1980).

A more complete picture has been obtained of developmental changes in the conventional domain. Table 9-1 shows that the development of social-conventional concepts reflects the person's underlying conceptions of social organization and moves toward an understanding of convention as constitutive of social systems and as important for the coordination of social interactions. Development follows an oscillating pattern between periods affirming the importance of convention and phases negating it. This oscillation indicates

Table 9-1
Major Changes in Social-Conventional Concepts

	Approximate Ages
1. *Convention as descriptive of social uniformity.* Convention viewed as descriptive of uniformities in behavior. Convention is not conceived as part of structure or function of social interaction. Conventional uniformities are descriptive of what is assumed to exist. Convention maintained to avoid violation of empirical uniformities.	6 – 7
2. *Negation of convention as descriptive social uniformity.* Empirical uniformity not a sufficient basis for maintaining conventions. Conventional acts regarded as arbitrary. Convention is not conceived as part of structure or function of social interaction.	8 – 9
3. *Convention as affirmation of rule system; early concrete conception of social system.* Convention seen as arbitrary and changeable. Adherence to convention based on concrete rules and authoritative expectations. Conception of conventional acts not coordinated with conception of rule.	10 – 11
4. *Negation of convention as part of rule system.* Convention now seen as arbitrary and changeable regardless of rule. Evaluation of rule pertaining to conventional act is coordinated with evaluation of the act. Conventions are "nothing but" social expectations.	12 – 13
5. *Convention as mediated by social system.* The emergence of systematic concepts of social structure. Convention as normative regulation in system with uniformity, fixed roles, and static hierarchical organization.	14 – 16
6. *Negation of convention as societal standards.* Convention regarded as codified societal standards. Uniformity in convention is not considered to serve the function of maintaining social system. Conventions are "nothing but" societal standards that exist through habitual use.	17 – 18
7. *Convention as coordination of social interactions.* Conventions as uniformities that are functional in coordinating social interactions. Shared knowledge, in the form of conventions, among members of social groups facilitate interaction and operation of the system.	18 – 25

Source: From Turiel 1983

the difficulty children have in accounting for the function of arbitrary social norms and illustrates the slow process of reflection and construction that precedes the adolescent's view of convention as important to the maintenance of the social system.

Issues of Domain Overlap

Early criticism of the domain model of social development focused on issues of overlap between the two domains (Rest 1983). Critics argued that such instances of overlap falsified the claim that morality and convention constitute distinct areas of social knowledge. Those criticisms, however, reflected an incomplete understanding of the model. The existence of analytically distinct structures of social knowledge does not preclude their conjoining or coordination in reasoning about social events. To illustrate how social judgment might entail coordination of knowledge from more than one conceptual system, consider the situation of four children trying to decide how to divide up the ten dollars they earned delivering newspapers. On the one hand, this is a mathematical problem entailing an understanding of how to divide ten into four parts. On the other hand, this is a moral problem requiring an understanding of equity and fair distribution. No mathematics teacher would reduce his subject matter to ethics, nor would an ethicist confuse her subject matter with mathematics. Yet, in this example, we can see that the problem solution requires knowledge from both domains.

Similar situations arise in the context of multifaceted social situations. Turiel (1983) has suggested that such multifaceted situations take at least three forms: (1) those in which conventional concerns for social organization and coordination entail injustices (as in a caste system,); (2) second-order events in which violation of a convention results in "psychological harm" to persons who adhere to the convention (e.g., failure of a young white man to address an older black man by the title "Mister"); and (3) ambiguously multidimensional events, such as abortion, in which significant discrepancies exist in their domain attribution by different people. Reasoning about multifaceted events entails the coordination (or failure of coordination) of both the moral and the conventional features considered. In research on subjects' reasoning about multifaceted events (Smetana 1982; Turiel and Smetana 1984), three modes of domain relations emerged: (1) a predominant emphasis on one domain, with subordination of the other; (2) conflict between the two, with inconsistencies and the absence of resolution of reconciliation of the two components; and (3) coordination of the two components, so that the two are taken into account in the solution to the problem. (In chapter 8 in this volume, Turiel employs the construct of domain overlap to account for public disagreements over the nature of morality.)

The picture of social reasoning that emerges from the distinct domains view indicates that we cannot take a global approach to values education. Indeed our current understanding of the domain nature of social knowledge is consistent with reinterpretation of earlier global theories of social development, such as Kohlberg's stages of moral development, as an approximation of the age-related changes in the development of domain coordinations.

MORALITY AND RELIGION

Before proceeding to a discussion of educational applications, I want to review some of our recent research on children's concepts of morality and religious rules. One question frequently raised by those concerned with moral or values education is whether moral values can be taught independently of religious values. The current request by fundamentalists to put God and prayer back in the classroom derives from an old and enduring belief that extends beyond the parochial scope of specific religious groups. That belief is that morality and religion are inseparable. The constitutional issues this request raises have already been alluded to. A thorough treatment of those legal issues has been presented in a booklet by Patricia M. Lines of the Education Commission of the States (Lines 1981). Although further discussion of the constitutionality of religious education is beyond the scope of this chapter, wc will add to the public debate our findings examining whether Christian children's concepts of morality are independent of religion (Nucci 1985).

Moral and Conventional Values as Seen by Catholics

The subjects in our study were Catholic sophomores attending a Catholic urban high school and devout undergraduate Catholics at an urban public university. Each of these two hundred subjects was asked to make judgments regarding a series of actions now considered sins by the Catholic Church. We classified actions that entailed harm or injustice toward another, such as stealing, killing, rape, and slander, as matters of morality. Other actions, such as failure to attend religious services on Easter or Christmas, failure to fast prior to receiving communion, the use of contraceptives, masturbation, premarital sex between consenting adults, divorce, and ordaining women, entailed violations of worship patterns or social behavior prescribed by the institution of Catholicism. We classified these actions as nonmoral and akin to matters of social convention. It should be pointed out that nonmoral religious prescriptions are not, strictly speaking, conventions, since they are derived presumably from scripture and are not considered by the devout to be the products of social consensus. With Catholicism this issue is complicated by the existence of Church authorities (i.e., the Pope and cardinals) empowered to determine and interpret such issues for members of the Catholic faith. We still assumed, however, that the Catholic subjects would not treat such issues as matters of morality.

These subjects were asked to make several judgments, two of which I will discuss here. First, subjects were asked whether it would be wrong or all right for the Pope, in conjunction with the bishops, to remove the attendant moral and conventional rules, and if it would then be all right for Catholics to engage in the actions once the rules were gone. Second, subjects were asked whether it would be wrong or all right for members of another religion to engage in the behaviors if the other religion had no rules or standards regarding the acts.

Briefly, findings from this study were as follows. With respect to questions regarding the removal of Church rules, the overwhelming majority of the subjects (92 percent high school; 98 percent university) viewed it as wrong for the Church authorities to remove rules governing moral transgressions such as hitting and stealing. In contrast, less than half of the high school (41 percent) and university (33 percent) Catholics viewed it as wrong for the Pope to remove the rules regarding nonmoral (conventional) behaviors such as fasting prior to communion, the use of contraceptives, engaging in premarital sex, and so forth. The subjects' responses regarding whether or not it would be wrong to engage in the various actions once religious prohibitions were removed essentially paralleled the findings regarding the removal of the rules themselves.

With respect to relativity questions (i.e., questions about other religions), it was found that Catholics tended to universalize only the moral issues. On average, 91 percent of high school subjects and 97 percent of the university subjects viewed it as wrong for members of another religion to engage in acts entailing moral transgressions (e.g., stealing, slander), even if the other religion had no rules regarding the acts. In contrast with moral issues, less than half of the Catholic subjects (on average, 34 percent high school, 18 percent university) were willing to universalize Catholic conventions and treat as wrong the engagement in such actions by members of religions that do not regulate those behaviors. The tendency of the subjects to acknowledge the relativism of their Church's conventions is highlighted by findings that the percentages of subjects viewing the acts as wrong for members of another religion were significantly less than the percentages of subjects who viewed it as wrong for Catholics themselves to engage in the behaviors if the Pope removed the governing rules. In sum, the findings from this aspect of the study indicate that most Catholics distinguish between Church conventions, which serve to organize the behaviors of persons who define themselves as Catholics, and those moral acts that have an intrinsic effect on the rights or well-being of others, Catholic and non-Catholic alike. For those acts that bear directly on the well-being of others, the fact that changing religious doctrine would not make such acts acceptable to the overwhelming majority of Catholics indicates that morality, at least for most Catholics, is independent of religious doctrine.

Moral and Conventional Values as Seen by Christian Fundamentalists

That study was followed up with an interview study of Christian fundamentalist children. Subjects in the study were sixty-four Amish and Conservative Mennonite children, ages ten to seventeen, from rural northern Indiana. The subjects were notable for their strict adherence to biblical commands and for their disavowal of any Church hierarchy empowered to intercede between scriptural rules and their own actions. Among the strictures they adhered to was a prohibition against the use of either radio or television in the home.

Each child was individually interviewed regarding four moral issues: hitting, stealing, slandering, and damaging another's property; and six nonmoral issues: day of worship, work on the Sabbath, women's head coverings, baptism, interfaith marriage, and women preaching. Adolescents over the age of fourteen were also interviewed regarding a seventh nonmoral issue: premarital sex between consenting adults.

With respect to questions regarding whether it would be all right for the congregation and its authorities to remove or alter the various religious rules, the fundamentalists responded quite differently from the Roman Catholics. While many more subjects on average objected to the removal of rules governing moral (98 percent) than nonmoral (65 percent) actions, on some specific nonmoral items, such as the prohibition against work on Sunday, nearly as many subjects (91 percent) objected to the removal of that religious rule as objected to the removal of rules governing moral actions. The primary reason given by the subjects for objecting to the alteration of prohibitions against nonmoral religious rules was that the given rule was commanded by God. The difference between the Catholics and the fundamentalists seems to reside in the fact that Catholics, but not the fundamentalists, believe that a temporal authority, the Pope, has the power to interpret matters of doctrine. Without such a belief, the fundamentalists rely on literal statements in the Bible, such as Paul's admonishments that women wear head coverings (I Corinthians 11), as direct commands from God.

With respect to relativity questions, the fundamentalists responded very much like the Catholics. Considerably fewer (25 percent) of the subjects felt that it was wrong for members of other religions to engage in actions contrary to nonmoral Mennonite religious rules than to engage in actions such as slander, which constitute moral transgressions (94 percent). The primary reasons subjects gave for saying that it was all right for others to engage in acts counter to Mennonite rules governing nonmoral acts (e.g., women wearing head coverings) were that such nonmoral religious rules were a function of particular religious systems or that others were ignorant of God's laws. In contrast with the relative tolerance shown regarding nonmoral issues, the fundamentalists, like the Catholics, viewed it as wrong for members of other religions to engage in moral transgressions. Their primary reasons for treating such actions as universally wrong was that they resulted in harm or injustice to others.

Our most dramatic findings, however, came in response to an additional set of questions we asked of these fundamentalist children. In that portion of the interview we asked: "Suppose Jesus (God) had not given us a law about (some particular act), would it be all right for a Christian to do the act in that case?" In response to that question, on average, only 1 percent of the subjects said that it would be wrong to engage in the nonmoral actions. In contrast, 85 percent of the children said it would continue to be wrong to engage in actions entailing moral transgressions (e.g., slander, stealing). That such actions entail harmful or unjust consequences for others was the reason each child gave for this position.

The responses of the Amish children in our study are illustrated in the following excerpts from an interview with an eleven-year-old boy. The excerpts also serve to illustrate the more general distinction we have made between morality and societal convention. The first portion of the interview deals with the Amish convention that women wear head coverings. The boy's responses are given in the context of a story that tells of an Amish/Mennonite girl who attends a local public junior high school where none of the other girls wears a head covering. In order not to be different the girl decides not to wear the head covering to school. The second excerpt presents the same subject's responses to questions regarding a moral issue, stealing. The two excerpts follow.

Religious Convention: Women wearing head coverings.

(*Was Mary right or wrong not to wear a head covering at school?*) Wrong, because the Bible says you should, the women should have their hair long, and have it covered with a covering and the men should have their hair short. (*Do you think it really matters whether or not a Mennonite girl wears a head covering?*) It depends on if you are baptized or not. If you are baptized, you should. (*How come?*) Because that's the way God wants it. (*Can that rule about head covering be changed?*) Yes, I suppose it could. (*Would it be all right for the ministers to remove the rule about women wearing head coverings?*) No. (*Why not?*) Because God said that's how he wants it, and that's how he wants it. (*If the ministers did remove the rule about head coverings, then would it be all right for girls not to wear the head coverings?*) If they were obeying the minister and not God, it would be, but if they were obeying God and not the ministers, then it wouldn't. (*Suppose it wasn't written in the Bible that women are supposed to wear head coverings, God hadn't said anything about head coverings one way or the other, would it be all right for women not to wear head coverings then?*) Yeah, it would be o.k. then, because if God didn't say so it wouldn't matter. (*The other girls at Mary's school belong to religions that don't have the rule about head coverings. Is it o.k. that those religions don't have the rule?*) It's all right if that's the way their church is, believes. (*Well, then, is it o.k. for those girls not to wear the head coverings?*) Yeah. (*Why is it o.k. for them but not for Mary?*) Because she goes to a Mennonite Christian Church, she should obey the Mennonite laws. (*Could a woman still be a good Christian and not wear a head covering?*) It depends on her, it depends on if she is really a good Christian and has accepted Christ. It depends on her, if she cannot find a head covering that suits her, but she thinks she should be able to wear it, then I'd say it would be all right to go without one, put your hair up. (*Well, then, why wear a head covering?*) Because if you are around people more often, like if one person doesn't have one and the other one does and they are both real good Christians and one goes, they are both walking and a guy comes up and says man, I can tell which one's a Christian out of them. This one over here has a covering and I can tell she is, but over here I don't know for sure because she doesn't wear one. I would have to do some questioning before I know for sure.

Moral Issue: Stealing.

(*Is it o.k. to steal?*) No. (*Why not?*) Because that is one of the Ten Commandments that God put in the law and gave to Moses and he expects us to obey these laws and if we don't obey these laws, we can know for sure that we will not go to heaven, we will absolutely go to hell. (*What's wrong with stealing?*) Having something that does not belong to us and taking it from someone else, it would just irritate you. Like, one time my sister stole my radio batteries. I didn't know where they were and then I found out that she had them in her tape recorder and I thought that these were the exact ones so I took them back. Actually, she had them in her drawer and she saw these were missing so she came back four hours later while I was in bed sleeping and she just grabbed them right out of there and put mine back in. By this time, she had worn mine down and they weren't working so I thought for sure that she had just wore hers out and so I went and stole mine back which were really hers. My conscience just bothered me until I returned them and took the other ones and I found out that these were the correct ones to be having anyway. (*Should the rule about stealing be followed?*) Yes, or else we will go to hell. And all of those will know, and those who are on earth already know that hell is a bad place. There's fire and brimstone and you could die down there! And everybody that goes there, they know that they are a sinful person. (*Suppose all the ministers decided to drop the rule about stealing so that there was no rule about stealing. Would that be all right?*) No. (*Why not?*) Because God said that it wouldn't be expected of us and he expects us to obey him. (*Would it be all right for a Christian to steal if the ministers dropped the rule?*) No, because you still wouldn't be able to go to heaven, you'd have to go to hell. (*Suppose the people of another religion don't have a rule about stealing. Is that all right?*) No. (*Why not?*) Because if they have their Bible, then they know about the law. (*Suppose they don't use our Bible, they have a different religion and it doesn't have a rule about stealing. Is that all right?*) No, because God said that thou shalt not steal and that goes for everybody. (*If they didn't know about that rule, would it be o.k. for them to steal?*) No, because it would still make everybody unhappy. (*If God hadn't said anything about stealing one way or the other, would it be all right to steal then?*) No. (*Why not?*) Because then if people would steal, then the world wouldn't be very happy. (*Could you say more about that?*) Like when my sister stole my batteries, it really irritated me. If everybody's stuff kept getting stolen, everyone would be mad and say, "Hey, where's my stuff?" It would be terrible; nobody could keep anything that was theirs. I wouldn't like it.

What we can see in this eleven-year-old boy's responses is that he acknowledges that the rule about head coverings is based on the word of authority (God), that it is relative to a particular interpretation or view of that authority's norms, and that it serves a social organizational function of distinguishing boys from girls, and Christians from others. In contrast with his views about head coverings, this Amish boy treated stealing as universally wrong, and wrong even if God did not have a rule about it. The wrongness of stealing, according to our subject, is that it leads to hurtful or unjust consequences. Thus, we see in him an early objective morality that differs from his understanding of nonmoral religious prescriptions.

Summary of the Findings on Morality and Religion

Taken as a totality, I interpret the findings from our studies with religious children to mean that children's moral understandings are independent of specific religious rules, and that morality is conceptually distinct from one's religious concepts. We also seem to have found that morality for the secular child, as well as for the devout Christian, focuses on the same set of fundamental interpersonal issues: those pertaining to justice and compassion. For the public schools, this means that there can be moral education compatible with, and yet independent from, religious moral doctrine. Such moral education would focus on the development of children's conceptions of justice, fairness, and concern for the welfare of others. Such an educational aim as Kohlberg (1981) and Dewey (1909) have stated is well within the constitutional framework of our democracy. Let us turn, then, to a discussion of some principles for values education that stem from the distinction between morality and societal convention.

FROM THEORY TO PRACTICE

Arithmetic and morality may both be said to deal with right and wrong. Yet, as we noted earlier, no teacher would use arithmetic worksheets in which students computed sums as a means of teaching moral values. This is because it is obvious that arithmetic and morality are different domains of knowledge. It has been less obvious to educators that morality and societal convention constitute distinct conceptual and developmental dimensions. What we have seen, however, is that the child's natural epistemology is consistent with the moral-conventional distinction. One clear educational implication of this research is that values education should differentially address the development of concepts in these two domains. This does not require that we start completely from scratch in our approach to values education. Instead it means that current developmental approaches to values education, such as those offered by Kohlberg and his colleagues (Power, Higgins, and Kohlberg in this volume), need to be modified to make them "domain appropriate" (Nucci 1982).

In common with the Kohlbergian approach, domain-appropriate values education would attempt to coordinate educational practice with students' developmental levels. This practice acknowledges that a student's interpretation of values issues will differ according to the level the student has reached in a developmental sequence, and that activities likely to foster development at one level will be unlikely to succeed at another. It also acknowledges that social growth is not simply a process of learning society's rules and values, but a gradual process in which the student actively transforms his or her understanding of morality and social convention through reflection and construction. That is, the student's social growth is a function of meaning making rather than mere compliance with externally imposed values.

In contrast with the traditional Kohlbergian educator, however, the teacher attending to the research reviewed in this chapter would recognize that social conventions are not a subset of morality but constitute a distinct values dimension. Such a teacher would also recognize, therefore, that the students' conceptions of social conventions form an important component of their social understanding, and should not be ignored as part of a values education program.

The first step toward such an approach entails the teacher's analysis and identification of the moral or conventional nature of social issues employed in values lessons. Such an analysis would be necessary to ensure that the issues discussed are concordant with the domain of the values dimension they are intended to affect. A discussion of dress codes, for example, would constitute a poor issue from which to generate moral discussion, since mode of dress is primarily a matter of convention. Likewise, consideration of whether it is right to steal to help a person in need would be a poor issue with which to generate a lesson intended to foster students' understandings of the function of social conventions.

A corollary function of the teacher would be to focus student activity (verbal or written) on the underlying features concordant with the domain of the issue. Thus, students dealing with a moral issue would be directed to focus on the underlying justice or human welfare considerations of the episode. With respect to conventions, the focus of student activity would be on the role of social expectations and the social organizational function of such social norms. As was noted earlier, not all issues of social right and wrong fall neatly into one domain or the other. Many issues overlap the two domains and can provide rich opportunities with which to involve students in reasoning that necessitates the coordination of knowledge from more than one social dimension.

Research on the Domain Approach to Values Education

The basic premise of the domain approach to values education was recently investigated in a study examining whether differentially attending to the domain of social issues has any greater impact on the development of students' moral and conventional concepts than does a unitary approach to values education (Nucci and Weber 1988). The study entailed integrating moral and social values discussions and written activities into an eighth-grade American history course. Together with the classroom teacher, the investigators identified a series of issues from American history that were primarily either moral or social-conventional in character as well as events and issues that involved domain overlap. Examples of the moral issues are slavery and the forced removal of Indians from their lands. Illustrative examples of conventional issues are those pertaining to the assimilation of immigrants into mainstream American society, such as differences in modes of dress, work habits, and dating patterns. Changes in laws permitting women to vote is an example of a mixed-domain issue employed in the study.

Students participated in small-group discussions of these issues once each week for a period of seven weeks. In addition, each student wrote essays on related moral, conventional, or mixed-domain issues in an English composition course associated with their American history class. Students were assigned to one of three conditions. In one condition, students were directed in their small-group discussions and essays to treat all issues as if they were matters of convention. The focus of their activities was on the norms pertaining to the issues under consideration. The emphasis was on the function of the norms in structuring society and the impact that altering or violating the norms would have on the social order. In the second condition, students were directed to treat all issues as if they were matters of morality, and they were asked to consider the justice and welfare implications of the issues under consideration. The third condition fit our definition of domain-appropriate values education; the focus of discussions and essays was concordant with the domain of the issues being studied. In the case of mixed-domain issues, students were asked first to consider the social-normative and the justice features of a given issue, and then to integrate or coordinate the moral and conventional aspects of the event.

Following the seven-week instructional period, students were assessed for their levels of moral development and concepts of societal convention. Moral level was assessed by means of a group measure, The Defining Issues Test (DIT) (Rest 1979). The DIT produces an index called the "P" score that is a measure of moral growth indicating the extent to which the subject employs principled (justice) reasoning to render moral decisions. The level of reasoning in the conventional domain was assessed through individual clinical interviews (Turiel 1978, 1983). All subjects in the study were either at Level 4 negation, in which social conventions are viewed as the arbitrary and unimportant dictates of authority; Level 5 affirmation, in which conventions are understood to be constitutive of social systems; or at a point of transition scored as 4/5 (see Table 9-1 for descriptions of levels).

With regard to moral reasoning, subjects in the moral-only condition and subjects in the domain-appropriate condition had significantly higher P scores than subjects in the convention-only condition (moral only P score = 38.80; domain-appropriate P score = 37.12; convention-only P score = 25.37). With regard to development in the conventional domain, the outcome was the inverse. Subjects in the convention-only condition and subjects in the domain-appropriate condition obtained significantly higher levels of development in the conventional domain than did subjects in the moral-only condition. Mean level scores by condition were as follows: convention only = 4.80; domain appropriate = 4.72; moral only = 4.37.

The findings from this study have two sets of implications. First, these results provide additional evidence for the claim that morality and convention constitute distinct conceptual systems. If it were the case that normative/moral issues formed a single system, then raising students' level of understanding in one area (e.g., convention) should have resulted in a corresponding increase in their conceptual level in the other (i.e., morality). In this study precisely the opposite situation was observed in both conditions where educational intervention focused on only one domain.

Second, the study sustained the proposition that social development is optimized by experiences concordant with the domain of the social knowledge system. In this study activities concordant with moral issues served to develop students' moral level but not their understanding of convention, and vice versa. Only those students engaged in activities concordant with each domain exhibited growth in both moral and conventional reasoning. Thus, the results of this study lend support to the arguments for domain-appropriate values education, and call into question unitary approaches to values education, whether they emphasize justice issues, as in some versions of Kohlbergian moral education, or social norms and the social order, as in traditional character education.

Classroom Management

Each aspect of values education discussed thus far is embedded within the more general social climate of the classroom: the rules, structure, and sanctions that make up what Philip Jackson (1968) calls the "hidden curriculum." Interactions in the context of this hidden curriculum constitute an integral part of the contribution schools make to students' social development. In studies of naturally occurring classroom transgressions it has been found that both children and teachers respond differently to moral and conventional events (Nucci and Turiel 1978; Nucci and Nucci 1982). Moral transgressions tend to evoke responses that pertain to the harmful or unjust effects of acts. Breaches of social convention, as would be expected, generate responses that focus on social rules, expectations, and the social order. Despite these findings there have been no studies that have systematically examined the developmental impact of domain-appropriate versus domain-undifferentiated responses to transgression. What have been studied, however, are students' conceptions of moral and conventional school rules, and teachers' responses to transgression.

Children expect schools to have rules governing actions such as hitting and hurting, or stealing personal property, and state that it is wrong for schools or teachers to permit such behaviors because they result in harm to others (Weston and Turiel 1980; Laupa and Turiel 1986). In addition, teacher fairness and impartiality constitute important criteria for children's judgments of teacher adequacy (Arsenio 1984; Veldman and Peck 1963; Lee, Statuto, and Kedar-Voivodas 1983.) Thus, within the moral domain, it is less the case that teacher authority and rules establish what is right or wrong as it is the case that teacher authority stems from the extent to which the rules they establish and the actions they engage in are consistent with the child's conceptions of justice and harm. In the area of convention, however, students acknowledge that school authorities may legitimately establish, alter, or eliminate school-based norms of propriety (e.g., dress codes, forms of address) and the rules and procedures for academic activity (Blumenfeld, Pintrich, and Hamilton 1987; Dodsworth-Rugani 1982; Nicholls and Thorkildsen 1987; Weston and Turiel 1980). Indeed, it is not until age nine or ten that children consistently respond to their peers' transgressions of school conventions; before then children leave response to such norm violations to the adults (Nucci and Nucci 1982).

The findings regarding students' conceptions of school rules and authority are paralleled by studies of children's judgments of teachers' responses to transgression. It has been found (Nucci 1984) that students are sensitive to whether teachers' responses are concordant with the domain (moral or conventional) of the breach. Students evaluate not only the teachers' responses but also the teachers as respondents. Students rated highest those teachers who responded to moral transgressions with statements focusing on the effects of the acts (e.g., "Joe, that really hurt Mike"). Rated lower were teachers who responded with statements of school rules or of normative expectations (e.g., "That's not the way for a Hawthorne student to act"). Rated lowest were teachers who used simple commands (e.g., "Stop it!" or "Don't hit!").

As one would expect, students rated highest those teachers who responded to breaches of convention with rule statements or with evaluations of acts as deviant, and they rated lower those teachers who responded to such transgressions in terms of their effects on others (e.g., "When you sit like that, it really upsets people"). The use of simple commands was rated the least adequate, as it was with moral transgressions.

This research suggests that students attend to the informational content of teachers' responses to transgressions. It also suggests that the domain of teachers' responses to transgression may prove to be an important variable for future studies of the relations between classroom management techniques and social development in children.

CONCLUSION

The philosopher Alasdair MacIntyre (1982) has characterized the current historical period as one of moral dissensience. Yet in the midst of this moral Babel, the majority of parents expect schools to contribute to the moral development of children. The research indicates that morality is centered on universal concerns for justice, fairness, and human welfare that are available even to young children. Those findings provide a basis for moral education that is both nonindoctrinative and nonrelativistic.

The research also makes clear that values education should not be reduced solely to concerns for moral development. A substantial and integral part of students' social values are within the domain of social convention. Understanding the necessary social organizational function of convention equips the student to understand his or her own sociocultural system as well as to interpret and interact with the cultural and social systems of others. Concepts of convention, rather than being a subset of morality, provide the necessary knowledge base for cultural tolerance and a critical perspective on one's own society. Thus, it is the development of both the student's moral reasoning and the concepts of social convention that is the aim of the domain approach to values education.

REFERENCES

Arsenio, William. "The Affective Atmosphere of the Classroom: Children's Conceptions of Teachers and Social Rules." Paper presented at the Annual Meeting of the American Educational Research Association, New Orleans, 1984.

Blumenfeld, Phyllis; Pintrich, Paul; and Hamilton, V. Lee. "Teacher Talk and Students' Reasoning about Morals, Conventions, and Achievement," *Child Development* 58 (October 1987): 1389–401.

Carey, N., and Ford, M. "Domains of Social and Self-regulation: An Indonesian Study." Paper presented at the meeting of the American Psychological Association, Los Angeles, 1983.

Damon, William. *The Social World of the Child.* San Francisco: Jossey-Bass, 1977.

Damon, William. "Patterns of Change in Children's Social Reasoning: A Two-year Longitudinal Study," *Child Development* 51 (December 1980): 1010–17.

Dewey, John. *Moral Principles in Education*. Boston: Houghton Mifflin, 1909.

Dodsworth-Rugani, Kathy Jean. "The Development of Concepts of Social Structure and Their Relationship to School Rules and Authority." Doct. dissertation, University of California, Berkeley, 1982.

Enright, Robert; Franklin, Christina; and Manheim, Lesley. "Children's Distributive Justice Reasoning: A Standardized and Objective Scale," *Developmental Psychology* 16 (May 1980): 193–202.

Gallup, George. "Eighth Annual Gallup Poll of Public Attitudes toward the Public Schools," *Phi Delta Kappan* 58 (1976): 37–50.

Hollos, Marida; Leis, Phillip; and Turiel, Elliot. "Social Reasoning in Ijo Children and Adolescents in Nigerian Communities," *Journal of Cross-Cultural Psychology* 17 (September 1986): 352–76.

Irwin, D. Michelle, and Moore, Shirley. "The Young Child's Understanding of Social Justice," *Developmental Psychology* 5 (November 1971): 406–10.

Jackson, Philip W. *Life in Classrooms*. New York: Holt, Rinehart, and Winston, 1968.

Kohlberg, Lawrence. *Essays on Moral Development, Vol. 1: The Philosophy of Moral Development*. San Francisco: Harper and Row, 1981.

Kohlberg, Lawrence. *Essays on Moral Development, Vol. 2: The Psychology of Moral Development*. San Francisco: Harper and Row, 1984.

Lapsley, Daniel. "The Development of Retributive Justice Reasoning in Children." Doct. dissertation, University of Wisconsin, Madison, 1982.

Laupa, Marta, and Turiel, Elliot. "Children's Conceptions of Adult and Peer Authority," *Child Development* 57 (April 1986): 405–12.

Lee, Patrick C.; Statuto, Carol; and Kedar-Voivodas, Gita. "Elementary School Children's Perceptions of Their Actual and Ideal School Experience: A Developmental Study," *Journal of Educational Psychology* 75 (December 1983): 838–47.

Lines, Patricia M. *Religious and Moral Values in Public Schools: A Constitutional Analysis*, Report No. LEC-1. Denver, Colo.: Education Commission of the States, 1981.

MacIntyre, Alasdair. *After Virtue*. Notre Dame, Ind.: University of Notre Dame Press, 1982.

Nicholls, J., and Thorkildsen, T. "Distinguishing Intellectual Conventions from Matters of Logic and Fact." Paper presented at the biennial meeting of the Society for Research on Child Development, Baltimore, 1987.

Nucci, Larry P. "Conceptual Development in the Moral and Conventional Domains: Implications for Values Education," *Review of Educational Research* 49 (1982): 93–122.

Nucci, Larry P. "Evaluating Teachers as Social Agents: Students' Ratings of Domain Appropriate and Domain Inappropriate Teacher Responses to Transgressions," *American Educational Research Journal* 21 (Summer 1984): 367–78.

Nucci, Larry P. "Children's Conceptions of Morality, Societal Convention, and Religious Prescription." In *Moral Dilemmas: Philosophical and Psychological Reconsiderations of the Development of Moral Reasoning*, ed. C. Harding. Chicago, IL: Precedent Press, 1985.

Nucci, Larry P., and Nucci, Maria. "Children's Social Interactions in the Context of Moral and Conventional Transgressions," *Child Development* 53 (April 1982): 403–12.

Nucci, Larry P., and Turiel, Elliot. "Social Interactions and the Development of Social Concepts in Preschool Children," *Child Development* 49 (June 1978): 400–7.

Nucci, Larry P., and Weber, E. "An Experimental Test of the Domain Approach to Values Education." Unpublished manuscript, University of Illinois at Chicago, 1988.

Nucci, Larry P.; Turiel, Elliot; and Encarnacion-Gawrych, E. Gloria. "Children's Social Interactions and Social Concepts: Analyses of Morality and Convention in the Virgin Islands," *Journal of Cross-Cultural Psychology* 14 (December 1983): 469–87.

Piaget, Jean. *The Moral Judgment of the Child*. Glencoe, Ill.: Free Press, 1932, 1948.

Rest, James. *Revised Manual for the Defining Issues Test*. Minneapolis: Moral Research Projects, 1979.

Rest, James. "Morality." In *Handbook of Child Psychology, Vol. III: Cognitive Development*, ed. John H. Flavell and Ellen Markman. New York: John Wiley, 1983.

Smetana, Judith. *Concepts of Self and Morality: Women's Reasoning about Abortion*. New York: Praeger, 1982.

Song, Myung-ja; Smetana, Judith G.; and Kim, Sang Yoon. "Korean Children's Conceptions of Moral and Conventional Transgressions," *Developmental Psychology* 23 (July 1987): 577–82.

Turiel Elliot. "Social Regulation and Domains of Social Concepts." In *New Directions for Child Development, Vol. 1: Social Cognition*, ed. William Damon. San Francisco: Jossey-Bass, 1978.

Turiel, Elliot. *The Development of Social Knowledge: Morality and Convention*. Cambridge, Mass.: Cambridge University Press, 1983.

Turiel, Elliot; Killen, Melanie; and Helwig, Charles C. "Morality: Its Structure Functions and Vagaries." In *The Emergence of Morality in Young Children*, ed. Jerome Kagan and Sharon Lamb. Chicago: University of Chicago Press, 1987.

Turiel, Elliot; Nucci, Larry; and Smetana, Judith G. "A Cross-cultural Comparison about What? A Critique of Nisan's (1987) Study of Morality and Convention," *Developmental Psychology* 24 (January 1988): 140–43.

Turiel, Elliot, and Smetana, Judith. "Social Knowledge and Action: The Coordination of Domains." In *Morality, Moral Behavior, and Moral Development: Basic Issues in Theory and Research*, ed. William M. Kurtines and Jacob L. Gewirtz. New York: Wiley, 1984.

Veldman, Donald, and Peck, Robert. "Student Teacher Characteristics from the Pupil's Viewpoint," *Journal of Educational Psychology* 54 (December 1963): 346–55.

Weston, Donna, and Turiel, Elliot. "Act-Rule Relations: Children's Concepts of Social Rules," *Developmental Psychology* 16 (September 1980): 417–24.